Parsi Fiction

Volume 1

Parsi Fiction

Volume 1

edited by

Novy Kapadia
Jaydipsinh Dodiya
R.K. Dhawan

PRESTIGE

Published by
PRESTIGE BOOKS
3/28, East Patel Nagar
New Delhi 110 008
e-mail: prestigebooks@greatindian.com

Vol. 1 ISBN: 81-7551-107-9
Vol. 2 ISBN: 81-7551-108-7

Rs. 1000

Composed by Vivek Mathur, Delhi 110 006 Ph. 3981867
Printed at Chaman Offset Press, New Delhi 110 002

Contents

The Parsis and the Novel

Firdaus Kanga

Dina Mehta

Ardashir Vakil

Farishta Murzban Dinshaw

Foreword

Parsi novelists have been in the forefront of Indian writers in the English language for the past few decades and many have become household names amongst the literati. The settings and characters in their books have a degree of the exotic which catches the imagination, especially of the western readers. Too often, however, the idiosyncracies and extreme individualism of the Parsis make their characters almost caricatures. Galling as it may be to the community in India, it has enhanced the reputation and often the coffers of the writers, many of whom are now residing in the West.

Some of us may be aware of the long tradition of writers who have had an impact in their own times on the social, political and economic scenes arousing the consciousness of their readers in India and abroad. These were the towering personalities of India's freedom struggle, who created an atmosphere of change—social and political. Dadabhai Nowroji, Dinshaw Vacha, Phiroze Mehta, Kabraji, Khabardar and others wrote both in Gujarati and English. What we now have in the present writers is technical craftsmanship and felicity of prose which have caught the modern reader's fancy. It is almost as if a new genre of writers has emerged on the literary scene.

Professors Novy Kapadia, Jaydipsinh Dodiya and R.K. Dhawan have put together two volumes of critical evaluation of the Parsi novels. Their case studies of Bapsi Sidhwa, Rohinton Mistry, Firdaus Kanga, Dina Mehta and some of the new novelists are highly illuminating. Others are covered in a wide sweep of time and experience. Pride of place has however been given to those of the period of the Parsi diaspora of the Sixties of the twentieth century and later.

The present book should be of value to students of English literature all over the world where Indian writing in the English language is increasingly studied. The early chapters related to the philosophy and character of the Zoroastrian faith practised by the Parsis would give the reader a better understanding of the novels which are discussed subsequently in the book.

We, at the Delhi Parsi Anjuman, have always encouraged publications on life, literature and culture. I have a great pleasure in writing this Foreword to the book which brings to bear literary criticism of the Parsi fiction. I congratulate the editors for the stupendous task undertaken and the publishers for bringing out the volumes expeditiously and so elegantly.

New Delhi

Lt. Gen. A.M. Sethna
President
Delhi Parsi Anjuman

In memory of

Shri Mansinh Rajabhai Dodiya
Former Research Scholar
Department of Hindi
Saurashtra University
Rajkot

The Parsis: An Introduction

NOVY KAPADIA

Who are the Parsis? They are an ethno-religious minority in India, living mostly on the west coast of the subcontinent, especially in Mumbai. In Pakistan, most Parsis reside in Karachi and Lahore. The word Parsi means a native of "Pars" or "Fars" an ancient Persian province, now in southern Iran. The Greek word for this province was Persepolis. The Parsis left their homeland over twelve hundred years ago to save their religion, the teachings of Zoroaster, from being Islamized by the invading Islamic Arabians in the seventh century A.D. The Parsis are followers of Prophet Zarathushtra. Their religion known as Zoroastrianism was founded around 2000 B.C.

Historians dispute the date. Some like Annie Besant claim the Zoroastrian religion was founded in 7000 or 8000 B.C. Aristotle places the date of the prophet at 9,600 B.C. In his book Zoroaster, L.H. Jackson claims that the prophet was born in 660 B.C. and died in 600 B.C.

The origins of this small community of around 90,000 go back to the Indo-European branch of the Aryans. They are said to be descendants of the Aryan tribes which migrated from the Pamirs of central Turkistan to West Asia, particularly Iran.

The religious texts of the Parsis are collectively known as the *Avesta.* The essence of the religion can be found in the five *Gathas* or Divine Songs of Zarathushtra (there are many more *Gathas,* but they are not traceable). The *Gathas* are basically Zarathushtra the prophet's dialogue with God which reveals the ethical nature of the gospel. Other religious texts are *The Yasna,* a collection of seventy-two psalms which forms the chief liturgical work in the *Avesta* and *Vendidad* which is a code of conduct, with laws on purity and behaviour in twenty-two chapters.

So the religion of the Parsis is Zoroastrianism. The word Parsi is really an ethnic term or identity for this minority community. They should really be called Parsi-Zoroastrians. Present day Zoroastrians who have migrated to USA or Canada or Britain can be distinguished in two groups. Those who have migrated from the Indian subcontinent are referred to as Parsi-Zoroastrians whereas others who have come from Iran are known as Iranian Zoroastrians.

The Parsi-Zoroastrians are famed for being a very adaptable minority community. Since they have settled in the Indian subcontinent they have adapted Gujarati as their main language. With the advent of the British and the spread of the British Empire, the Parsis were the first Indian community to learn English. Nowadays Parsis learn how to speak, read and write in both Gujarati and English. Parsi families residing in different regions of India, also learn the regional language or Hindi. So most Parsi families in the Indian subcontinent speak at least three languages.

The scriptures of religious texts of the Parsis are written in the ancient Avestan language or the Pahlavi script. However these languages are now extinct and are used only by priests for prayers.

In the 1997 census by the Government of India, the Parsis were only about 75-80,000 in number, 0.016 per cent of the total population of India. Yet their feeling of group identity and active participation in the social, cultural and economic life of both India and Pakistan is immense. Eminent jurist Nani A. Palkhiwala observes in his book *We the Nation: The Lost Decades*: "History affords no parallel to the role of Parsis in India. There is no record of any other community so infinitesimally small as Parsis, playing such a significant role in the life of a country so large." (317)

Are Palkhiwala's views just a case of euphoric back-patting? Let us examine the facts. As a community, the Parsis are well-off and urbanized (about 95%). In shipping industry, aviation, banking, catering, canning and dairy products, the Parsis have been pioneers in India. There have also been numerous legal luminaries and many notable Parsis like Rustamji Jivanji Gorkhodu, a close associate of Mahatma Gandhi, K.F. Nariman, an ardent promoter of the swadeshi movement, Dadabhai Naoroji, one of the founders of the Indian National Congress, Sir Dinshaw Eduljee Wacha, president of the Indian National Congress at its 1901 session and Sir Pherozeshah Mehta, Vice-Chancellor of Bombay University and member of the Municipal Corporation of Bombay, to mention a few, played a prominent role in the Freedom Movement. Another significant feature is that despite being a minuscule minority, the Parsis have never asked for any form of reservations in jobs or entrance to colleges in post-independent India. Yet, despite such a progressive attitude and comparative prosperity, the Parsi community still maintains very strong sense of group identity and cohesiveness.

Now that we have a reasonable insight about the Parsi community, let us try and understand some of the motivating factors, which make this smallest religious minority in the world strive for identity and behave in a particular manner. To understand the motivating factors even better, it is important to get some knowledge about the basic tenets of Zoroastrianism.

The religion founded by Zarathushtra or Zoroaster (the more commonly used Greek form of his name) is in its original form, a monotheism. In contrast to the innumerable gods and demons (devas) of his time, Zoroaster proclaimed the sole, absolute, omnipotent, eternal God, called *Ahura Mazda* or "Wise Lord." Ahura Mazda is both the creator as well as the judge on the day of the Last Judgement. Zarathushtra was born in the city of Arak, in Azerbaijan. At the age of fifteen, Zarathushtra turned away from all worldly pleasures and devoted himself day and night to the worship of Ahura Mazda. When he was twenty years old, he bade farewell to his parents and went to meditate in a cave. Like Gautama Buddha and Mahavir, Zarathushtra wanted to unravel the mystery of life. His queries dealt with eternal problems like why there was death and suffering in the world and how did evil come into the world and why were some hungry and poor and others rich and well-fed.

According to historical legends, Zarathushtra lived alone in a cave, high on Mount Ushi-daren eating roots and berries and drinking goat's milk. On Mount Ushi-daren which means "bestowing awareness," Zarathushtra received enlightenment and conversed with Ahura Mazda in a vision. At the age of thirty, Zarathushtra went back to the world of men and taught them the wisdom he had learnt. He and his first disciple Maidhyomaongha became wandering preachers. However, many of the nearby tribes listened to but rejected his teachings. After many trials and tribulations, he first succeeded in the small kingdom of Bactria in eastern Iran. His missionary labours continued for thirty years, after which he settled at Balkh the capital of Bactria, the Greek name for Afghanistan. Eminent Parsi historian Piloo Nanavutty's book *The Parsis* (1977) gives detailed information on the life of Zarathushtra and his teachings. According to her, Zarathushtra was killed when he was seventy-seven years old. The prophet was stabbed in the back, whilst praying at the Fire Temple at Balkh, by Tur-bara-Tur, leader of the Turanians, a tribe hostile to the concept of monotheism.

Zarathushtra preached the monotheistic religion of the One Supreme God, Ahura Mazda *(Wise Lord)*. His message is a positive, life-affirming, active-principled one, which demands not so much belief, as reason and action on the part of every individual. According to the prophet Zarathushtra, the whole universe is dominated by two primal forces, Good and Evil. The task of mankind is to choose between them. *Spenta Mainyu* the power of light and good are the good spirits opposed in this world by the evil spirits *Angra Mainyu*. The supreme god Ahura Mazda thus combines with Spenta Mainyu to become the principle of good represented as *Ohrmazd*. The personified evil spirit is *Ahriman*. Life is seen as a classless struggle between the forces of good and evil. There is no concept of earthly renunciation or asceticism. The moral demands on Parsi-Zoroastrians are "Hvarshta (Good Deeds), Hukhta (Good Words) and Humata (Good Thoughts)." (Eckehard Kulke, p. 18) The conflict between good and evil will continue until Evil is routed. After the destruction of Evil, according to Zarathushtra's teachings, there will be a general Resurrection, a Final Judgement and then an endless era of Universal Peace. On earth, human beings must make their own choice. A choice of the forces of good is a personal responsibility. It involves a life of active benevolence. The views on life after death are similar to Christianity. The good people will enter paradise, the rest will be ushered into Purgatory or be plunged straight into Hell. Keki B. Shroff in a presentation made to Vision TV of Canada on 26 May 1995 showed how Zoroastrian ideas have played a vital role in the development of western thought. He listed some theological concepts shared by Zoroastrianism with Judaism and Christianity. The similarities are as follows:

1. Belief in one supreme and loving god.
2. The concept of Heaven and Hell and individual judgement.
3. The ultimate triumph of good over evil. A strict moral and ethical code.
4. The messiah to come for the final restoration.
5. The concepts of resurrection, final judgement and life everlasting.
6. The Zoroastrian origin of words like Satan, paradise, pastor and amen.

A historical perspective is essential to understand the dilemmas, identity crises and problems of the Parsi community in India which is aptly reflected in Parsi literature. The Parsis are the descendants of the Persian Zoroastrians who had sought refuge in India in the eighth century A.D. when Persia, now Iran, was conquered by Arab invaders. After the collapse of the Persian empire at the battle of Nahawand in 642 A.D., the defeated Persians who practised the ancient monotheistic religion, Zoroastrianism, were converted to Islam by the conquering Arabs. Consequently, many Zoroastrians fled from Iran and sought refuge in India.

Several history books dealing with the exodus of the Parsi Zoroastrians to India have stated that after fleeing from Madyan in Iran, they first arrived at the Port of Diu in the eighth century A.D. After their stay for about 19 years, they set sail towards the south and landed at the port of Sanjan in Gujarat around 785 A.D. Sanjan was then ruled by the liberal monarch, King Jadhav Rana.

The Dastur (Priest) who was heading these refugees approached King Jadhav Rana, narrated their tales of woe and sought permission to settle down in Sanjan. At a public assembly in an open maidan, the Dastur gave details of the basic tenets of Zoroastrianism in sixteen Sanskrit shlokas. It is learnt that initially Jadhav Rana was hesitant about giving shelter to the refugees from Persia, as he was uncertain about the reaction of his own citizens. The king's first response was a sorrowful inability to accommodate the Zoroastrians on a permanent basis at Sanjan due to inadequacy of space.

At this crucial juncture, the Dastur requested that an urn filled with milk to the brim be brought to the assembly. When the same appeared, he took off his ruby studded gold ring and dropped it into the urn. Using symbolic gesture, the Dastur showed that just as the contents of the urn had not spilt over but become richer by the insertion of the precious ring, similarly the Parsi-Zoroastrians would bring further prosperity to that area if granted shelter. Moved by the reasoning of this pious priest, King Jadhav Rana asked the Dastur to narrate their actual requirements. The Dastur replied that they desired freedom of worship, freedom to bring up young children in their own traditions, and land for cultivation so that they became self-sufficient. Jadhav Rana agreed to these demands but imposed five preconditions for allowing the Zoroastrians to settle in Sanjan. The five stipulations were:

1. To adopt the Gujarati language. (The Parsis have adopted this language faithfully, have forgotten their traditional dialects and in all modern day census reports indicate Gujarati as their mother tongue).
2. The women would wear the Sari. (This sartorial custom has also been faithfully followed and the Parsis in India have adopted sari as the dress of the community. Traditional Parsi women wear the 'Sidhi' sari in the Gujarati fashion, draped over, the right shoulder, with one end tucked at the

back and the other end falls in the front.

3. Men should handover their weapons.
4. Venerate the cow. (Due to this condition, traditional Parsis still do not eat beef, through there are no religious taboos against the eating of beef).
5. The marriage ceremonies shall be performed at night only. (This condition was imposed so that the local population is not attracted by such a ceremony and hence the danger of conversion is minimized. The Parsis in the subcontinent still follow this tradition and do not allow outsiders in their Fire Temples, which is a further guarantee that they will not attempt any conversions to their religion.)

After accepting these stipulations, the fragile but learned Dastur made one more symbolic gesture to assure the king of their loyalty and diligence. He stirred a spoonful of sugar in a brass bowl full of milk and said, "we shall try to be like this insignificant amount of sugar in the milk of your human kindness." Emotionally moved by such sincere commitment, King Jadhav Rana granted asylum to the refugees in Sanjan. The Dastur then appeared before the king and on behalf of the community pledged these words:

> Hame hinustan rayr bashim.
> We shall be the friends of all India.
>
> (*Dipanjali*, June-December 1996, 11)

The words of the Dastur remained the basic credo or article of faith for Parsi Zoroastrians throughout their stay in India. It also reflects the characteristic spirit of adaptability of this minority community which enabled it to thrive in a country of such diverse cultures and religions.

However, eminent Parsi literary critic Nilufer Bharucha views that the conditions and restrictions like adopting the local languages, costumes, customs and not inter marrying with the local population and never proselytizing led to feelings of alienation within the community. She writes:

> These unequal conditions provided fertile breeding ground for feelings of ambivalence and alienation from the host country. This ambivalence and alienation became exacerbated during the colonial period, when the Parsis were among the first to embrace English language education and become the most westernized Indian community. Most Parsis, thus felt bereft at the end of the Empire and the resultant loss of the special/elite status they had enjoyed during the colonial period. Several migrated to the west in the 1950s and 60s. (358)

However as is evident in Parsi literature, both the Parsis who sought greener pastures in the west and those who stayed on in India have experienced identity crises and confusion. In the West, the Parsis face the dilemma of being branded as just another community of subcontinental Asians, an identity they sought to escape. In India, as is reflected in the works of Rohinton Mistry, Dina Mehta, Firdaus Kanga, Bomen Desai and Bapsi Sidhwa, this minority community has to cope with the hegemonic forces of the dominant community. The struggle to create their own space in the West as well as in India and the identity struggle of what it means to be a Parsi Zoroastrian and all the major problems, aspirations, hopes, ambitions and prejudices of the community are reflected in Parsi literature.

Madhavankutty Pillai in an investigative article in the *Asian Age* of 13 May 1997 reveals that due to prosperity, extreme individualism, urbanization, late marriages, low birth rate and antique laws about not accepting the children of Parsi women married outside the community into the fold is taking their toll on the Parsi community in India. Statistics show that Parsis are the most urbanized community in India. Ninety-four percent of the Parsi population is urbanized as compared to 16.4% of Hindus. Also the Parsi population in India has declined from about 1,14,890 in 1941 to about 70-80,000 in 1997. Madhavankutty Pillai quotes the Parsi demographer Kersi Limathwala about the declining population of the community: "Though there are no definite figures available at present, a rough estimate is that in a year there are 1,000 deaths and 500 births."

Given these conditions and factors the laws of statistics dictate the eventual annihilation of this race. If attitudes do not change, it seems unlikely the Parsis will see another millennium change. Under these circumstances, as Rohinton Mistry has indicated in a recent interview, fiction such as his will record the history of the Parsis for the ages to come. This is true not only of Mistry's fiction, but also that of the fiction of Bapsi Sidhwa, Dina Mehta, Firdaus Kanga, Farrukh Dondy and other Parsi writers.

Bibliography

Dodiya, Jaydipsinh, ed. *The Fiction of Rohinton Mistry: Critical Studies* (New Delhi: Prestige, 1998).

Kapadia, Novy, ed. "Kaikhushru Pallonji Katrak Dar-E-Meher," *Silver Jubilee Celebrations Journal, 1961-1986* (Delhi: Parsi Anjuman, 1986).

Kapadia, Novy and A.G. Khan, ed. *The Parsis: Madyan to Sanjan* (New Delhi: Creative, 1997).

Kavarana, Roxanne. "The Parsis in India: A Community under Stress," *The Times of India Research Foundation Journal* (April 1989).

Khullar, Ava and Shanker Bose. "The Parsis: A Socio-Economic and Demographic Survey," a monogram prepared for the Centre of Study of Developing Societies, Delhi, 1978.

Kulke, Eckehard. *The Parsees in India: A Minority as Agent of Social Change* (Delhi: Bell Books, 1978).

Nanavutti, Piloo. *The Parsis* (Delhi: Delhi Parsi Anjuman, rpt. 1992).

Palkhiwala, A. Nani. *We the Nation: The Lost Decades* (New Delhi: UBSPD, 1994).

Polly, Chenoy N. *Angicisation of the Parsis cited in Mainstream,* 1 April, 1989, pp. 1-9.

Sahukar, K. Adi, ed. *Dipanjali,* June-December 1996, Journal of the Delhi Parsi Anjuman.

Singh, Arun. "The Parsis: The Faith and the People," cited in *The Parsis: Madyan to Sanjan.*

Taraporewala, I.J.S. *The Religion of Zarathushtra* (Bombay: India House, rpt. 1979).

Teachings of Zarathushtra

HOMI D. SETHNA

Zarathushtra or Zoroaster as he is commonly called in Greek and other languages lived in the midst of antiquity around 3,500 years ago, long before the Christian or the Buddhist era. Zarathushtra calls God, the one God, Ahura Mazda, the Lord of Wisdom. Zarathushtra received a revelation from Ahura Mazda. The first revelation is that there is only One God. Zarathushtra is the first known prophet to have proclaimed Monotheism. Zoroastrianism provides us with a comprehensive view of life, of the Unity of One God and of all Creation. To promote the welfare of human kind and all the things created by nature was his ethic.

To convey this totality, Zarathushtra composed a number of Poetic Hymns called the Gathas, which contain a well-formed theology. The Gathas were originally recited by Zarathushtra in the ancient Avestan language, and were handed down in an oral tradition for many centuries. Only about the fourth century A.D., they were first put down in Pahlavi Script, and were transcribed from the Pahlavi into the Avestan Script in the sixth century A.D., the Script we know today.

In all, there are 238 verses, put into Gathas. Each verse conveys a wealth of wisdom and all the 238 verses carry the essence of the teachings of Zarathushtra.

Zarathushtra's philosophy encompassed not only the life of the spirit but of our day-to-day living. He never advocates isolation, rather he says we should be involved with the world around us. He advocates action. In one Gatha he recites:

This precious reward of Thine O Mazda
Thou givest by way of the Good Mind
Thou givest to vigorous bodily life to him who works for and tends to Thy Creation,
Who furthers Thy beneficent plan by the power of his understanding
Guided by Thy spirit of Truth.

World can be saved only if man responds to the needs and sufferings of his fellow-men in accordance with the principles which emanate from Ahura Mazda. Man must uphold these principles with determination and in spirit. This is the Message of Zarathushtra. In one Gatha he says, "Happiness unto him who brings happiness unto others."

The notion of Religiosity in Zarathushtra has been insightfully expressed by Dr. Stanley Insler of Yale University, U.S.A., the well known scholar of Avesta, the language in which the Gathas are written. "The extraordinary contribution of Zarathushtra is the profound realization that man can both serve and honour God more meaningfully in the enactment of the lordly principles of Truth and good feeling among his fellow-men than in the awesome reverence founded upon fear and dread. It is true that God merits praise and worship but chiefly so because He created and offered to his people those instruments of God which can in turn offer dignity and happiness in the world of man."

In the teachings of Zarathushtra, as expressed in the Gathas, there is always emphasis on the ethical or moral aspect of existence and he sees the good in all life. Even trees and plants have life and they must be loved and cared for. There is divinity in every atom of the universe. All living things are interdependent. And any disturbance of the ecological balance in our world is a lapse from the perfect creation of Ahura Mazda. In Zoroastrian ethics, natural law is characterised as the principle according to which all things come to their full realization. It brings satisfaction to all living beings, happiness to human beings and harmony to social existence.

As Zarathushtra said to his own daughter on the occasion

of her marriage:

> These words do I address to you maidens who are being married.
> These counsels do I give to you.
> Keep them in your mind and lay them to heart.
> Let each cherish the other with righteousness.
> Then surely the reward of a happy life shall be yours.

Zarathushtra could give this advice to his daughter, only because he knew, like all of us should and do, that Man is the only 'creature' created by God who has been given this great gift of God, the faculty of 'Reason,' or a rational mind or to put it simply, the ability to 'choose' our own way, or a mind that can think and reason out which path to take. All other 'creatures' have been given the gift of 'instinct.' They do what they feel instinctively. Therefore the question of reasoning and choosing does not apply to them.

By the same logic, human nature has freedom as an essential ingredient in it, thus making it possible to choose between good and evil, between peace and violence. Violence and evil are characterized by intolerance and inhumanity.

In his teachings, Zarathushtra laid emphasis on the relationship between means and ends and repeatedly spoke against violence of any kind. In our times, men like Mahatma Gandhi personified this belief.

"Freedom is a fundamental value in Zoroastrian ethics. The humanity of a moral agent requires that he be free to choose and then be held responsible for that choice. Not only is the value emphasised in moral notions in the Gathas, it is made the basis, the full basis of the judgement of human behaviour."

Justice is not blind. Justice is impartial. In Zarathushtra's philosophy, God is omniscient and just, but man must not assume that He is omnipotent.

Most men believe that God 'controls' all men's actions and if anything goes wrong in their lives, they say "That was my Fate, my Destiny, what could I do?"

Man must work with honesty and determination and take

every step using his faculty of Reason and then he will be writing his own Destiny and not blaming God—as he often does!

> The man of devotion is beneficient to all.
> He is beneficent because of his wisdom,
> Because of his realisation of Truth,
> Because of the goodness in his thoughts,
> in his words, in his deeds.
> Unto him Ahura Mazda shall grant the
> Kingdom of the Good Mind
> And verily this blessing I too long for.

Zarathushtra's philosophy and his ethical concepts, enunciated 3,500 years ago and as recited in the Gathas are not only relevant in this day and age, they also form the basis of great men's thinking and actions. Mahatma Gandhi's life was based on "Truth, Love and Justice" and so are the lives of Saints and Sages through the ages. To think that a man was born thousands of years ago when paganism and primitive concepts of life were rampant, to give the world a Philosophy, a Way of life that is not only so positive but relevant today, you have to ponder how Zarathushtra could have done it in that day and age. The teachings of Zarathushtra give us the answer.

Getting to Know Parsi Zoroastrians

Compiled by
The Zoroastrian Association of Metropolitan Washington, Jashan

In the recent years, many Zoroastrians have emigrated to the United States, Canada, Britain, Australia and other countries. They are living amidst alien cultures and are in the process of finding their roots.

The local populations, amongst whom these Zoroastrians are living, are coming more and more in contact with them and are showing increasing interest in their background.

The objective of this article is to present a few basic facts about the history, beliefs, values, customs, and achievements of a small but outstanding group that has not only managed to preserve its ancient religion—believed by some scholars to be the oldest in the world—but has also made very important contributions wherever its members have lived.

This article is meant for Zoroastrians, who have felt the need for a brief description of their history and faith, as well as for non-Zoroastrians who wish to know something more about the Zoroastrians.

Who are the Zoroastrians?

Once the state religion of the mighty Iranian empire—which at one time extended from Africa to China, from the Danube in Europe to the plains of Judea in the Middle East, and up to the Punjab and Sindh in India—its followers today number less than 150,000 worldwide. After Iran was conquered by the Moslem Arabs in the seventh century, those Zoroastrians who refused to convert to Islam either sought refuge in isolated areas of Iran or fled to India, China, present-day Afghanistan and Russia, and other countries.

The largest surviving group, about 91,000, is to be found in India where its members are known as the 'Parsis.' The second largest is in Iran with about 30,000 according to the 1976 census. There are sizable groups in the U.S.A., Canada, Britain, and Pakistan, and smaller ones in Hong Kong, Singapore, Sri Lanka, Australia, East Africa and other places. A few Zoroastrians can be found in almost all English-speaking countries and even in some non English-speaking countries.

Why did the Zoroastrians flee to India?

India was chosen for many reasons. It was not only close geographically, but also had cultural and commercial ties with Iran. Both the Iranians and the people of North India belong to the same Aryan race, and the languages of Avesta and Sanskrit have much in common. Some historians even believe that there were Zoroastrians in India before the refugees came by sea in the seventh century.

Since their arrival in India, the Zoroastrians have been known as the "Parsis." The name derives from the Iranian province of "Pars" or "Fars" from where the fleeing Zoroastrians started their long journey to India.

How were the Zoroastrians received in India?

The only source of information relating to the early history of the refugees who came to India by sea is the "Kisseh-i-Sanjan," a Persian poem of 864 lines written around 1600 A.D. by a Zoroastrian priest, Bahman Kaikobad, of Navsari. According to this poem, when the Zoroastrians decided to make their first settlement in Sanjan, the chief priest of the party asked the local Hindu King, Jadi Rana, for permission to settle in Sanjan. In reply, the Hindu ruler is said to have made five conditions.

> The high priest of the Zoroastrians would have to explain their religious beliefs to the king.
> The refugees would have to give up their native Persian language and learn the local language.
> The women would have to adopt the sari, the traditional Hindu dress.
> The men would have to lay down their weapons.
> The Zoroastrians would have to hold their wedding processions only in the dark.

While accepting these conditions, the chief priest is said to have replied by reciting 16 Sanskrit "slokas" or stanzas pledging loyalty to the Hindu ruler. Although some of the facts stated in the "Kisseh-i-Sanjan." have been questioned by some historians, the account narrated in the poem explains some of the present-day customs and values of the Parsis. For example, the wedding ceremony is performed even today after sunset, and at least a part of the ceremony is repeated in Sanskrit. Parsi women wear the sari like Hindu women, and loyalty to the ruler of the day is a strong trait among the Parsis.

One may well ask: "How come the Zoroastrians managed to preserve their faith and identity in India whereas those who fled to other countries did not?" They could preserve their faith thanks to the tolerant attitude of the Hindus, and they could maintain their identity because the Hindu caste system prohibited intermarriage.

Who was Zarathushtra?

Zarathushtra was born in Iran, probably in the region that is a part of present-day Russia. He was married and had children. His father was Pourushaspa and his mother was Daghdova. Long before the coming of Zarathushtra, the people of Iran followed the Mazdayasni religion. By the time Zarathushtra was born, the true teachings of this religion were forgotten and the people believed in many gods. This caused a good deal of distress to Zarathushtra. To seek a message from God, he withdrew himself from the material world at an early age and spent several years in solitude. When he knew that he had heard the voice of God, he set out to preach. For ten years, no one paid any heed to him; in fact, he was denounced as a heretic and sorcerer. The tide turned when he was received by King Vishtasp. So impressed was the King by Zarathushtra's message that he publicly embraced the new religion which spread rapidly throughout Iran and neighbouring countries. The success of the new religion was not liked by his opponents who succeeded by slander and deception in having him imprisoned on a charge of sorcery. Undaunted, he continued to spread his faith after his release from prison. His enemies, however, continued to persecute him. He died a martyr's death, at the age of seventy-seven, at the hands of one of his enemies while praying in a temple.

There is controversy about the time when Zarathushtra lived. At one time western scholars believed that he lived around 600 B.C., but today some scholars believe that he lived around 1500 B.C. or even earlier. This would make Zoroastrianism the oldest of the prophetic religions.

What are the Principal Teachings of Zarathushtra?

The principal characteristics of the religion taught by Zarathushtra are: its stress on ethics, its positive approach to life, optimism about the future of the world, its emphasis on free choice and its catholicity.

According to Zarathushtra, the world is a battleground between the forces of good and evil. Ultimately, good will prevail over evil. Our mission in life is to so conduct ourselves that this ultimate victory is achieved. He urged his followers to live a full and useful life in this world, to appreciate all things that are good and beautiful in creation, not only to do good and desist from evil but also to fight evil, and to make others happy. He assured his followers that the strength of God would be given to those who fought evil, and stressed that an evil deed could be offset by a good one. As for happiness, the way to seek happiness was by making others happy.

He pointed out that in each of us there is a divine spark. It is up to us to recognize this divine spark of essence within us, to understand its capabilities and to try and so conduct ourselves that we reach the state of perfection in this world. As a practical guide in daily life, his prescription was very simple.

> Think good thoughts.
> Speak good words.
> Do good deeds.

Zarathushtra emphasized free choice. In one of his first sermons, he preached: "Ye who seek knowledge, please listen carefully to what I say, and perceive the truth in the light of reason, because it is possible for each man to have a separate creed."

He also taught that one should be liberal in thinking and to respect all that is good, true and beautiful. Here is a passage that brings home this point: "We reserve and love all good thoughts, words and deeds that may have been presented here or elsewhere, now or at any future period, because we are on the side of goodness."

Some scholars believe that some of the important concepts found in other religions—such as the concepts of monotheism, of heaven and hell, of the end of the world, of the resurrection of the dead, and of the coming of the Savior—originated with Zoroastrianism.

What are the Most Important Zoroastrian Values?

Every religion puts more emphasis on some aspects than others. It is important to know the values stressed in Zoroastrianism because these values influence the daily life of the Zoroastrians.

Zoroastrianism stresses truth more than anything else. The very first prayer a Zoroastrian child learns is devoted to truth. A free translation of that prayer—called Ashem Vohu—is: "Truth is the greatest virtue. It is happiness. Happy is he who is truthful for the sake of truth."

According to the Greek historian, Herodotus, every young

man in ancient Iran was instructed in three things—to ride a horse, to shoot with bow and arrow, and to speak the truth. Lying was considered the greatest disgrace. It is, therefore, not surprising that the Parsis of India and the Zoroastrians of Iran have earned a reputation for honesty.

Another cherished value is charity. In the very second prayer a Zoroastrian child learns—the "Yatha Ahu Vairyo"—there is a line which says: "He who gives assistance to the poor acknowledges the kingdom of God."

There is so much stress on charity in the Zoroastrian way of life that in India there is a saying "Parsi, thy name is charity." This tradition is also to be found in Iran.

Zoroastrianism also puts value on purity—purity of the body as well as that of the mind. This is why a Zoroastrian is expected to take a bath before any important ceremony. Zoroastrians also take pride in keeping their homes clean.

Zoroastrianism also stresses hard work and dignity of labor. In the "Gathas" which are a record of the prophet's conversations with God, we find this passage. To the question: "What is the way of furthering the Mazdayasni religion?" Ahura Mazda replies: "Incessant cultivation of corn, O Spitama, Zarathushtra. Who cultivates corn cultivates righteousness."

What are the Sacred Books of the Zoroastrians?

All the existing scriptures propounded by Zarathushtra as well as the religious writings of his followers are collectively known as the "Avesta." (Avesta is also the name of the language spoken in Iran at one time.) The "Avesta" consists of two parts—the older Avesta and the later Avesta (or "Khordeh Avesta"). The most important part of the scriptures is the "Gathas" or Divine Songs. These are dialogues between the prophet and God, and they are ascribed to Zarathushtra himself.

The "Avesta" is written in a number of languages. The "Gathas" were written in a language that was Pre-Avestan. later scriptures were written in the Avesta language and in the Pahlavi and Pazand dialects.

What exists today is only a fraction of the original scriptures, many of which were burned when Alexander destroyed Persepolis.

The Zoroastrians still recite their prayers in the language in which the scriptures were written. Some reformers argue that they should be recited in the mother tongue of the believer or in English so that the person offering the prayers can understand what he or she is praying. Others, who want to continue the old practice, argue that saying prayers in the old languages is more effective on account of the sound vibrations produced by these languages.

Do Zoroastrians Believe in One God?

They do. There is a mistaken belief among some western scholars that Zoroastrians believe in two Gods—a God of good and a God of evil. This is not true. In fact, some scholars claim that Zarathushtra was the first prophet to preach monotheism, the concept of one God. Zarathushtra talked about two opposing forces—the forces of good personified by 'Hormuzd' and the forces of evil personified by 'Ahriman.' According to Zarathushtra, the forces of good will ultimately prevail over the forces of evil, and the purpose of life is to help this process.

Do Zoroastrians Believe in Life after Death?

They do. Besides one day in each month, the last ten days of the Zoroastrian calendar are set aside for remembering the dead. There is also a special day each year when the departed are supposed to visit the earth. This corresponds to the All Souls Day observed by Christians. It is also believed that the soul hovers over the dead body for three days after death.

Do Zoroastrians Believe in Heaven or Hell?

They do. In the "Gathas" Zarathushtra often refers to life after death, and to the "Chinwat Bridge" where the good deeds done on earth are weighed against the evil deeds. Many Zoroastrian scholars believe that the descriptions of heaven and hell in

Zoroastrian scriptures are purely allegorical, that heaven and hell are not places but conditions. Some Zoroastrians believe that the reward or punishment for good or bad deeds is often given in this world itself rather than in the next.

Do Zoroastrians Believe in Reincarnation?

Few scholars have found any evidence of this belief in Zoroastrian scriptures.

Do Zoroastrians Believe in the Coming of the Final Savior?

They do. Some scholars believe that the concept of the Final Savior originated with Zoroastrianism.

What is the Zoroastrian View of the Nature of Human Beings?

Zoroastrians do not believe that human beings are born in sin. They believe that there is potential for good as well as evil in every human being. There is a divine spark or essence in each of us. We should recognize it and utilize it to its fullest potential. This divine spark ("Fravashi" or "Farohar") is depicted in architecture as a bird with outstretched wings.

What Kinds of Temples or Churches do the Zoroastrians Have?

For a Zoroastrian, communication with God is essentially an individual experience. He or she can pray at home or in a "fire-temple."

Are Zoroastrians "Fire Worshippers"?

No, they are not. They do not "worship" fire. The fire is a symbol of the Zoroastrian faith just as the cross is a symbol of Christianity. In a Zoroastrian temple, the only symbol before which prayers are said is the fire which is tended by a priest five times a day. The fire stands for a number of things. It is a symbol of purity, for fire purifies everything. It also stands for the "inner fire" or divine spark in a human being. The fire burning in the Zoroastrian temple or at home is a constant reminder that we should always keep our "inner fire" alive.

There are three "grades" of temples, depending upon the process of consecration and who is allowed to tend the fire. The first and second grades of fire can only be tended by the priests, whereas the last can be tended even by laymen.

Are there Other Symbols of Faith?

There are two symbols that Zoroastrians wear. One is the "sudra," a white, muslin shirt. In the center of the front neck opening is a small "pocket" into which all good deeds are "inserted." This is, of course a daily reminder that one must perform good deeds. The garment's color is white, because white is a symbol of purity.

The other symbol is the "kusti" a sacred thread tied three times around the waist while saying a prayer. It is tied three times to remind one of the three basic principles of the faith—good thoughts, good words, good deeds. The "kusti" is woven out of 72 threads of sheep's wool. These threads symbolize the 72 chapters of the scriptures, called the "Yasna," which include the "Gathas."

The first time a Zoroastrian wears the "sudra" and the "kusti" is when he or she is formally inducted into the faith, usually between the ages of 7 and 11.

What is the "Navzote" Ceremony?

The "Navzote" is the name of the ceremony during which a Zoroastrian child is formally initiated into the religion. In India, it is usually performed at the age of 7, 9 or 11. Tradition says it should be an odd number, and the ceremony must be done before the onset of puberty. After a bath (to signify purity of body), the boy or girl is made to wear the "sudra" for the first time. After a short prayer, he or she ties the "kusti" around the waist. During the ceremony, the child recites a few simple prayers, receives benedictions from the priest, and declares his or her acceptance of the Zoroastrian religion in the following words (freely translated):

> I follow the Mazdayasni religion, the religion of Zarathushtra. I love and accept this religion. I love and accept the very mind of good thought. I love and accept the very utterance of the good words. I love and accept the very action of the good deeds. I love and accept the good and true Mazdayasni religion which stops all quarrels and wars, teaches us to die for others, and leads us to Asha, the truth of God. The Mazdayasni religion is for me the greatest, the best and the finest of all religions which are or which shall be, because it is God's religion shown to us by Zarathushtra. I believe all things good come from Ahura Mazda. Such are the boons of those who follow the Mazdayasni religion.

What Kind of Marriage Ceremony do the Zoroastrians Have?

In India the marriage ceremony, is preceded by preliminary ceremonies three days before the actual ceremony.

Before the actual marriage ceremony the couple individually takes a bath to signify purity of the body. Then both sit down silently on chairs facing each other. A screen of cloth is held between them, and they hold their right hands in a clasp below the screen. This signifies that henceforth they will be united. To reinforce the idea of unity, the priest passes a thread round the couple seven times, while reciting prayers. When the screen is lifted, each throws rice on the other. The popular belief is that the one that throws the rice first will be the dominating partner. After that, the couple sits on chairs side by side. During the prayers recited by the priest, both the parties are asked three times if they are willing to be married. Each party has a "witness" standing behind the chair and the priest also asks the witnesses to confirm the agreement. If either party says "no," the wedding ceremony is ended. Finally, the priest recites blessings and gives advice. Although divorce is allowed among the Zoroastrians, the priest stresses the permanency of the marriage tie.

It is interesting to note that the actual ceremony is performed after sunset. Also, part of the ceremony (sometimes the entire ceremony) is repeated in Sanskrit—as a reminder of the pledges given to King Jadi Rana who gave refuge to the Zoroastrians when they landed in India about 1300 years ago.

What did the Zoroastrians Achieve in Iran?

The history of pre-Islamic Iran is usually divided into five periods—pre-Achaemenian, Achaemenian, Greek, Parathion, and Sassanian.

The Achaemenian period (550 B.C. to 330 B.C.) was the most glorious in the history of Iran. This was the time of Cyrus and Darius, two of the most illustrious rulers not only in the history of Iran but also in the history of the world. This was also the period of the crucial wars between the Persians and the Greeks. Although Iran lost militarily in the end, the contacts between the two nations had great cultural significance. Iran's literary works were translated into Greek and her culture had a powerful influence on Greek thought, and through Greece on Western civilization.

Cyrus, the founder of the Achaemenian dynasty, is sometimes called the first world emperor in history for he united all the West Asia into a vast empire. He is also remembered for his sense of justice, his humane treatment of subjugated nations, and his respect for other religions which were allowed to flourish in his empire. The Jews in particular have a high regard for Cyrus who is mentioned several times in the Bible. After conquering Babylon in 538 B.C., he freed the captive Jews and allowed them to return to Jerusalem and rebuild their temple. It is not surprising that Cyrus as a personal name is to be found not only in the countries of the Middle East, but also in Europe and North America.

Under Darius the Great, the Iranian empire reached its zenith, extending from Africa to China, from the Danube in Europe to the plains of Judaea in the Middle East, and up to Punjab and Sindh in India. Darius was not only a conqueror. He was also a very able administrator and a great builder. He is believed to be the first emperor in history to divide his empire into a number of provinces, each ruled over by a governor, a general, and a secretary of state, each of whom was appointed directly from the capital and was independent of the others. (We see that the doctrine of separation of powers, such as the one prevailing in the USA, is a very old one). As a builder, Darius constructed a canal linking Iran with the Mediterranean and a 1500 mile royal road from Sardis to his capital at Susa, and built many palaces and cities including beautiful Persepolis which was burned by Alexander.

Under Darius, the Iranians controlled a third of the Greek population. When some of the Greek cities revolted, the Iranians attacked Greece, but lost. Darius's second son, Xerxes, who succeeded him began another invasion against Greece but after a series of battles, the Iranians again lost. It is interesting to speculate that, if the Iranians had won, the Zoroastrian religion might have spread to Greece and later to much of Europe. That is why Zoroastrianism is sometimes called "the religion that almost became the religion of Europe."

The achievements of the Zoroastrians of Iran are not restricted to the period of the Iranian empire. Many Zoroastrians have achieved success in modern Iran also. They have held important positions in the government, in the armed forces, in education and other fields. Among them are Dr. Farhang Mehr who was appointed President of Shiraz University and who also held important posts in the government, and the late Arab Rustom Guiv who donated generously to many causes.

What have the Parsis of India Achieved?

The Parsis number less than a hundred thousand in a total Indian population of nearly 750 million. In relation to their numbers, their achievements in recent times can truly be described as outstanding. Consider some facts:

> The foundation of the industrialization of India was laid by a Parsi, J.N. Tata, founder of the House of Tata. The Tatas established, among other institutions, the first steel

mill in India, the first technological teaching and research institute, the first airline, the first school of social work, the first cancer hospital, the first institute for nuclear research.

Long before the Government of India started awarding scholarships for studies aboard, the J.N. Tata Trust enabled scores of Indians—Parsis and non-Parsis—to study abroad and occupy eminent positions in the country on their return.

Parsis have occupied top positions in the government, including the armed forces. They have been appointed cabinet ministers in the government, governors of states, ambassadors and chiefs of staff of the army, navy, and airforce. The first and only Field Marshall in India's history is a Parsi, Sam Manekshaw.

The first chairman of the India Atomic Energy Commission was a Parsi. Dr. Homi Bhabha, who was also elected President of the first Atoms for Peace Conference convened by the United Nations.

Parsis have played a prominent part in India's fight for freedom. The first flag of freedom was designed and flown in Paris by a Parsi lady, Madame Cama, who lived in exile in France in the last century. Parsis like Dadabhai Naoroji, Pherozeshaw Mehta, Dinshaw Wacha and K.F. Nariman, are among those who made a very significant contribution to the struggle for independence. It is worthy of note that all three Indians who got elected to the British Parliament from England—Dadabhai Naoroji, Muncherjee Bhownagree and Shapurji Saklatvala—were Parsis.

The Parsis are also the pioneers of the textile and shipbuilding industries in India.

A Parsi born in Bombay, Zubin Mehta, is the Conductor of the New York Philharmonic.

Why are there So Few Zoroastrians Left Today?

There are many reasons why there are so few followers of one of the great religions of the world.

In the first place, when the Arabs conquered Iran, not everyone who wanted to flee from Iran could do so. Those who fled to countries other than India inter-married with the local populations and got assimilated.

As for the Zoroastrians who fled to India, the birth-rate among the Parsis has been actually falling in recent years (whereas the birth-rate in India as a whole has been rising). Among the reasons for this are late marriages and the desire to have small families.

While children of Zoroastrian fathers married to non-Zoroastrians are accepted into the faith, there is opposition—especially in India—to the acceptance of children of Zoroastrian mothers married to non-Zoroastrians and to the acceptance of non-Zoroastrians who wish to follow the religion.

Zoroastrianism: An Introduction

DINA G. MCINTYRE

Nobody knows exactly when Zarathushtra lived. Opinions range between 6,500 BC and 600 BC. Nobody knows for sure where Zarathushtra lived, except that it was somewhere around ancient Iran. And for many hundreds of years, the language in which Zarathushtra composed his Gathas was not known or understood. The Gathas are the only extant work in that language, which is why the language is called "Gathic."

You may wonder how such precious knowledge has been lost! Part of the reason may have been that with the passing of time, the religion for many centuries was in the hands of souls who were not enlightened, who made political compromises, who turned it into a profit-making institution, a control mechanism, and who were not able to grasp, and therefore maintain, the pure, spiritual truths that Zarathushtra taught.

But the major reasons for this loss of knowledge were two devastating invasions which included the burning of our religious texts, and the killing of learned teachers. The first occurred when Alexander (mistakenly called 'The Great') defeated the Persian empire around 330 BC (the Persian emperor whom he defeated was no beauty either). It is reported that Alexander sent one copy of the Zoroastrian texts to his teacher Aristotle, and burned the rest. An ancient Zoroastrian work states that he "took away and burned those scriptures, . . . which had been written in gold water on prepared cowhide, and deposited in Stakhr i Pabagan in the Fortress of Writing. He killed many of the high priests and the judges . . . and the upholders of the religion, and the able ones and the wise men of Iran."[1]

Some of the Greek philosophers are so close in their thinking to Zarathushtra's ideas that I have often wondered if those learned men of Iran who were not killed, but who were sent to Greece as slaves along with the Zoroastrian texts, may have transmitted this knowledge to their Greek masters, wanting it to survive, even if it meant that it would survive as Greek thought.

It is interesting that Plato called Zarathushtra the father of philosophy. "Philosophy" means love of wisdom. The ancient Iranian name for the Zoroastrian religion is "mazdayasna" which means "worship of wisdom," which in Zarathushtra's view means to serve it with love. (Y51.22) And Zarathushtra's name for God is *Ahura Mazda*—the Wise Lord (or Lordly Wisdom).

Because learning was not universal in those days and was limited to a few, Alexander's actions in killing the learned dealt a devastating blow to the knowledge of religion in those who were left in Iran, where it survived (in a somewhat corrupted form) during the Parathian and Sassanian empires.

The second loss occurred when the Sassanian empire was defeated by the Arabs around 650 AD. An early historian writes that after the invaders "had killed their learned men and priests, and had burned their books and writings, they became entirely illiterate."[2] In waves starting around 900 AD, some Zoroastrians fled to India to avoid religious persecution and death at the hands of the new rulers.

Long after Zarathushtra, the Gathas were incorporated into other, later, texts (now called the Yasna[3]), which were preserved (at first verbally, later in writing) because they were recited by the priests from memory as part of the rituals of worship. As centuries passed, even though the priests no longer understood what they were reciting, they faithfully continued to memorize and recite these ancient texts, passing them down from one generation to the next. This is how the Gathas have survived down to our time.

It is only within the last fifty to hundred years that western scholars have succeeded in decoding this ancient language so that we now understand perhaps 80 per cent of it, although there are still many differences both in translation and interpretation.

Part of the problems of interpretation have stemmed from the view that such lofty thoughts could not possibly have existed in such ancient (read primitive) times. Therefore, with noble exceptions, the Gathas have been interpreted with little understanding of their metaphorical, multi-layered and deeply spiritual meanings.

But the ultimate betrayal has occurred at the hands of some present-day Zoroastrians who expound the view that the Gathas are "mere poetry" and "just ethics" which indicates how little they understand them.

In the Gathas, Zarathushtra shows a very intense, personal relationship with God. He talks to God, he argues with Him, he complains to Him, he asks questions of Him, he praises Him, he worships Him, he loves Him, he commits to Him, he asks for help. (Zarathushtra himself was the object of intense persecution because of his views). And he believes that prayers are always answered if they have two ingredients—good purpose and love. He says to God: "For I know that words deriving from good purpose and from love are not to be left wanting by you."[4]

NOTES

1. As written in the *Arda Viraz Namag,* [not one of my favourite books] as translated by Fereydun Vahman, and provided to me by my friend Farrokh Vajifdar of London.
2. Mirza, *Outlines of Parsi History,* p. 362, quoted from the historian Al-Biruni.
3. The Gathas appear as Yasna Chapters 28 through 34, and 43 through 51, and 53.
4. As translated by Insler, in *The Gathas of Zarathushtra* (Brill, 1975).

Published as Introduction to Dina G. McIntyre's book *Three Prayers and the Name of God,* Gatha Studies Trust, Glenshaw, U.S.A.

The Sacred and Reverent Fire of Zarathushtra

PESI MUNCHERJI

The "Avesta" teaches that every Fire, whether it be the fire giving warmth to the poor pavement-dweller, or the fire producing goods in a factory, contains the divine energy "athra," which connects every object in this world with "Ahura Mazda."

With the second millennium drawing to a close, one's thoughts go back to centuries past when our prophet Zarathushtra was born, and for all Parsis the world over 'Khordadsal' continues to be a day of prayer and rejoicing.

Zarathushtra is said to have been born nearly 3,300 years ago in Azerbaijan in Western Iran. Unlike other newborns, it is said, he smiled at his birth. He was the third of five children of Porushasp and his wife Dughdova. At the age of 7, Zarathushtra was sent to a learned teacher where he studied not only religion but also farming, cattle-raising and medicine. He spent his time in divine meditation on top of a mountain called "Ushidarena." But religion always dominated his mind.

During his life-time, he worked and looked after the poor and needy, was not afraid to go to the battle-field and attend on the wounded soldiers, always finding ways and means to remove the sufferings of his people.

It was on Mount Sabalan, at the age of 30, that Zarathushtra received his first revelation—FIRE—to be followed by six more, Sky, Water, Earth, Plants, Cattle and Man from "Ahura Mazda." The "Avesta" says: "athro Akumhe Mazdao puthro," which means "Fire is the son of Lord Ahura Mazda." Fire is respected in mostly all religions, and is considered the greatest and the most worthy of all worship. It is the divine energy which is the cause of all motion.

Just picture Zarathushtra, the mighty one, as he first spoke to the people, and taught them the truths that the FIRE had revealed to him. Picture him standing by the altar, speaking of what the FIRE had revealed to him. In one of the Oracles, it is said: "When thou beholdest a sacred fire, formless, flashing dazzlingly throughout the world; Hear thou the voice of the FIRE." As Zarathushtra spoke, there was at first no fire, only sandalwood in fragrant heaps. As the prophet stood there, he held a rod. As he raised that rod towards heaven, the heavens burst into fire, and some of these flames darted down below and the altar at his side was aflame, and the living fire round him made him a mass of flame as he spoke the "Words of the Fire" and proclaimed the everlasting truths. To the modern Zaroastrian, the "sacred fire" is the fire within oneself with a burning desire to always succeed. The "sacred fire" is something that propels a Zoroastrian into action. That "sacred fire" lets him rest only when his mission is accomplished.

Coming back to the life of the prophet, it is said, for 10 years Zarathushtra succeeded in getting only one follower, Maidhyoi Maonha—a lesson in the virtue of patience—and so he decided to go to the court of King Vishtasp in Iran, bearing the sacred fire called "Adar Burzin," and explained to him the way of the Wise Lord, "Ahura Mazda." He told the King: "Learn the rites and doctrines of the religion of excellence. For without religion there cannot be any worth in a king." The King's wise men, priests and magicians, questioned Zarathushtra for 3 days and 3 nights on every subject under the Sun, to which he had a ready answer. King Vishtasp was very much impressed, and decided to accept the doctrine of Zarathushtra. But his courtiers became jealous, and told the king, that Zarathushtra was a sorcerer and had him imprisoned.

At this time the king's favourite horse, "Aspa-Siha" (black horse), got paralyzed and could not move. The king's physicians and magicians failed to heal him. When Zarathushtra came to know of it, he sent word to the king: "If I cure your horse, will you do what I say?" When the king agreed,

Zarathushtra imposed 4 conditions on him: (1) The King must accept the new faith. (2) The Crown prince Asfandyar must defend it. (3) The Queen Hutaosha must accept the tenets of the new faith. (4) Those who had Zarathushtra imprisoned, must be banished from Iran. And as each leg of the horse straightened out, each of the 4 conditions were fulfilled.

Frashaoshtra, the King's trusted Minister, gave his beautiful daughter, Havovi, in marriage to Zarathushtra, who was by now forty-two years old. They had three sons and three daughters. The sons were named Isatvastar, Urvatatnar and Khurshid-Chichar. The three daughters were Freni, Thrity and Paoruchista.

Zarathushtra's teachings of the sacred scriptures from the "Zend Avesta" spread far and wide for 30 years, even to distant Tibet and China. Zarathushtra was the first prophet in human history to preach of one God, "Ahura Mazda," Lord of Life and Wisdom, based on Truth, Righteousness and Justice, Love and Compassion, and asked his people to always lead a charitable life, which the Parsis have practised over the centuries till today. Freedom of choice was his doctrine and teaching throughout his life.

When he was seventy-seven, Zarathushtra's death was sudden and tragic. While praying in the Fire Temple at Balkh, the Turanians entered the city. Tur-I-Baratur sought out the prophet and stabbed him in the back. The soldiers burnt the entire "Zend-Avesta," and set fire to the Fire Temple and the Palace, even the eighty priests who were praying in the temple at that time were slain. Zarathushtra threw at Tur, the assassin, the rosary (prayer beads) held in his hand, and there emanated from it such a splendid flood of light that its flame fell on Tur-I-Baratur and consumed him with Zarathushtra's last words: "May Ahura forgive you even as I do."

So ended the life of a great prophet, a great teacher whose philosophy of life, like the "sacred fire" always flies upwards with utterances of three simple words "humata, hukhta, havashtha," purity in thought, word and deed.

The Persian poet Firdausi, speaking of Zoroastrians in his famous epic, the "Shah Namah" wrote: "Maa gui ke atash parastaan budand. Parastandeh-e-pak yazdaan budand." Translated, it reads: "Do not call them fireworshippers. For they are worshippers of Ahura Mazda through fire."

Today the one question which is important in our daily lives is: "Who can tell what lies immediately ahead of us?"

Few in our small community realize what a dominant and big part religion plays in the lives of the few of us as compared with the millions of others in this world. Few we are, because our earlier Zoroastrians were converted; besides Zoroastrianism does not allow people to be converted to our religion. We are confronted with the question, particularly today, "How to keep this great religion of ours alive?" Any human being will agree that Prayer is the biggest and strongest branch of any religion, and if you neglect prayer, you are apt to break that strongest branch and fall headlong. Prayer is a relationship with the divine expressed in words and also in silence. It is a habit of life. Prayer keeps us at peace not only with ourselves, but with others as well. With prayer we are living in the awareness of God's presence.

In the "Zend-Avesta," which is attributed to the authorship of Zarathushtra, it is said: "Ahura Mazda, Lord of Wisdom (Ormuzd) the god of the Sky, who is symbolized by the Sun, or the Fire or light, is eternal justice and righteousness (Asha), and with him are the 'Amshaspande,' the immortal saints, personifications of the virtues which Ormuzd has created in Man. Against him is 'Ahriman,' the prince of darkness, who sprang from the spirit of Evil, 'Angro-Mainyu.'"

In no way are we idolaters or fire-worshippers, we Parsis revere the Sun and Fire only as a symbol of divine majesty.

Religion is for the masses, and religious sentiments are common in all individuals. Just as we have popular poetry, and the popular wisdom of proverbs, so do we have religion, or religions too, and one of them is Zoroastrianism. Just as mankind needs an "Interpretation of life," so do we. There is as much reason today as there ever was for believing that our religion will never die. What is it that brings God and Man together? It is prayer. In the words of Shakespeare:

> My words fly up, my thoughts remain below:
> Words without thoughts, never to Heaven go.

If there is wisdom, there must be the source from which it comes. Ralph Waldo Trine in his book *In Tune with the Infinite* says: "All is from God and in Him, and there is nothing that is outside." For true worship, only God and the human soul are necessary, but a place of worship like an "Agiari" or "Atash Behram" brings in the true atmosphere and adds light to your prayer.

In our "Agiari" or "Atash Behram" burns a fire night and day; the fire which is the supreme symbol of God, a symbol of divine life, and that which is called the Son of "Ahura Mazda." Our prayers are addressed to the Fire thus:

> Happy is the man to whom thou cometh mightily, Fire, son of Ahura Mazda. More friendly than the most friendly, more worthy of adoration than the most worthy of honour. Mayest thou come helpfully to us at the greatest business. Fire, thou art acquainted with Ahura Mazda, acquainted with the heavenly. Thou art the holies of the same (the fire) that bears the name Vazista. Oh Fire, son of Ahura Mazda, we draw near to thee. ("Yasna" XXXVI. ii 4-10. Trans. Prof. Speigel)

In every religion, fire has been the symbol of significance, and has been revered by all religions, in one form of the other. "Ahura Mazda" is fire. Brahma is fire. The Jews worship their God as a pillar fire. And the Christians proclaim: "Our God is a consuming fire."

Courtesy: *Zend*, Quarterly House Magazine of Shree Parsi Panchayat, Vadodara, Vol. 2, No. 3, September 1999.

The Role of Parsi Entrepreneurs: 1750-1850

AMALENDU GUHA

Urbanization of the Community

Linked with the medieval trade routes between the northern plains and the Deccan as it was, the seaboard of the Gujarat region offered the most favourable sites for navigation and maritime trade in pre-British India. This partially explains the ascendancy of various Gujarati trading communities in India's entrepreneurial history. But while the Bania, Bhatia, Khoja, Bohra and other Gujarati caste groups had been traditionally associated with their banking and/or trading occupations, the Parsis were rather late comers into these fields. In the seventeenth century, some of them were, of course, engaged in supplying timber and water to anchored ships and in various handicrafts like carpentry, shipbuilding, weaving, brewing and perfumery. But by and large, theirs was an agricultural community.

Families with an artisan background were increasingly moving towards the townships of Surat, Bombay, Daman and Broach where the European East India Companies had located their early factories and could offer them skilled jobs. Some of them also entered trade and commerce in due course. By the end of the eighteenth century, they were already economically a viable community in these townships. At the same time, the recurrent famines in Gujarat during the year 1780-1840 forced thousands of Parsi villagers to take refuge in the city of Bombay, where they were provided with relief and job opportunities by the opulent Seths of their own blood. By 1850, about half of the Parsi community had become urbanized through a process of pull and push. This denoted a profound structural change in the Parsi society. Their new home, Bombay—an island producing within itself no articles of commerce—was, under British protection, ideally suited for enterpot trade, with an accent on foreign markets. From trade to industry was but another leap.

China Trade in Opium

The transformation of the Parsi artisans into merchant entrepreneurs during the first half of the nineteenth century is interesting in more than one respect. Under colonial constraints, the ship-wrights and other artisans could not emerge straight as independent capitalist shipbuilders from their handicraft base. It was necessary for them to enter the lucrative field of export trade in raw cotton and opium for primitive accumulation under British patronage. Thus, the rapid growth of Parsi mercantile capital, right from the beginning, was tied primarily to their sharing of foreign, particularly Chinese, markets with the British and secondarily to selling British goods in the home market.

When the trade with China was interrupted temporarily by the Opium War of 1839-42, several Parsis of Bombay committed suicide. Parsi opium traders became increasingly dependent on a single monopolistic European Agency House of China, Jardine Matheson and Co. Together with Remington Crawford and Co. and Jamsetji Jijibhai and Sons as partners, it had already formed the Malwa Opium Syndicate to control the market. Sir Jamsetji Jijibhai (1783-1859) who had been thus transacting more than one million pound worth of business with China and remitting 1,50,000 pounds worth of foreign exchange annually to London through this deal, became opulent no doubt. But the smaller traders found themselves cornered.

China Trade in Raw Cotton

China was the biggest purchaser of Indian raw cotton. But Manchester was interested in increasingly directing export towards Great Britain to build up stocks against exigencies of

American cotton supplies. It may be noted here that raw cotton exports to China from the ports of Bengal and Madras used to be subjected to an export duty of 8 annas and 9 annas, respectively, per mound until 1859, while those to UK or Europe from any Indian port had to pay no such duty. This discriminatory measure particularly affected the Parsi trading group as they had relatively a stronger position in the China trade. During the period 1833-46, Great Britain received on average only 40 per cent of India's exportable raw cotton surplus, the remaining portion going mainly to China.

Neither Indian nor British legislation had yet provided for limited liability before 1858, this could only be obtained through the medium of a Crown Charter, granted after a joint stock bank had met the requirements of the Colonial Banking Regulations. These circumstances forced the Oriental Bank Corporation, an Anglo-Parsi Joint concern, to shift its head office in 1845 from Bombay to London, much to the detriment of Parsi interests. It was then that it could at least obtain a Charter in 1851. However, the bank thereby ceased to be subject to the Indian legislation and to its Indian shareholders.

Moreover, the Parsis too could not escape from racial discrimination. The Canton Chamber of Commerce, established in 1834, did not even admit Parsi traders to its membership on the plea that the natives of India were not sufficiently qualified for negotiations with the Chinese. They were represented on the Bombay Chamber of Commerce by one or two members only. Even after the passage of the so-called "Black Act" of 1836 which had abolished racial discrimination in the civil courts throughout India, the European British subjects continued to be tried only by European magistrates and judges, in all criminal courts. This discrimination in the realm of justice made no exception of Parsis. Like other Indians, Parsi entrepreneurs too were second class citizens vis-a-vis their European commercial rivals.

Business Leadership and Caste Factor

How is it that the Parsis were in advance of other well-knit Western-Indian communities who had a much long experience of trade, insurance and banking and who had equally shared with the former the same advantages and disadvantages of a common habitat and environment? It has often been naively suggested that it was their freedom from the rigidities of a caste-society alone that helped them to seize economic opportunities as and when they came, for betterment of their lots. Their occupational mobility, unrestricted by caste factors, was no doubt an advantage.

The ascendancy of the Parsi business community could not be explained in terms of the caste factor alone. Other Gujarati trading castes, as reservoirs of accumulated business acumen for centuries, showed as much zeal as the Parsis in overseas trade.

Wadias and Banajis descended from shipcarpenters' families; Sir Jamsetji Jijibhai and Jijibhai Dadabhoy (1786-1849) were sons of a weaver and a master-tailor, respectively. But all of them had to go up the ladder via accumulation through overseas trade. Shipping and export-import trade were as much open to the Parsis as to others in Western India. Caste considerations did matter for a few occupations like brewing, sale of liquor and shoe-making so far as the Hindus were concerned. But they affected the overall supply of business leaders only marginally in these or other fields.

Parsis and Sanskritisation

Even the Parsis, despite their early British contacts and concomitant involvement in a Westernization process, were themselves a closed caste-group vis-a-vis the outer society. They constituted a rigid endogamous group with a Panchayat at its hand as the custodian of a strict Parsi way of life. Anyone not obeying the social code could be turned "out of caste." In the practice of child marriage, bigamy and several other superstitious rituals, they had already been aping the more dominant Hindu society, according to Panchayat's own assessment of the early nineteenth century situation. Thus, to a limited extent, the Parsis too were exposed to a process of Sanskritisation, while facing a challenge from Westernization. They were not partaking of food cooked by non-Parsis, nor did they intermarry or interline with the later. But they had already overcome their prejudices against occupations, such as smithy, involving use of "sacred" fire.

Parsis's Success Explained

Parsi success has therefore to be largely explained with reference to their greater ability to adjust themselves to European power under changed political circumstances. The strength of the Parsis lay in their relative non-involvement in earlier civil and military administrations run by Hindus and Muslims and the concomitant advantages, such as a claim to special favour from the new masters.

To sum up, the Parsi ascendancy in business and industries was caused by a combination of factors. They shared with other Gujarati trading communities the advantages of belonging to the economically most advanced region of India under given geographical and historical circumstances. Secondly, the fact that they had greater occupational mobility than others was also a factor so far as this small community was concerned.

Parsis were, on the other hand free from diverse social commitments. As demands on their leaders were not many-sided, they could devote their entire energies to economic self-help. They could continue to do so at last until 1850, undisturbed by political and social power struggles. They had no politics, and their public spirit and philanthropy were oriented more to the relief of their own people than of the society at large. And yet, despite their concern for group welfare, their business organisation could effectively accommodate the spirit of individualism, on the one hand, and that of co-operation with other groups, on the other. They were able to integrate their interests particularly with those of the British, without any reservations whatsoever. This largely explains their achievements.

Methods of Business Organisation

In the beginning, business was organised on family basis. Later, two or three members of the same extended family would run a formal partnership for limited purposes. By the early nineteenth century, such partnerships were no more limited to closed family circles. Partnerships with Europeans, Hindus and Muslims were quite common. Muncherji Jamsetji Wadia (1780-1872) was a partner of J.A. Pope in one field and of Motichand Aminchand in another field. After the dissolution of the partnership with Pope, he had a Portuguese partner for some time. Sorabji Mancherji Readmoney had Muhammad Ali Bin Muhammad Hussain Rogay, a Konkani Muslim as a partner for a long time. Sir Jamsetji had his father-in-law as his partner till 1818 and Motichand Aminchand thereafter till around 1835. These are a few examples. When a son came of age, he generally ran business on his own account. That is, he was taken into the family business as a working partner and was, at the same time, free to start new firms in partnership with others.

A Parsi capitalist normally started his career not in his own family firm, but as an employee of a European firm. This apprenticeship provided him with a training in European business methods which he could make use of, later, in his own independent business career. This innovation made all the difference between Parsi business leaders and those emerging from traditional trading groups. Moreover, amongst the Parsis, there were deliberate attempts to channelise inherited capital into fewer hands.

In the eighteenth century, Manokji Nowroji Seth is said to have tried to introduce primogeniture in his family. Taking advantage of the absence of a written code of Parsi customary law, attempts were kept up till 1837 to interpret Parsi inheritance according to English Law, so that landed property in the Island of Bombay could pass undivided to the eldest son. But consequent upon the mass petition dated November 20, 1835, the Government passed Act No. IX of 1837, bringing an end to these attempts and establishing an equalitarian inheritance as was customary. However, by enactment of Wills, entrepreneurs often circumvented the customary division of property. Besides, inbreeding to a fantastic scale as well as the institution of adoption of a near relative as son (in the absence of one) also helped to postpone division of family property.

Philosophy of Collaboration

Lastly, our study of the Parsi capitalists to 1850 reveals that the entire Parsi community was undergoing profound changes simultaneously in several fields—social, religious and economic. They seized every opportunity to have Western education, general as well as vocational. On the one hand, a socio-religious reformation movement cum renaissance stirred them up into self-consciousness and on the other, they allowed themselves to be Anglicised at other levels. These developments were simultaneous with their search for new avenues of business for money-making and self-assertion.

Other Gujarati trading communities did not undergo such a multi-dimensional process of change. Yet, it is important to note, they did not lag far and long behind the Parsis. Despite a more conservative social outlook and a lack of modern education, they were not very late in following suit and becoming constituents of the Indian industrial bourgeoisie. The Parsi lead in industries was undoubtedly there, but it need not be exaggerated. Nor should the explanation of this lead be sought in terms of social division and caste orientation of the Indian capitalist class. Even the first Indian-owned cotton textiles enterprise, founded by C.N. Davar (1815-1873), a Parsi, was in a way a joint venture of the capitalists of western India. D.R. Gadgil has rightly pointed out that, despite dissimilarity of behaviour patterns, Indian businessmen belonging to different communities were seen to act together or operate as a single pressure group.

Courtesy: *Dipanjali*, January 2000.

Zoroastrianism and Parsis in India

S.D. NARGOLWALA

The subject itself can be divided into two parts (1) an explanation of the religion itself and (2) the history of Zoroastrianism and Zoroastrians down through the ages.

Zoroastrianism is not a religion in the sense in which the term is commonly understood. Zoroastrianism does not contain the ingredients which are ordinarily supposed to form part of religion viz., dogmatism, compulsions from without, blind faith, the fear of punishment and the expectation of future reward as the impelling forces in our daily life. Zoroastrianism is rather a scientific and rational explanation of existence, of reality as a whole, of man's place in it, his duties while in this life and the high destiny which he can achieve by establishing his conduct in accordance with the eternal and immutable law of Nature which Zarathushtra called the Law of Asha. Zoroastrianism is essentially based upon knowledge and illumination, therefore, our emblems are the Fire and the Sun, the latter being the source of all light and illumination. Far from discouraging enquiry and questioning, Zarathushtra welcomes a spirit of rational enquiry and is fully competent to offer a rational and scientific explanation. Therein lies the glory of this religion. The word, Zarathushtra, is composed of 'Zarath' golden, and 'Ushtra,' light, so Zarathushtra means "He of the Golden Light."

The era of Zarathushtra is a matter of some controversy amongst scholars. Western scholars are tempted to place Zarathushtra as late as in 650 B.C., but this view is based upon equating Hystapes, the father of King Darius of the Achaemenian Dynasty (558-330 B.C.). with Vishtaspa who ruled in the Kyanian period (2,000-700 B.C.), and in whose time Zarathushtra really lived. From the internal evidence of the five *Gathas* (hymns) the work of the Prophet himself, philologists today put the date of Zarathushtra at about 2,000 B.C. or earlier.

"Zarathushtra is said to have been born probably in Rhages, now Rae, near Teheran." He went up the mountains of that province for meditation and preached his faith for many years among hostile tribes till he came to the court of Kava Vishtaspa, King of Bactria in the north-east of Iran which is today Balkh in Afghanistan. Tradition says that Zarathushtra laughed when born in contrast to all children who cry. All Nature rejoiced in that there was born one who would conquer evil and teach mankind the way to righteousness and happiness. Many attempts were made on the life of the child by black magicians but without success. As a young boy, he was placed under able teachers, but they soon found that he was more advanced than they. Zarathushtra spent several years in meditation and study pondering over the fundamentals of life and existence trying to find a rational explanation based upon the Law of Nature, *Asha*. We find in his writings questions and answers as to who sustains this earth, according to what laws do the sun, moon and the stars move in such harmonious order, what are good and evil, the relative and the absolute, the fleeting and the eternal? Finally he discovers the perfection which lies in the Absolute as possessing perfect wisdom, which Reality he calls Ahura Mazda, Lord of Life and Wisdom.

The religion of the Iranian peoples of his time was a primitive form of polytheism of Indo-Aryan origin based in part upon the *Rig Veda*. There were many deities who were worshipped each of whom had his priests claiming special tribute. Each family had sacred idols to ward off disease and ill fortune. The life of an Iranian in Zarathushtra's time, and indeed, of all the peoples of India, Babylonia and Assyria consisted in trying to wrest a bare subsistence from the soil and from their herds, trying to placate the many gods so as to avoid their wrath, and in meeting the demands of various kings and rulers.

Each tribe had different rituals, sacred obligations and customs. Feuds were frequent. No explanations were given to inquisitive minds other than to follow ancient mandates and taboos. To this Eastern World, Zarathushtra brought a new, universal concept of religion. His religion was not a set of superstitious rituals based on fears, but a universal call to a better life to be achieved with the aid of an *invisible* God of wisdom, truth, light and goodness. To those who enquired about the nature and the source of evil, he had an answer which, in essence, was adopted by most religions that followed his.

The tenets of the Zoroastrian religion are basically contained in the *Gathas*. Man is free to determine his life and faith. Through good thoughts, good words, good deeds, and purity of body and soul, he pays homage to and collaborates with Ahura Mazda, Lord of Life and Wisdom, in fulfilling the "divine purpose of His Holy Creation." By falsehood and wickedness, he increases the forces of Ahriman the Spirit of Evil. The creed of Zarathushtra was an optimistic one, for it predicted the triumph of good over evil. The Zoroastrian religion spread rapidly in the time of Kava Vishtaspa, and in subsequent conquests which extended the Persian Empire from India and Babylon to the Greek frontiers. The "Laws of the Medes and the Persians" were known everywhere as the personification of the wisdom of the East, as can be seen in the writings of Plato, Pliny and Plutarch. It is said that Zarathushtra himself, still active in the affairs of state at the age of seventy-seven, was killed by a Turanian soldier during an attack on the city of Balkh.

There can hardly be any question that Zarathushtra was the first man we know who gave a definitely moral character and direction to religion, and at the same time, preached the doctrine of monotheism which offered an eternal foundation of reality to goodness as an ideal of perfection. Zarathushtra showed the path of freedom to man, the freedom of moral choice, freedom from blind obedience to unmeaning injunctions, freedom from the multiplicity of shrines which draw our worship away from the single-minded chastity of devotion. Zarathushtra preached that the moral worth of deed comes from the goodness of intention, and the value of his religion was in upholding man in his life of good thoughts, good words and good deeds. Zarathushtra was the first prophet in history who emancipated religion from the exclusive narrowness of the tribal god, and offered it to the universal man. Without doubt, such a high conception of religion of the ultimate ideal of perfection which must be revealed to all humanity, even at the cost of martyrdom, is unique in the history of any religion belonging to such a remote dawn of civilization.

The active, heroic aspects of the Zoroastrian religion reflect the character of the people themselves. They had zest in life, and confidence in their own strength. They accepted this word in all seriousness. By force of will and deeds of sacrifice, they tried to achieve *Haurvatat,* wholeness, well-being, in this world, and *Ameretatat* immortality, in the next.

The religion of Zarathushtra is enshrined in the *Gathas,* sacred songs divided into stanzas and strophes. According to Iranian tradition, Zarathushtra composed around 100,000 such strophes, but only a few hundred are left with us today. Even from these, we are able to glean the philosophy of Zarathushtra and the great truths he taught. The five *Gathas* which have come down to us are:

(1) *Gatha Ahunavaiti,* on freedom of choice;
(2) *Gatha Ushtavaiti,* on supreme bliss (ushta);
(3) *Gatha Spenta Mainyu,* on the Holy Spirit;
(4) *Gatha Vohu Kshathra,* the gatha of the Good Kingdom;
(5) *Gatha Vshishtoishti*, the gatha of Sovereign Desire, the gatha of fulfilment.

The name given to each Gaṭha gives us a clue to its contents. The word, 'Ahu,' means life, energy, the moving force which operates in Nature, so the *Ahunavaiti Gatha* deals not only with the laws which operate in Nature, but also with freedom of choice, the creation of the world and the origin of evil. A study of the laws underlying the universe gives rise to a sense of sublimity. Hence, the second Gatha, the *Ushtavaiti* leads the reader to religious ecstasy showing the way to keep joy and happiness. The *Spenta Mainyu Gatha* deals with the essence of the absolute, the Spirit which permeates all existence and moves it. It unfolds the perfect wisdom which activates the Divine Plan. Man cannot comprehend this perfection and wholeness until he develops his own mental faculties and acquires moral strength. This is the gist of the fourth Gatha, the *Vohu Kshathra.* The fifth gatha, the *Vshishtoishti,* is the gatha of fulfilment wherein a series of admonitions are laid down for man to follow.

With Ahura Mazda, the supreme Creator and Ruler of the Universe, six other Beings are associated in the Gatha. These Beings were later named the *Amesha Spenta,* Holy Immortals, or Immortal Shining Ones. They are aspects of the God-head, and are considered as divine energies radiating from Ahura Mazda in streams of light, as we find in the description of Asha, the Divine Law, given in the *Haptan Yasht.* These six Divine Powers or Energies are:

Asha, the Divine Law, Truth, Righteousness and Justice;
Vohu Mana, the Good Mind, representing Divine love that transcends all bounds of time and space;
Kshathra, the Power and Majesty of Ahura Mazda, His Choice Kingdom;
Kshathra vairya, the creative activity in the service of mankind;
Kramaiti, Divine Devotion, stability, loyalty, the love of God in our hearts. She reveals to us the Bhakti Marg, as in the *Gita.*
Hauvatat—Wholeness, Well-being, Perfection;
Ameratat—Immortality;

With Ahura Mazda at their head, the Seven Amesha Spenta are collectively known as the *Hafta Amshashpands.*

The language in which the *Gathas* are written is not known, but is loosely termed Gathia Avestan. It bears a strong affinity with Rig-Vedic Sanskrit. Scholars are led to surmise that both languages appear to have been derived from a common language which was in existence amongst the Aryans before they separated into different groups. The Avestan language in which most of the Zoroastrian scriptures have come down to us came into existence some three hundred years after the era of Zarathushtra, according to earlier scholars. However the recent thinking of scholars on this subject of difference in the language of the Gathas and most of other Avesta is explained by the difference in locale. The Gathas were written, at least most of the Gathas (Divine Songs), when Holy Zarathushtra was meditating in a mountain (Ushidaren awakening), probably Demavand, whereas other Avesta were written, very likely by his immediate disciples, in Eastern Iran (Bactria). Lengthy commentaries were written on the *Gathas* and on the main principles of the religion. During this period, the *Yashta,* long poems of praise, and *Nvaeshes,* shorter poems of praise, were composed. In the Zoroastrian calendar of thirty days, every day of the month has a name, and it is likely that one Yasht was devoted to each day. Only a few of the Yashts, however, have survived.

Zarathushtra preached his religion in the Kyanian period of Iranian history. After the overthrow of that dynasty, c. 700 B.C., there were centuries of darkness and unsympathetic rule till Cyrus the Great established the famous Achaemenian Empire 2,500 years ago. There was a sudden revival of the Zoroastrian religion. Ancient texts, like the *Gathas,* and later Avesta writings were thrown together in one omnibus book named the *Yasna* or *Yezashne,* each chapter thereof being known as a Ha. In this Book of Worship, the *Gathas* are not placed in running order, but interspersed twice by other chapters. The *Vispered* and *Vendidad* are writings of this period.

Upon the conquest of Iran by Alexander the Great in 330 B.C., there ensued another long and dark period for Iran. The entire library at Persepolis, containing a mammoth collection of books, manuscripts and other writings of learning along with the entire Avesta writings were burnt to ashes by Alexander. Legend has it that this was done by Alexander in a drunken state at the instance of his courtesan Thafs who was enraged with the Iranians as her advances had been rejected by a respectable Iranian General. The Zoroastrian scriptures were once again neglected and disjointed until another great Zoroastrian, Ardeshir Papakan, founded the last Zoroastrian empire in Iran called the Sassanian Empire (226-651 A.D.). During this period, the Scriptures were once again gathered together, chiefly through the zeal of the great Dastur, Tansar, and recast. The court language of the Sassanians was Pahlavi, while the spoken language of the common people was Pazand from which modern Persian is derived. It was during this period that a concise prayer book was composed, called the *Khorda Avesta,* or more popularly, *Khordeh Avesta,* the Little Avesta. It contains not only Avestan papers, but passages in Pazand also, with commentaries on astronomy (*Behram Yasht*), medicine (*Ardibehesht Yasht*) and cosmogony (*Farvardin* and *Zamved Yashts*).

The Sessanian Empire succumbed to the Arabs at the Battle of Nihavand in 641 A.D. The last Sassanian King, Yazdegard III, fled to Merv where he lived in hiding for ten years till he was discovered by one of his own generals and assassinated by a lowly miller at the instigation of the Governor of Merv, Mahwi Suri, also pronounced Mahui Suri, on Roj Aneran, Mah Khordad, English date 10th September 651 A.D. The Arab conquest was complete. Those who wished to remain Zoroastrians went to the mountains of Kohistan in Khorasan where they eked out a miserable existence for nearly one hundred years. Others were forcibly converted to Islam.

As Zarathushtra insisted upon acting good to one's fellow men, the motto of the religion became "Good thoughts, good words, good deeds." The two great emblems of the faith are *Hvare kshaeta,* the glorious Sun, and *Atar khvareh,* the radiant Fire. Ahura Mazda is said to have "the most luminous of all luminous bodies" which is "clothed in the most glorious of all glorious lights, the Sun." (*Haptan Yasht*) Fire is called "the holy sign" of Ahura Mazda, and is "the son of Ahura Mazda." (*Haptan Yasht*) Just as physical fire burns up any filth flung into it, but itself remains pure and bright, even so, the Fire of Thought must burn up the Lie, the *Drui*, in our hearts and minds so that thought, word and deed may be dedicated to *Asha,* the Truth. Hence, Zoroastrians build Fire Temples as places of worship. There are three grades of Fire Temples: *Atash Behram, Atash Adaran, Agvary* or *Dar-e-Meher* and *Atash Dadgah* or the household fire in every Zoroastrian home. The first *Atash Behram* was consecrated in 790 A.D. in Sanjan, from the Alat (instruments) which the Parsis had brought with them from Khorasan. It was this Sacred Fire kindled after their coming to India, the Iran Shah, which is to this day held in special reverence by the Parsis of India. After many vicissitudes, the Holy Iran Shah came to rest in 1742 A.D. in Udvada, a small village about 100 miles from Bombay to which the Parsis make pilgrimages from India, and from other countries of the world.

As Zarathushtra laid such emphasis on freedom of choice, a child born of Zoroastrian parents is not considered a Zoroastrian till initiated to the fold by the *Navjote* ceremony. The word 'Navjote' means a new initiate who offers Zoroastrian prayers. The Navjote Ceremony in Iran is known as Nozad (a new birth) ceremony, on the supposition that the soul is now born into a new life of spiritual activities. The ceremony of initiation consists of the investiture of the child with the sacred shirt called *Sudreh* and a sacred thread called *Kusti.* The Navjote ceremony among the Parsis corresponds to the conformation ceremony among the Christians, except that with Zoroastrians, the Navjote is obligatory. It is performed at any time after attaining the age of seven and before completing the age of fifteen, and usually performed at the age of seven or nine or eleven. Thereafter, the child continues to wear the *Sudreh* and *Kusti,* and perform the Kusti ritual with the prescribed prayers, throughout life. The sudreh is made of pure, white muslin or cotton, while the Kusti is woven of seventy-two threads of fine, lamb's wool; representing the seventy-two chapters of the *Yasna,* the most sacred of our texts because it contains the *Gathas* of Zarathushtra. In the Pahlavi texts, the *Sudreh* or *Sudra* is described as "Vohu Manik Vastra," the Garment of Good Mind. It has a very small pocket in front called the *Kisseh-i-Kerfeh,* or pocket of good deeds. This is intended to be a constant reminder to every Zoroastrian to offer up to his Maker, every night, at least one square inch of good he has tried to perform during the day. The word 'Kusti' means a waist band. Being tied thrice round the waist, it points to the trinity of good thoughts, good words, good deeds. These form a barrier insulating the individual from all that is evil.

After the Navjote, the next most important ceremony in the life of a Zoroastrian is usually that of marriage. In former times, the ceremony began with the young couple sitting facing each other. The officiating priest would then place a cloth between them and tie the ends round their chairs. He would then take the bride's right hand and place it in the groom's right hand and tie their hands seven times with a piece of twine. An assistant priest, holding the *Afarghan,* would stand beside the senior priest. Prayers would then be recited. At a signal from the officiating priest, the assistant fed the fire with sandalwood and incense. At this point, the cloth curtain between the young couple was removed and everyone clapped their hands. The bride and groom threw a fistful of uncooked rice which they had been holding in their left hands on each other. This action symbolized prosperity. After this, the marriage ceremony continued as prescribed.

Today, the bride and groom sit side by side during the marriage ceremony. The parents and relatives of the couple sit behind their respective children. Beside them stand the witness to the marriage. Two priests stand in front of the couple and the ceremony begins. During the recital of the legal formula, the priest asks the witness on behalf of the groom's family, the following: "In the presence of this company that has met together in the city of.............on.............day.............in the year.............of Emperor Yazdegard of the Sassanian Dynasty of auspicious Iran, say whether you have agreed to take this maiden.............by name, in marriage for this bridegroom, in accordance with the rites and rules of the mazdaysnans promising to pay rhe 2,000 *dirams* or pure white silver, and two *dinars* of real gold of the Niapur coinage?" Then the witness from the bride's side is asked: "Have you and your family with righteous mind, and truthful thoughts, words, and actions, and for the increase of righteousness, agreed to give for ever this bride in marriage to..........?" The witness replies: "I have agreed."

Next follows the most crucial part of the ceremony. The priest turns first to the groom, then to the bride and asks: "Have you chosen to enter into this contract of marriage up to the end of your life with righteous mind?"

The entire formula is repeated thrice, and thrice both bride and groom must reply: "Pasande Kardam" (I approve). If either party refuses to answer, the marriage ceremony is interrupted there and then, and no priest dare marry the couple against their wish.

Next follow some beautiful admonitions and benedictions in Pazand and Avesta. The entire ceremony is recited even in Sanskrit, recalling the early days of the Parsi settlers in India when Sanskrit was the language of educated Hindus. While reciting these benedictions, the priests throw grains of uncooked rice on the couple to symbolize prosperity and plenty. The ceremony concludes with a final blessing.

The priests are then presented with beautiful Kashmir shawls and some cash. After embracing their parents, the couple leave and go to the Fire Temple to pay their homage to the sacred fire. Again, prayers are said and sandalwood and incense offered to the fire, and the *Atash Nvaesh* recited.

The couple now return to the assembly where they meet their guests.

When the guests have departed, and the family have had their dinner, the bride goes to the groom's house, accompanied by members of her family. She holds a small wick lamp in a protective silver vase. The light should not go out on the way to her new home. At the threshold, her husband awaits her. He lifts her over the lintel, or else she crosses it, right foot first. The little wick lamp is kept burning in the bridal chamber all night.[1]

Some of the most beautiful prayers are connected with the funeral ceremonies of the Zoroastrians which continue for four consecutive days. Again, on the tenth day after death, certain papers are recited both in the home and in the Fire Temple. After a month, prayers are again recited, and then annually on the death anniversary. The dead body is disposed of in Towers of Silence on the top of a hill. The flesh is devoured by birds of prey, and after a few days, the bones are lowered into deep wells at the bottom of which are layers of charcoal, lime and other minerals which slowly dissolve the bones. Thus the moral remains of the individual are disposed of in a most hygienic manner.

There are various other religious ceremonies, such as the consecration of a Fire Temple, purificatory ceremonies like the *Riman,* ceremonies in commemoration of the righteous dead such as the *Muktad,* and elaborate ceremonies like the *Izashne.*

The term 'Parsi' is derived from *Parsa,* the name of a province in south-western Iran in ancient times. *Parsa* was used also for the people of the province and the adjectival form *Parsik* is used for the people as well as the language of the province of Pars. When Cyrus, a celebrated resident of Pars, rose to power in his home-province in the 6th century B.C. and later extended his sovereignty over the whole of Iran, the term 'Parsis' was applied to the whole of the country. As explained above, the word 'Parsi' literally means 'a resident of Pars.' It is, therefore, originally an ethnic term and it was generally applied to the people of Pars. After the downfall of the Sassanian Empire and the Arab conquest of Iran, the term 'Parsi' was used for those residents of Iran who remained faithful to their ancestral Faith, namely Zoroastrian Religion. The term was specially used for the Zoroastrians of Iran to distinguish them from those Iranians who discarded their ancestral Faith and embraced Islam. Since those days the term 'Parsi' refers to the original residents of Iran and their descendants professing the Zoroastrian Religion, and living in Iran, India and elsewhere.[2]

Let us now turn to the Parsis in India. Around 766 A.D., a small group of Iranian Zoroastrians set sail in open sailing vessels, and landed at Div or Diu, a tiny island at the tip of the Kathiawar coast. There they settled for nineteen years to practise their faith in peace. For some obscure reason, they again set sail in open sailing vessels and landed at the fishing village of Sanjan where Jadi Rana or Jadhav Rana gave them refuge.

The Parsis spread in small colonies all along the west coast of Gujarat as we learn from the only written document on the early history of the Parsis, the *Kissa-i-Sanjan*, the Story of Sanjan, a chronicle in Persian couplets by Behman Kaikobad Sanjana, a Dastur or High Priest of Navsari, and dated 1600. Despite its late date, and some discrepancies, the *Kissa* is a very valuable document, more so as we have no earlier testimony on the subject. Between the 8th and 15th centuries, the Parsis settled in various small towns on the Gujarat coast.

The Parsis settled down as farmers and agriculturists, fruit growers, toddy planters, carpenters and weavers. Not only were they excellent weavers, they also gave India three of her most ancient crafts, namely the *Surti ghat*, the *garo* and the *tanchoi*. The *Surti ghat* is a soft silk with a satin finish on one side. In the past, the thread was woven by little children, aged four to six years, in damp, half-lit cellars, after which the thread was slowly exposed to light. The hand-woven silk was then dyed in vegetable dyes concocted from powdered roots and herbs, the favourite colours being a vivid tomato red, Tyrian purple, bright pink, dove grey and saffron. The material thus woven was so strong that it was known as *Surti ghat*, the Surat mountain, the weavers coming from the town. Today, textile factories in Surat and Ahmedabad produce *Surti ghat* by the yard, but the texture is not so fine, nor the colours as rich as the ancient handwoven specimens.

The *garo* and the *tanchoi* are both crafts originally imported from China. The *garo* is a fine silk with elaborate Chinese embroidery all over the sari. The motifs are birds, animals, flowers, pagodas and Chinese gardens. The *sali garo* gives the impression of fine twigs being woven into the material. Hence its name, *sali* meaning a twig. This effect was produced by removing a single thread every twentieth of an inch. The *sali garo* was usually plain, with beautiful, silk embroidered borders, often worked in *petit point*. The word *garo* means to strain through a cloth or sieve. The secret of this craft seems to be lost, for today, the only *garos* that exist are fifty to eighty years old, having come down from grandmother to grandchildren in Parsi families whose ancestors once had a lucrative trade with China. Like the *Surti ghat*, the *garo* is also found in deep, rich tones, such as purple, wine red, black, russet, though white cream coloured *garos* also exist.

The *tanchoi* is a fine, silk brocade with floral designs woven in. Three Parsi brothers learnt the secret of its weaving after a prolonged stay in China. They started a weaving centre of their own in Surat. They were known locally as *tanchoi* the three Chinamen, from *tan* meaning three, and *choi* meaning Chinese. Their surname was Joshi, and for years the weaving centre was known as Joshi-ni-haveli, the Joshi mansion. Their descendant, Kaikhushrau Sorabji Joshi (d. 1958), had his weaving centre in the Turkwadi suburb of the Moglisarai district of Surat. Saris woven in this rich brocade were worn only on auspicious occasions such as Navjotes and weddings. Joshi looked after his craftsmen as if they were members of his family. His fame, and that of his craftsmen, spread all over India and reached the ears of Gandhiji. He immediately set off on foot to visit the humble weaving centre. He was so gratified with what he saw that he patted Joshi on the back and announced that when Independence had been won, Joshi would be invited by the Indian Government to organize *Tanchoi* weaving centres throughout the country. Gandhiji kept his promise. By 1948, Joshi was employed as a senior official of the All Handicrafts Board. Before he died, Joshi lived to see the *tanchoi* sari woven in ever new and lovely designs in the finest of fine brocade in weaving centres which stretch from Kashmir to Kanya Kumari. Surat and Hyderabad, however, take the lead in this handicarft.

A new era in the history of the Parsis begins with the rise of British and Portuguese power in India and the development of Bombay. The Parsis became entrepreneurs and leading businessmen and industrialists.

The three Parsis most closely associated with the Indian National movement in the nineteenth century were Dadabhai Naoroji (1825-1917), Sir Pherozeshah Mehta (1845-1915) and Sir Dinshaw Wacha (1844-1936).

The first Parsi woman to carve for herself an honoured niche in the national movement was Bhikaji Cama (1861-1936). The turning point in her life came when she attended the first historic session of the Congress in Bombay. From that moment, she became an ardent patriot. Another well-known freedom fighter was Rustomji Jivanji Chorkhodu (1864-1924). Rustomji joined the Satyagraha movement in Africa, started by Gandhiji in 1894, and became an ardent follower of the Mahatma.

The greatest service Rustomji performed was saving the life

of Gandhiji. On his second visit to Durban, when Gandhiji was in imminent danger of being lynched by an irate mob, Rustomji sheltered him and smuggled him to safety at the risk of his own life and property. The history of the political freedom movement in India is studded with Parsi names, too numerous to mention individually.

In commerce and industry, the names of the Wadias, the Banajis, the Jeejeebhoys, the Petits, the Jehangirs, the Tatas deserve mention. They were the pioneers of the ship building industry, the textile industry, the iron and steel industry. the hydroelectric industry, the banking industry, etc. After the House of Tata, the next largest Industrial organisation run by Parsis is the Godrej organisation which was the first Indian manufacturer of a fireproof lining for safes, and of soaps etc.

In the professions, several Parsis have excelled. In the legal profession, Sir Dinshah F. Mulla rose to be a Member of the Judicial Committee of the Privy Council in England in 1930. Mr. Nani Palkhiwala is another famous Parsi name in the legal profession. In the Civil Services, many Parsis have held and continue to hold high offices. In the Armed Forces at one time or the other, the Chiefs of the three Services have been Parsis, the most famous of them being Field Marshal Sam Manekshaw. In medicine and science, there are famous names like Dr. Homi Jehangir Bhabha, Dr. D.N. Wadia, Dr. Homi Sethna, Dr. Jal Paymaster, Dr. Rustom Jal Vakil, Dr. Adarbad Irani, Dr. S.P. Shroff, etc. Parsis provided three well-known painters in Shiavax Chavda, Jehangir Sabawala and Homi J. Bhabha. Amongst sculptors, there are widely known names, such as the late Ardeshir M. Davierwala and Piloo Pochkhanawala. Parsis have also played a prominent role in the development of western music in India. A Parsi with an international reputation in the world of western music is the young conductor, Zubin Mehta. The Parsis were once again pioneers in the development of the theatre in India, as also the development of the cinema. Similarly, in literature and journalism, there are many widely known Parsis.

Thanks to the tolerance and hospitality of the people of India, the Parsis have been able to preserve their ancient religion and their own individual way of life for nearly 8,000 years. According to the 1977 Year Book of *Encyclopaedia Britannica,* there were, in June 1976, around 228,480 Zoroastrians in the world. Of these 224,700 are in Asia, 3,000 in Europe, 250 in North America, and 530 in Africa. The Parsi population in India is estimated at about 80,000 to 85,000. Pakistan has around 6,000 while Iran has 25,000 Zoroastrians.

Today, the community faces many serious problems. In a secular democracy after Independence, the importance of religion has diminished. There is a decline in the population to about 85,000 in the whole of India. Emigration accounts for only a small fraction of the dwindling numbers. Late marriages, inter-marriages and conversion to other faiths account for the rest. Centuries of inbreeding have also reduced the fertility rate among the Parsis. An acute shortage of low cost housing is aggravating the situation. There is a need for overhauling the laws governing the Parsis. There is also the need for broadening the franchise for election to the Trustees of the Bombay Punchayat. The indifference and ignorance prevailing among the Parsis regarding their spiritual heritage must be replaced by a deep and full understanding of the teachings of their Prophet Zarathushtra. Only then will Parsis be able to contribute their best to their great land which has been their home for nearly 1400 years.

NOTES

1. See Piloo Nanavutty, *The Parsis* (National Book Trust, India, New Delhi, 1977), pp. 25-27.
2. Dr. Mirza, *Outlines of Parsi History*, pp. 2-4.

Courtesy: *Dipanjali*, Dar-E-Meher Silver Jubilee Celebrations 1961-1986.

Causes and Effects of Decline in Parsi Population

RUSTOM S. GAE

In 1930s, the population of Parsis in India was more than 110,000. At the commencement of the millennium, it will be less than 70,000. Demographic study predicts that by the year 2025 when the population of India will be 125 million, the population of Parsis will dwindle to 25,000. The Parsi community has more persons as senior citizens over the age of 65 years than those under the age of 18. Death rate is more than twice the birth rate, leading thereby to gradual decline in the population every year.

Parsis: An Endangered Species

Parsis' contribution in fields like commerce, science, industry, medicine, law, arts etc. at one time evoked pride and admiration for the minuscule community of Parsis in the country. Even at present, the small but talented community has produced industrialists like Ratan Tata and Jamshed Godrej, jurists like Farrokh and Tehmpton Udwadia, composers like Zubin Mehta, novelists like Rohinton Mistry and poets like Keki Daruwalla. These distinguished persons have achieved good name and fame by their sheer ability and integrity. In spite of all these achievements, the diminishing population of Parsis depicts an alarming and gloomy picture for the entire community.

Fear is entertained that Parsis are an endangered species just like tigers and lions in India and their survival is at risk. Our inability to come to terms with the same is threatening to tear apart what was once a close-knit community in the country. Alarmed by the steady demographic decline of the Parsi population, the Bombay Parsi Panchayat, the apex body of the community in India, decided to sponsor the third child of every Parsi couple and look after all the material and educational needs of such children. However, this sop did not produce desired results towards increase of the population.

Inter-Caste Marriages

It is well accepted that marriage within the community has many advantages and should be encouraged, since it brings together couples brought up in the same environments and tradition of a common religion, culture and way of life. However, inter-caste marriages primarily of Parsi women marrying outside the community is the main cause of gradual diminution of Parsi population. With almost 25% of such women and almost as many not marrying at all, the patrilineal bias is being challenged by many Parsis. Such women are ostracized and looked down upon by the orthodox lobby of the community, though there is no bar against such marriages in the holy scriptures. Old rituals and customs must undergo a change with the advance of time and should, where required, be discarded for the survival of the community.

Such marriages are usually performed as civil marriages under the Special Marriage Act, 1954, each spouse to the marriage continuing to follow his or her own religion. The number of such marriages is increasing every year, causing thereby a serious problem for the survival of the community.

Status of Children of Parsi Women Married Outside

At the core of the controversy is the crucial issue whether children of a Parsi woman married outside the community can be considered Zoroastrians. Bombay Parsi Panchayat has not yet given its unequivocal approval to recognition of such children as Zoroastrians. The orthodox lobby is strongly against their recognition. This materially leads to a gradual depletion of the population aggravated by the increase in the number of Parsi women marrying outside the community. The irony of fate is that children of a non-Parsi woman who marries a Parsi are not subject to any such bar in the matter. Even some Trustees of the Bombay Parsi Panchayat have also cautioned the community about the gravity of the matter.

It may be unequivocally emphasized here that just as children of a non-Parsi woman married to a Parsi are considered Zoroastrians by performing their "Navjote" ceremony, similarly children of a Parsi woman married to a non-Parsi should also be considered Zoroastrians by performing their "Navjote" ceremony with the consent of the parents. This is the sine-qua-non for the survival of the minuscule community of Parsis in India. Such Navjotes are being performed in Mumbai, usually on the sly, and openly in Delhi and places outside Mumbai and abroad. Children undergoing such Navjotes should be gracefully accepted by the community without any mental reservation or demur. It is considered that if the matter is agitated in a court of law, the judgement would very likely be in favour of recognizing such children as Zoroastrians, more so after the commencement of the Constitution of India providing for the equality of sexes. Every effort should therefore be made to ensure the survival of the small, but still unique, ethnic group of Parsi Zoroastrians in India by recognizing such children as Zoroastrians.

Some years ago, Trustees of the Bombay Parsi Panchayat passed a resolution allowing Parsi women marrying outside the community under the Special Marriage Act, 1954, to avail of Doongerwadi facilities on their death in Mumbai. In the same magnanimity, they should accept children of such Parsi-women as Zoroastrians on performing their Navjote ceremony. In the larger interests of the community, Trustees should give a lead in the matter and thereby open the door for increase of the Parsi population.

Other Causes of Diminution of Population

Other causes of diminution of population include (a) migration, (b) marriage of women at an advanced age, (c) falling birth rate and small families (d) unwillingness to leave Mumbai or live in joint family on marriage (e) economic independence of educated youth and (f) high standard of living by traditionally following Western styles and habits.

Marriage at an Advanced Age

Several economically independent Parsi women refuse to leave Mumbai on marriage and decide to marry after they are well established in profession or business. This virtually results in promising young men marrying outside the community. Craze of living in that over-crowded city, having serious housing problem, should be given up by the youths to improve their future prospects of life in India.

Opportunities Available to Youths

Ample opportunities are available to the educated youths for work or employment in places outside Mumbai. Gujarat is fast developing and new industries have started in Vapi, Atul, Surat and other places in South Gujarat not far from Mumbai. If the youth get proper guidance and help for self-employment in cottage and small scale industries or for work in factories in these places, it will be an encouraging factor to increase the population of Parsis in the State of Gujarat.

Migration

In view of globalization and liberation policy adopted by the government of India during recent years, there are several attractive posts at handsome remuneration available to talented youth in the country. They should compete and avail of the same by giving up the glamour of foreign assignments and posts which in several cases is a mere hallucination. Restrictions imposed on emigrants are severe and job opportunities are on a decline. Higher education specially in technical fields like engineering, computer, medicine, etc. affords good opportunities to promising youth to prosper in our own country.

As an incentive to the promising youths of the Parsi community, the Bombay Parsi Panchayat may set up a venture capital fund, having money from various funds under its control, to encourage them to start business and industry in India rather than going abroad for the purpose. The spirit of entrepreneurship and zest which once prevailed in the community is now lacking and should be encouraged and developed.

Promising young boys go to foreign countries for higher education and subsequently migrate to those countries, reducing thereby the chances of Parsi women finding suitable spouses for marriage in India. Several women do not want to leave India and migrate abroad and that creates further problems in the small community. There is some substance in these grievances and this needs attention of the leaders of the community including the Trustees of the Bombay Parsi Panchayat.

Reservation of Seats in Educational Institutions

Difficulty in getting admission in colleges and other educational institutions experienced by the youths, specially in technical subjects and high speciality courses, is well known. For the purpose they have to run from one institution to the other in the city and at times to different cities. High percentage of reservation of seats for Scheduled Castes is a serious handicap. Fortunately, the Supreme Court has recently held that special provisions like reservations for Scheduled Castes, Scheduled Tribes and other backward classes are not permissible in terms of national interest for admission to super speciality courses in medicine and engineering, where merit alone should be the sole criterion for selection. In another recent case it held that employees recruited under the reservation policy cannot continue to claim seniority over the general category colleagues as a matter of right. This will serve as a booster to talented youth in getting admission to higher studies in educational institutions.

Reservation percentages at times even exceeding 50% followed by some states place members of minority communities to a great disadvantage, since only a very small percentage of seats is reserved for these communities. In spite of their obtaining very high percentages of marks, far in excess of the minimum qualifying marks prescribed for the general public, they find it extremely difficult to get admission in medical and engineering colleges in these states. Now that competitive merit will be the only criterion for selection, these youth will have wider base for admission. Above decisions of the Supreme Court will thus be really beneficial to the youth and they should take full advantage of the same. They should compete for admission in courses of medicine and engineering. This should be done before any legislative measures are adopted by the government to sanctify reservation percentages.

Reservation for Minority Communities in Educational Institutions

As regards the small quota reserved for minority communities, educational institutions usually want proof at the time of admission of the candidates that they are members of the minority communities. Notification dated 23 Oct. 1993 issued by the Ministry of Welfare, Government of India, under section 2 C of the National Commission for Minorities Act, 1992 notifies Muslims, Christians, Sikhs, Buddhists and Zoroastrians (Parsis) as the minority communities. Members of minority communities should take full advantage of this Notification, while seeking admission in Educational Institutions.

Benefits of Gujarati as Mother Tongue

Youths having Gujarati as their mother tongue have one more benefit for getting admission in colleges and other educational institutions in Mumbai, Pune and other places in Maharashtra administered and managed by Gujarati Trusts and Institutions. Gujarati educational Institutions enjoy reservation up to 50% of the seats for candidates in Maharashtra having Gujarati as their mother tongue. In the case of Parsis, the BPP issues certificates as required by colleges that the mother tongue of Parsi candidates is Gujarati. This will also encourage Parsis to have workable knowledge of Gujarati which seems to have been neglected in some quarters in the community. This will further enable them to read and understand religious books written or transliterated in Gujarati. It is strongly recommended that Parsi youths should avail of the above facility, while seeking admission to colleges and other educational institutions.

Optimism for Survival of Parsi Community

All these causes regarding diminution of Parsi population threaten to erase Zoroastrianism, the world's oldest prophetic religion, and its followers from the map of India. The community is facing the prospect of extinction, which should be well arrested and controlled by maintaining unity among its members. The gulf between those adopting the orthodox interpretation of Zoroastrianism and those clamouring for reform must be narrowed down by closing ranks and forging unity in the community. Customs and traditions, even old and time honoured, must change with advance of time. Those which have become redundant must be discarded, specially in the new millennium. The community must keep abreast of changes in the fast moving world.

Conclusion

The matter needs serious thought and consideration by the Trustees of the Bombay Parsi Panchayat and leaders of the community as well as wide discussion by way of full-fledged debates on the subject by the entire community in India as well as outside India. In spite of heavy odds, optimism needs to be entertained that the small but talented community, having become a part and parcel of India since last thirteen centuries, will survive by overcoming all these difficulties and hurdles and remove the grim prospect of extinction.

First published in *Dipanjali*, January 2000.

Zarathushtra in the Millennium

PILOO NANAVUTTY JUNGALWALLA

We are living in an age of extreme consumerism. Technological advances have outstripped moral values. Mother Earth is ravaged as never before. Her mountains and lakes, rivers and oceans, her forests and fields are polluted to such an extent that it is difficult to undo the damage. Communication between countries and individuals is now so close that every one desires a place in the sun. What value has Zarathushtra's teachings in such a ruthless world?

Zarathushtra is the first prophet in history to preach of one supreme God, Ahura Mazda, Lord of Life and Wisdom. Moreover, Ahura Mazda and the Truth or Asha are one (Ys. 28.8; 29.7). He rules Man and the Universe through His six Powers, the Amesha Spenta, Immortal Shining Ones. These are Asha, Truth, Justice, Law and Order, Vohu Mana, Good Mind, embodying Ahura Mazda's loving goodness and care for all beings; Kshathra, Power, Sovereignty, Armaiti, Love and Devotion, and lastly, the twins, Hauvatat, Perfection, and Ameretat, Immortality. Traditional teaching explains this working in a beautiful image, the rainbow. "Just as a rainbow has seven colours, but is one rainbow, so Ahura Mazda and His Powers are one."

They dwell in Man and in the Universe. They can be invoked through prayer, embodied in our Mantras, Sacred Words of Power, found in our scriptures, the Avesta. Ahura Mazda created a perfect world wherein plant, animal and mankind lived in harmony. How then did Evil come into existence?

To explain this situation, Zarathushtra uses the legend of the Twin Mainyu or Twin Spirits, the sacred and designed for the fulfilment of both husband and wife. In his last Gatha which celebrates the marriage of the Prophet's youngest daughter, Paoruchista, the officiating priest says: "better and the bad. They are in opposition to each other in thought, word and deed. They come together and create gaya, or mortal life, and ajyaiti, non-life, that is, physical death. Gaya has to be distinguished from ahu, eternal life which cannot be destroyed. Now one of the Twins chose to do evil. Immediately, there sprang up Aishma, Wrath, and the Druj the Lie. They poisoned the whole of existence. So we live in this dualistic world of Good and Evil. Which do we choose?"

Choice is at the heart of Zarathushtra's teachings, and this is very much a part of the Millennium world, where each desires to gain fulfilment individually. Zarathushtra does not mince words when making his choice.

> Down with Wrath!
> Crush Cruelty,
> You who would maintain through Truth
> The widespread penetration of the Good Mind
> In whose company walks the just man . . . (Ys. 48.7)

He insists that every one must take full responsibility for his/her actions. He makes no distinction between the sexes: "Forth with them all (man and woman) will I cross the Bridge of Judgement." (Ys. 46.19)

Moreover, Zarathushtra claims that getting, the physical world, and menog, the mental world are one world, the two sides of the same coin, and both are sacred, and to be enjoyed. Our bodies are sacred and so must be kept clean and in perfect health. Food is sacred and to be relished but not to the point of disgorging what one has eaten. Sex is sacred and meant to be a thrilling experience, and therefore, not to be desecrated. Marriage is "May each of you strive with the other to attain truth." (Ys. 53.5) This will lead the couple to "a blessed existence." Friendship is sacred and not to be betrayed. Zarathushtra longs to be a friend of Ahura Mazda, so that hand in hand both may achieve the Frashokereti, the wondrous renewal of existence which will come about at the end of Time.

Not only are human relationships sacred, but Mother Earth

and all her creatures, plants and animals, rocks and stones, all are sacred and meant to be nurtured. This links Zarathushtra with current theories on ecology. In our Yashts and Nyaeshes, the concluding paragraph always mentions "the sacred Waters and Plants." Man is responsible for the prevention of vegetable and animal life and even of mountains which should not be blasted out of existence. The beauty of a landscape also demands to be preserved so as to be enjoyed by all. Hence one may conclude that Zarathushtra is, par excellence, the prophet of the Millennium.

Interview with Mrs. Piloo N. Jungalwalla
by Narayani Ganesh

Q. For how long have you been working on the translation and commentary?

A. Officially, for the last seven years with Farrokh Vajifdar, a linguist who is also my guru. But unofficially, I began many many years ago. Way back in 1952, I did a translation with our High Priest, Dastur Bode. But then at that time, I knew too little in spite of which it was quite well received. You see, it was written straight from the heart.

Q. The book has a beautiful colour illustration of Zarathushtra holding a stick in his right hand and the left hand is half raised as though he is saying something. Is it stained glass?

A. Yes, it is indeed very beautiful. It is the stained glass window in the little Agyari in Bandra, Bombay. There is also a beautiful painting reproduced in the book that illustrates the beginning of Creation as conceived by Ahura Mazda, who has presented the legend of Creation in a unique manner, in a Blaze of Light. Man and the Universe are governed by Ahura Mazda through His six special Powers which emanate from Him—Asha, Truth, Justice, the Cosmic Order, and Vohu Mana, the Good Mind. Asha, is like the Vedic Rita—the Cosmic Order, Dharma, Righteousness. The range of God's Creation is fascinating, especially in the eyes of a child—He creates the mighty elephant as also the minute ant!

Courtesy: *Dipanjali*, Jan. 2000

Zoroastrian Community and Its Future

NOVY KAPADIA

In the afternoon they came unto a land in which it seemed always afternoon.
All around the coast the languid air did swoon.
Breathing like me that hath a weary dream.

The above-mentioned lines from Tennyson's poem "The Lotos-Eaters" aptly sum up the conditioning and attitude of mind of Zoroastrian community concerning its future and existence. Perplexity, uncertainty and doubt come to the forefront in any discussion on the future of the Zoroastrian community or religion. Like the sailors in Tennyson's poem, a languid air of uncertainty seems to have overcome many Zoroastrians as regards the future of their community. They seem to be plunged into a morass of self-doubt, hesitation and apathy in spite of the various controversies that envelop the religion and future existence of the community as a whole.

Amongst those who care, there is a sense of weariness in spite of the anguish of the possible extinction of the Zoroastrian community itself. However, amongst a large cross-section of Zoroastrian society, caught in the whirlpool of twentieth century western culture of materialism, individualism and splintered personality, the attitude to community and religion is indifferent and at times even negative. Such an attitude is especially prevalent amongst the younger generation of the Zoroastrian community. In the rational scientific world of today, to retain loyalty and affection towards something diffused and detached like the development of religion or the well being of a community, people have to muster up faith. However, because of the causality and reasoning behind all natural phenomena, people mostly retain faith only towards things tangible. As a result of this, many people neglect community and religion, because it does not affect their daily lives, as obviously as say money and commerce, for instance, do. Owing to this, a vicious circle of indifference creeps into the younger generation of Zoroastrians. Their attitude can be best summed up by the lines in Verse 65 of the Rubaiyat of Omar Khayyam in the Fifth and last edition of the Fitzgerald edition.

> The Revelations of Devout and Learn'd
> Who rose before us, and as Prophets burn'd.
> Are all but stories which awoke from sleep.
> They told their comrades and to sleep returned.

Perplexity, doubt and indifference are some of the major attitudes of mind that exist amongst the Parsis as regards the future of their community and religion. This leads to the broader question and inquiry of what then does the modern Parsi identify and align themselves with. As research in psychology indicates, very often the motivating power in a man is his faith and identity in a particular creed and ideology, community or vocation. Thus the Zoroastrian community and its future can be viewed from two aspects of whether the identity of the average Parsi is being lost in this modern scientific world of changing traditions, rationalism and materialism or whether the religion itself is being allowed to wither away in a bid for progress towards equality and brotherhood amongst peoples of the world.

The Parsis, to a certain extent, bear a resemblance to the Jews, as having been driven from their homeland, they have an instinctive knack of adequately adapting themselves to the social structure and environment of the country in which they settle down. With a lot of perseverance, shrewd foresight and skill, the Parsis, especially in India and Pakistan, have made a name for themselves in the field of business and industry, and other professional services and skills such as doctors, lawyers, contractors, teachers, musicians, cricketers and so on. Owing to this, the Parsis always come in contact with the modern world of changing conditions and are accordingly absorbed in a stimulating environment of change. However, a point to be stressed is that it is only evident in recent times that the identity of the present Parsi is losing itself in the modern world, so as to lead to his neglecting both his religion and his community. Even earlier on, Parsis have always allied themselves to progress and in many fields have given the lead in adopting new techniques and ideas to improve and embellish outmoded contentions and beliefs. So it can be seen that progress and improvement did not act as a deterrent towards faith and belief. Thus it can be said that the modern Parsi is drifting and is a victim of circumstances and environment by getting absorbed in the world of flux, of change in social relationships and understanding of reality. The future of the Zoroastrian community as a whole, in terms of numerical progress, is being imperilled by the modern day Parsis losing themselves to their surroundings and treading an individual path instead of merging with the community and seeking solace in unity, understanding of their religion and mature relationship with people for the betterment of both self and community.

The reasons for present-day Parsi struggling for identity in the modern world of changing value systems are their dual existence, namely aping of Western value systems, the pulls of tradition, confusion on whether to get 'Indianised' or Westernized or another identity and the splintered family. Many Parsi children do not receive sufficient attention and information about the religion and the past from their parents who tend to gratify their pleasures as individuals rather than sacrifice in order to bring up a unified family. Lack of proper parental guidance has made many Parsi children indifferent to religion and even worship at the Fire-Temple is a mere ritual.

Amongst the religions of the world, it is said that the Zoroastrians are the least in numbers, though it is difficult to have an accurate account of the exact number as they are scattered in many countries throughout the world. Statistics prove that the Parsis are amongst the smallest communities in India.

Also, the steady decline in their numbers may soon lead to a state where the Zoroastrian religion is the first major religion in the world to become extinct. There are numerous reasons for the steady dwindling numbers of the Zoroastrian community. First and foremost, being a small community, most Parsis are comparatively well-off, and few live below appalling poverty-line of the subcontinent. Thus, there is no population explosion amongst the Parsis as extreme poverty does not drive any member of the community to a condition where procreation is the only form of recreation. Also the Zoroastrian community tends to be status-conscious and as practically all Parsi children get a good education, they realize the necessity of a small family. Again, owing to an uncertain or rather unclear past, there has never existed a pugnacious fanaticism towards the Zoroastrian religion by members of the community. As a result of this, very few Parsis would attempt desperate measures to salvage the future of the community.

However, it must be stated that the effects of inter-faith marriages is the most prominent amongst the innumerable causes for the steady decline in numbers in the Zoroastrian community. This is primarily owing to the peculiar rule which states that if a Parsi girl marries outside the community, then her offspring cannot be initiated into the Zoroastrian community. The rule is reversed for the Parsi males, whose offspring can be accepted as Zoroastrians, even if they marry outside the community. So in most cases when a Parsi girl marries outside the community, then her children are lost to the folds of the Zoroastrian religion. This paradox exists because most Parsis are very effective in compromise, and as faith in religion is not a strong point now-a-days, even male Parsis, when they marry out of the community, tend to let their children free in choice of religion.

Inter-faith marriage has caused a steady decline in the numerical strength of the Zoroastrian community. Parsi women in the twenties or at a marriageable age are often earning more than any eligible male of her own community. So many Parsi girls tend to remain spinsters or marry people outside the community, who have an income to outdo or match their own.

Also, male Parsis often do not attempt to settle down when they are young and virile, because their independent spirit and ego feels hurt at earning less than women. Besides this, Parsis who excel in professions like medicine, teaching and engineering, often try to get their life partners from amongst those who are on a similar stimulated intellectual wave-length. As the Zoroastrian community is smaller in number than others, Parsis in professions often have to resort to inter-faith marriages.

If inter-faith marriages have led to a decline in the numerical strength of the Zoroastrian community, then divided attention in worship and prayer has resulted in a half-hearted approach to religion which does not augur well for the future of the Zoroastrian community. In this case, special attention must be focussed on the recent tendency of Parsis to adopt their modes of worship outside the community. This is primarily a psychological precept, which can be traced to the rigid attitudes towards religion adopted by Parsis about two generations ago. At that time, the modes of religious worship had become a fetish, and the Zoroastrian community was rigid in their taboos about religion. For instance, inter-faith marriages were severely frowned upon and often, if someone was still bold enough to marry outside the community, then he or she was invariably ostracized by members of their community.

The laxity in attitude towards the Zoroastrian community and religion is a direct result of the clannish attitude and rigid dogmatic religious beliefs of Parsis have reacted vehemently against any attempt to have a closed religion.

This has led to a divided attention in worship and prayer, and has led to Parsis's frequently adopting their modes of worship outside the community. The future of the Zoroastrian community, or any other community for that matter, depends on the modes of worship and norms of behaviour of members of the community. However, the members of the Zoroastrian community tend to get more and more diversified and individualistic in their approach to religion. The result of such an action is that the community and religion are getting diffused. As numerous Parsis have started borrowing and adopting and mixing their modes of worship outside the community, there is no central binding force for the Zoroastrian community and its future seems diffused and uncertain.

Conversion is not possible amongst Zoroastrians as the religion does not encourage it. The 'Peterson' controversy in U.S.A. is a recent example of this. On conversion to Zoroastrianism, there are many doubts. Scholars believe that not accepting converts is a sociological factor rather than a religious tenet. The Parsis were forced to adopt such a practice because when large numbers of them migrated to India, after fleeing from the Mohammedans (who had invaded their native land of Persia), they were allowed to dwell on Indian soil only if they promised not to try and convert the poor to their religion. Historical evidence states that the first Parsi migrants in India compromised with the native King, Jadhav, and as a condition for being permitted to stay, they promised not to accept converts to the Zoroastrian religion. As further assurance, the Parsi priests promised that no non-Zoroastrian will be allowed to enter the sacred Fire-Temple. Whether such customs and taboos were prevalent amongst the Zoroastrians in ancient Persia or whether they have arisen out of a sociological necessity, is debatable. The inconclusiveness of any accepted consensus on such an issue, has divided the community, some clinging to conservative view on parity and others favouring change.

The controversy over the entrance of non-Zoroastrians into the fire temple and other such religious dilemmas exist still and are unresolved, because of confusion about the basic tenets of Zoroastrianism. Scholars and experts have analyzed and dwelt in depth on the Zoroastrian religion, yet all research work and its evidence is not easily available to the public at large. The future of the Zoroastrian religion is uncertain as there exists basic ignorance about the essentials of the religion. This fact is best highlighted by means of an effective contrast. In Christianity, the problem of the Holy Trinity and Transubstantiation and the controversies that exist between the Protestant and Roman Catholic religions have been effectively displayed in the works of people like Milton, Swift and others. Besides, a large amount of literature available in Islam, Christianity and Hinduism can whet the appetite of even a layman. In contrast to this, the basics of the Zoroastrian religion have rarely been highlighted by any poet, dramatist or novelist of world renown as such. Also the significance of the basic essentials of the Zoroastrian religion is not revealed and explained properly or in an interesting manner to children and laymen so as to sustain interest about the religion. For instance, very few children doing their 'Navjote ceremony' know the actual significance of the 'Kusti' and 'Sudra.' Besides a mechanical recitation of the prayers, few people probe deep into the religion as such. Another drawback is that the prayers are in a language which is not spoken in general. So people do not contemplate and think on the words of the prayers as such. Also, an indifference to the rituals and customs of the Zoroastrian religion and absence of a fixed congregation like the Church on Sunday has imperilled the future of the community as there are few or no meeting points to stimulate interest amongst the youth about the Parsi community or religion.

Lack of interest in the Zoroastrian community which has made the future of the religion bleak as such, exists mainly due to insufficient parental guidance. A child is stimulated towards certain activities, because they are part of his environment and upbringing. If from early childhood, parents and his other peer group are indifferent or unenthusiastic about Zoroastrianism, then children remain indifferent to religion. Parental responsibility or the lack of it can thus be seen as the major factor for the confusion that exists about the functioning of the religion and has caused an uncertain future for the community as a whole.

Courtesy: *Dipanjali*, December 1986, special issue on Silver Jubilee of Delhi Anjuman's Fire-Temple

Of Parsis and the Novel

KEKI N. DARUWALLA

Creative writing by Parsis has evoked considerable interest lately. I did not realize this till I was asked to give a "Keynote Address" at a seminar on Parsi writing, organized by the Saurashtra University, Rajkot, in December 1999. The seminar was held in the bucolic environs of the Shardagram Ashram near Mangrol, formerly a mini 'native' state within Junagarh. Professors from as far as Kerala had come with their papers on Rohinton Mistry, Boman Desai, Meher Pestonji and the poets Gieve Patel, Adil Jussawalla et al.

I have sometimes wondered how others see us—the beak-nosed, pale-faced people with their outlandish ways, their eccentricities, their amazing head gears, their typical accent—no matter which language they speak in, and their names which seem to be getting more weird and piquant as the years go by, dug out of moth-eaten Persian chronicles. But everyone was very polite about us.

The first point that strikes the mind is nomenclature. Is this label of Parsi writing necessary? Just because a dozen people from a particular community are writing well, does it mean we label their literature? Isn't there around us an efflorescence of fiction writing in India in the English language? Aren't Parsis merely a part of this and should their writing be nailed to a sub-nationalistically oriented canon?

Labels cause problems. They are surface and catchy substitutes for the more profound phenomena of identities. Identities have roots hidden in the dark. Labels are billboards. I don't know whether we should foist on the Indian literary scene any arbitrary binarism—Parsi and Hindu and Muslim literatures.

Brahmin and Dalit binarism one can understand, both as metaphor and as a sociological outcrop. Literature, produced by minorities, shares its frustrations and aspirations with the rest of the Indian community. Yet it is conceded that each community can have its literary space, its own claustrophobias, its own mental ghettoes. If you are writing fiction you will write about your people, your milieu. Shashi Deshpande will write of Konkan, Allan Sealey of Christians, Anantha Murthy about his own particular Brahmin community. Each one burrows into his own cultural ghetto.

When we discuss poetry and fiction by Parsis, we come to a strange coincidence. The poets, possibly because they belong to an older generation, have stuck on to India. Gieve Patel, Adil Jussawalla, Kersy Katrak, and among the younger ones, Hoshang Patel—all live here. The novelists—Rohinton Mistry, Bapsi Sidhwa, Boman Desai, Firdaus Kanga—are all abroad.

Hence when we deal with fiction written by Parsis, we are dealing with expatriate writers who bring their own complexes and mental baggage with them. Rohinton Mistry emigrated to Canada in 1975, the year Mrs. Gandhi promulgated the Emergency. His imagination is still arrested in that time zone. He was just twenty-three years old, an impressionable age, in 1975 when the double trauma of the Emergency and his emigration took place. It was a bad time to leave your country. It has shadowed his look back. In both his novels *Such a Long Journey* and *A Fine Balance*, the Emergency exerts a perverse pull. He sees the bungling, the corruption, the lack of challenge to perverse authority, through the eyes of a hurt Indian and a Judgemental expatriate.

There are three facets to the Parsi novel as sociological tract, as a memory bank and as a look back on the city or the country one has left behind.

A novel aspires to give a flavour of reality, the mystery of lives as they are being lived. As in films, an entire era with its concerns, anxieties and beliefs comes alive on paper if not celluloid. But this mystery has to be achieved with deft touches. Sometimes Mistry lays it on thick, for instance, the funeral of Dinshaw, which could be easily mistaken for a paper commissioned by the Indian Council for Social Research. All in all, the Parsi novelists, including Mistry, paint the Parsi milieu excellently. Mistry brings out the cultural exclusiveness of a community living in a Parsi colony, symbolized by a surrounding wall, which the municipality (read the modern era, the spirit of the times) wants to break down. Outsiders urinate on the wall. One watches Mistry reaching out to other communities, other gods, with the pavement artist coming to the rescue by painting all the gods and apostles from all the pantheons on it. Immediately it becomes sacred and no one dirties the wall anymore till the state demolishes it during the Emergency.

His second novel, *A Fine Balance*, is unbalanced. It is a never-ending wallow in misery and a diatribe against the State. Politically, Mistry is a novice. He has woven the plot in his first novel on the implausible theory that the sixty lakh fraud perpetrated by Jimmy Bilimoria (read Capt. Nagarwalla) was in aid of the Mukti Bahini! The conman is made out to be the hero, and the PM (read Mrs. Gandhi) the villain who is siphoning off the funds meant for the liberation struggle of Bangladesh. Thus, the handling of one of the central episodes of the novel is juvenile. And Bilimoria in the RAW is positively a joke. Secret services do not operate through agents in the Chor Bazaar! And such money is not deposited in banks, as any Indian black-marketeer will tell you. The incident also smacks of bias—the Parsi conman has to be altruistic. As Meher Pestonjee told me the other day, some of us Parsis seem to think of ourselves as God's gift to mankind! Well said.

But if you are looking for a novel which you cannot slot easily in any of the categories I have mentioned (neither sociological, nor rooted in memory, nor a lookback on the city or the country one has left) and is still an excellent read, you can do no better than go to Bapsi Sidhwa's *Ice-Candy-Man*. If it is rooted in anything, it is rooted in the Partition, where you see the entire bloody drama of Lahore through an "objective" Parsi lens. As in Arundhati Roy's more famous *The God of Small Things*, the world is seen through the eyes of a child—in this case through polio-stricken Lenny Baby, who lives in Lahore. The servants's quarters with its myriad characters—the bomb-bellied Imamdin, the sweepress Maccho and her daughter Pappo, Hari the gardener who gets himself circumcised and takes on the name Himat Ali and the sweeper Moti, who becomes David Masih once it is clear that Lahore is going to Pakistan—these, along with the visitors to the servants's quarters, form the chorus. It is through their opinions and comments that the reader sees the fitful events of the Partition. They are both protagonists and chorus, for it is their lives that are metamorphosed in the end.

The novel as memory bank is exemplified in Boman Desai's *The Memory of Elephants.* He has used a splendid literary device to achieve his purpose: to place before the reader not just the story of the family of the two brothers Homi and Rusi Seervai, but a panorama of the entire history of the Parsis, especially after the battle with the Arabs. Homi is the best ever student in the University of Aqihana (USA) and experiments with a machine called Memoscan which activates the particular part of the brain. He started by stimulating the brain of rabbit, using an X-Ray instead of an electrode and thus exploring, localizing and recording the functions of its brain. (He later invented a trip wire mechanism for the memoscan so that he could set it on a repeat cycle.)

However, after his first major love-affair and coitus with Candace, he suddenly wants to relive the same experience, again and again, fiddles with his machines, goes bonkers and through a freak accident, if that is the word, he enters racial memory itself, sees and talks to his grandparents and great grandparents in a flash and even witnesses vividly events of the time of Xerxes and Yezdegard and the battle of Kudisia. When he is in this semi-demented yet strangely occult state, his fraternal grandmother, Bipaiji, tells him: "When you invented your memomachine you cut into the Memory of the Soul. What I showed you, the Arabs and the Persians, were scoops from this memory. I have heard you say so often that the brain is like an iceberg—the tip holding the living memory, the submerged Memory of the Soul. A drop of water can become lost in the ocean; it can also become the ocean; I am giving you the chance to become the ocean. You were so obsessed with reliving the times you spent with your American muddum that you didn't even care about the cost to yourself. You would have sacrificed your gift, the brain of an Einstein, for a muddum who slept with waiters and barkeeps." Trust an old Bapaiji to say all that!

Very few Indian experts write of anything but India. Parsi writers also home in on "apri Mumbai." The protagonist may belong to the hills of a village in Maharashtra, as in Mistry's *A Fine Balance*, but the drama will take place in Bombay, as happens in Hindi movies. The nostalgia for Bombay is overpowering. I can do no better than quote a poem by the great Greek poet, Constantine Cavafy who lived in Alexandria. The poem is called "The City."

> You said, "I'll go to a different country, another sea,
> Another and better city than this one.
> Here everything I do goes wrong
> And my heart is dead and buried as a corpse.
> How long should my soul suffer here?
> Wherever I turn, anywhere I look
> I see the burnt cinders of my life here
> Where I've spent too long doing nothing."
>
> You will find no new sea or land.
> This city will always dog you.
> You'll roam the same streets,
> Go grey in the same houses.
> You'll always end up here.
> Forget anywhere else.
> You've no ship, no road.
> The life you've wasted here
> You've wasted everywhere.

First published in *Dipanjali*, January 2000.

Problematising the Minority Discourse: Inlets to the Parsi Sensibility

R.S. PATHAK

Writers of the Indian subcontinent have made the most significant contribution in the area of fiction. Writing about the Indian English novel, Dorothy Spencer opines that it is a major source for "a systematic study of cultural contact and cultural change" and would enhance the readers's "knowledge of acculturation process."[1] The fiction written by minorities is of special importance, for it enables us to have an intimate peep into their psyche. The question of minority in the Indian subcontinent is highly complex, critical and in many ways unresolved. The political discourse of the 1990s has tried to bring into focus the problematic of social insiders and outsiders, but the minority literary discourse here does not seem to have received the attention it deserves. Its careful analysis and appraisal is essential to demystify the concept and to take proper care of the minorities's perceived feelings of their position in the subcontinent as well as their psychological vulnerabilities. The present paper aims at throwing some light on socio-psychological values of the Parsis, their problems and plight and their predicament as delineated in the novels written by them in English, with a particular reference to the works of Dina Mehta and Bapsi Sidhwa, the two well-known novelists from India and Pakistan respectively.

The Indian Parsi novelists have thrown significant light on the way of life of their community, which is remarkably different from that of other Indians. The attitude of these novelists is not different from that of Bapsi Sidhwa enshrined in the Preface to her novel *The Crow Eaters* (1978):

> Because of a deep-rooted admiration for my diminishing community—and an enormous affection for it—this work of fiction has been a labour of love. The nature of comedy being to exaggerate, the incidents in this book do not reflect at all upon the integrity of a community whose scrupulous honesty and sense of honour . . . are legend.[2]

The contributions of the Parsis towards making a better India, right from the days of her struggle for freedom, cannot be set aside. But notwithstanding their admiration and love for their community, the Parsi novelists have projected its preferences and priorities, problems and "eccentricities" reiteratively. They have also taken occasionally a crack at its excesses and angularities at the cost of their quixotically amorous young people and their dotty characters. Their work recreates their community, which takes pride in living together, sharing collective memories and perpetuating the value of its heritage.

Most Parsis, as delineated by these novelists, have a typical weakness for Western values and civilization and try their best to have a close connection with the English. Most Parsis in Dina Mehta's *And Some Take a Lover* (1992), for example, owe their allegiance to everything English. They would make a point to visit the summer-resorts, which was "a matter of pride and prestige" to them.[3] They would feel particularly at home in these hill stations which were "an English creation, with their deluxe shops and hotels and skating rinks, with their dressing-for-dinner, their parties, dances and beauty competitions." Here the Parsis would blissfully forget all about "the strings and freedom-agitations in the country." (136) Roshni, the main character in Dina Mehta's novel, is conscious of the Westernization affecting the Parsis including herself:

> The Parsee way of life was the most Westernized in India. More than the Anglo-Indians they could afford the tastes, the standards, the luxuries introduced by the alien rulers. She [Roshni] spoke English better than her adopted mother-tongue, Gujarati. She even thought in English. . . . She read no Gujarati books or papers. She did not know

> Persian, the language of her ancestors. . . . She did not know a word of Avesta, in which her prayers were written. She knew more about Christianity than of her own religion. . . . She was more familiar with the Bible than with the Gathas, with the Acts of Apostles than with the life of Zarathushtra. (188)

Roshni also admits that her home itself is patterned on the Western style, right from its Victorian mass and solidity to Venetian glass vases and Dresden art-pieces. The English language and other aspects of the English culture are thus an integral part of the way of life of the Parsis. This Eurocentric approach considerably determines their world view and attitude to life.

Originally, this Anglomania seems to have resulted from practical considerations. Faredoon Junglewalla or Freddie, in Bapsi Sidhwa's *The Crow Eaters*, spells out its advantages. He calls the Englishmen the Parsis "sovereigns." "Where do you think we'll be," he asks, "if we did not curry favour? Next to the nawabs, rajas and princelings, we are the greatest toadies of the British Empire! . . . Otherwise, where would we Parsis be? Cleaning our gutters with the untouchables—a dispersed pinch of snuff sneezed from the heterogeneous nostrils of India!" (12) Having arrived in Lahore, the first thing Freddie did was to go to the Government House to demonstrate his loyalty to 'Queen and Crown.' When he took his wife out, he expected her to greet and behave "like any bold English girl." (190) He himself "hobnobbed with Maharajas and Englishmen." (101) His command of the language was slippery and yet he "prided himself on his English." (156) He would even quote English proverbs and swear the way the English would. (51, 69) Then, we have in the novel Khan Bahadur Sir Noshirwan Jeevanjee Easymoney, the ex-military officer, who lost one of his eyes by an enemy bullet. Having been knighted, he "dressed and talked like an English lordsahib" and "drifted in a rarefied atmosphere of lords, barons and sirs." (194) His house was lighted by crystal lamps and had brocade curtains, a huge French tapestry and "the dull gold furniture . . . of Louis XIV style," its "overwhelming elegance" being enhanced by "embroidered chairs."

(199) "His suit was from Savile Row, [and] his patent leather shoes shone like mirrors." And yet, ironically enough, "Despite his *British affectations* he *looked* graciously and splendidly Indian." (212; emphasis added) When marriage negotiations for his daughter were being finalized, he took pains to "*demonstrate* that though he might be a sir, and accustomed to the ways of British aristocracy, he was first and foremost a loyal and down-to-earth Parsi." (221; emphasis added) His wife, Lady Easymoney, "tidy and meticulous," "washed tomatoes with soap." (199) Such was the craze for the English way of life that even Freddie's penny-pinching son Behram alias Billy and his fashionable wife, Tanya, evinced "a fanatical faith in the ways of English society in India, and a disciple's knack at imitation." Their "ability to converse in English" set them apart from the common people. (245) Not only that, Billy and Tanya "fought in English, with an odd Gujarati word or sentence thrown in," (248) and when Tanya was expecting a baby she was expected to contemplate the pictures of "chubby-cheeked English babies" and produce a "European style offspring." (249)

The Parsi novelists have given meaningful hints about other aspects of the Parsi way of life. Dina Mehta, for example, tells us that most Parsis are relentless eaters and have a remarkable passion for "elaborate food of most indigestible kind." (13) They are to Rustom, himself an influential member of the community, pretentious people "interested only in money and social advancement." (20) Any person who did not have "the decency to be born a Parsee" would be regarded by them as "a savage." (31) The Parsis's eagerness to remain a closed ethnic group has resulted in inbreeding, reduction in their number and other untoward repercussions. In *And Some Take a Lover*, "Jangoo Batliwala was one such example with his soft, clammy palms, over-fleshed pink lips and the pale pigment of inbreeding. And Gulestan was another example of what happened when a minimal ethnic group sealed itself in its own juices." (37) Roshni Wadia, the protagonist of the novel, finds socialite evenings nothing but "odds and ends of looks, snippets of smiles, [and] a string of inane sallies." (116) A possible "superior husband material" (37) is invariably the topic of discussion among matriarchs and an object of relentless pursuits for eligible young women of the community. To an ordinary person the Parsis would, on the whole, appear to be a "vapid, pleasure-seeking crowd," or an "imbecile crowd" given to a "complacent, fatuous life," the "facet of the stylish ensemble" presented by them being "a fashionable pose, nothing more." (136) Roshni is averse to what she calls "the slithering and sliding and gambolling, [and] the frantic promiscuity" (215) of their get-togethers, although she herself is encouraged to participate in them frequently and whole-heartedly.

Bapsi Sidhwa, in *The Crow Eaters*, has also highlighted some of the most distinguishing traits of the Parsis. In general, a Parsi's "reputation for honesty and propriety is a byword," (23) and his faith is "based on charity." (47) Freddie's son Yezdi gives away his share of the property to the poor. There are nevertheless exceptions like Freddie himself who would have no scruples in swindling in an insurance case and "no one would know how diabolically wily, unscrupulous, and false he really was." (104) The Parsis do not allow conversions or mixed marriages and maintain their exclusive identity. Freddie tells Yezdi, who wanted to marry an Anglo-Indian girl: "if you marry outside our kind, the spark so delicately nurtured, so subtly balanced, meets something totally alien and unmatched" and the children born "might look beautiful but they will be shells—empty and confused; misfits for generations to come. They will have arrogance without pride—touchiness without self-respect or compassion." (128-29) This kind of claustrophobic exclusiveness may be responsible for slow-thinking persons and archetypal cranks. Gluttony is another deadly sin which lures the Parsis in a big way. Freddie's mother-in-law is an inveterate over-eater. She would easily appropriate "huge quantities of chocolate, biscuits . . . and wines." (26) Freddie says: "she eats like a horse at meals, and then swallows enough sweet chutneys, candied fruits and liqueurs to give an elephant diarrhoea." (27) This mindless eating would give ultimately bloated dimensions to middle-aged prima donnas.

The novelist has also drawn our attention to the Parsis's

love for money and their enviable business sense. Freddie is presented as a "dulcet-voiced adventurer with so few scruples" and a "charming rascality." (9) According to him, the "sweetest thing in the world" is one's need—the mainspring of one's "wants, well-being and contentment." "Need," he would add, "makes a flatterer of a bully and persuades a cruel man to kindness." (10) There is not much scope for pride and arrogance in his system, and he would follow the dictates of his needs which "make one flexible, elastic, humble." In support of his stance, he would misquote Christ: 'The meek shall inherit the earth' and 'Sway with the breeze, bend with the winds.' (11) "Business is business" (181) was the guiding principle of his life. What he dreaded most was "ruin, disgrace, and business annihilation." (190) Billy out-Freddied Freddie in this respect. "He was suspicious," we are told, and "avaricious" and "cunning" and "had a simple vocation in life. MONEY!" "He existed to make, multiply, and hoard it. He was notoriously and devoutly penny pinching. . . . His frugality might have been inherited from an undiluted line of Parsi forebears." (192) He was "systematic" and his "mind worked in bracketed numerals." (230) Money was his real love. "Never was a man so parsimonious"; he was obliged to face "a gigantic conflict between his passion for his wife and his passion for money. Money, being his first love, triumphed." (247) His "commandments" directed at his wife included:

> Thou shalt not spend money!
> Thou shalt not waste.
> Thou shalt give me a minutely detailed account of expenses.
> Thou shalt obey thy husband, and jump to his bidding.
> Thou shalt bring up thy children to obey and to love me more than they do you.
> Thou shalt never require anything.
> Thou shalt not disturb me.
> Thou shalt switch off all lights and fans. (278)

The Parsi novelists have dealt with the themes of the Quit India Movement, the Partition, the Independence, the British colonial rule and other momentous events affecting the subcontinent. But their attitude is ambivalent. In *The Crow Eaters*, for example, Freddie vehemently protests against the nationalist movement and exhorts his children to be loyal to the British Empire. Anyone who goes against the wishes of the English would be unacceptable to him "Quit India! Quit India!" Freddie is expectedly "perturbed by the trend of events in India"; he is "stirred by [the] talk of rebellion, self-rule, and Independence from the British—and most of all by the role of a few Parsis in all this." (282) People like Naoroji, he feels, are "making monkeys of themselves." Others will benefit by breaking the country and the Parsis would nowhere be wanted.

In her later novel *Ice-Candy-Man*, Bapsi Sidhwa has revealed the Parsis's attitude to the imminent Partition and the concept of 'Swaraj.' Set in pre-Partition Lahore, the novel highlights vulnerability of human relationships. Here, again, the Parsis find it difficult to decide whether to support the 'Swaraj' or to continue their loyalty to the British Raj. At a special meeting organised at the temple hall in Warris Road, an acrimonious debate on the political situation takes place. Col. Bharucha advises the Parsis to keep away from the nationalist agitation. Dr. Mody, however, pleads for involvement in the freedom struggle for the simple reason that "our neighbours will think we are betraying them and siding with the English."[4] On the initiative of the banker Toddywalla, they resolve to follow their time-tested path of compromise and adaptability.

Dina Mehta's novel *And Some Take a Lover* also delineates the Parsis's apprehensions and political crises in the wake of the Quit India movement and the Naval Ratings Mutiny. Happy in their own orbits, most Parsis, we are told in the novel, would prefer not to remember about "the strings and freedom-agitations in the country." (136) Roshni's mother, who represents elderly members of her community, is convinced that once the English go, the country would go to dogs. Dina Mehta's is an absorbing work about the conflicting loyalties of a Parsi family enmeshed in the political and personal turmoil.

It is not surprising that some great Indian leaders have not fared well in such a paradoxical situation. To Roshni's mother and people like her, Gandhi is merely "that scoundrel and vagrant the arch-traitor, the unmentionable, except with abuse." (38) To Roshni's cousin Framroze, Gandhi's fasting is "political blackmail," and aunt Piroja feels that he is pro-Japanese and a fifth-columnist. After her failure to marry Sudhir, an indignant Roshni also begins to see Gandhi as a despot. Roshni has never met Gandhi but was "aghast when she thought of the strange, awesome power he wielded over other people's lives." (219) Nehru and Indira Gandhi have also not been spared. In Rohinton Mistry's *Such a Long Journey*, which hinges around the Bangladesh crisis of 1971, the subsequent Indo-Pak war and the Nagarwalla Bank Case, Nehru is taken to task for the "humiliating defeat" of India at the hands of the Chinese in 1962. The novel also mentions Nehru's frustration, ill temper, political intrigues that surrounded him and his "monomaniacal fixation" with "his darling daughter."[5] The successor of Nehru, Lal Bahadur Shastri, however, received unqualified praise because under his stewardship "the stagnant waters of government would at last be freshened and vitalized." (114) The Congress Party is alleged to comprise "crooks" (68) and is reduced to "a rogues' gallery." (325) And the country is no better than "a patient with gangrene at an advanced stage." (313) There may be some dissenting voices but the general drift remains unchanged.

The Parsi novelists have reflected through their works the dilemma of the minority community and its identity crisis. Understandably an anglicized community would find it extremely difficult to identify with other Indian communities. Roshni, in *And Some Take a Lover*, recalls her grandmother's views about the majority community. A Hindu, to her, "turned his world into a vast spittoon by ejecting streams of betel juice on walls, staircases, roads, pavements; his bathrooms stank of urine and kitchens of heeng; he was dishonest in his business practices and mean with his money." (38) In the pre-Independence India they felt, to use Nissim Ezekiel's phrase, 'natural outsiders' at times deliberated "whether or not Parsees should return en masse to Iran, the land of their forebears thirteen hundred years ago." (29) Even the younger generation is not free from the dilemma. Roshni represents their challenges faced by them in varying degrees. Her lover Sudhir finds her "cut adrift in the circumstances she scarcely understood." (136) After Sudhir's departure, in retaliation she "allowed herself to be manoeuvred into an ugly trashy affair" with Rustom Bharucha and consequently "was lost for ever, the scarlet letter her companion for life." (23) The most frightening thing in her life now was her isolation, her "citadel of aloofness" (62) only leading her on to a "hinterland of confused values." (42) She feels "a terrible alienation . . . rather like a prisoner arraigned before the Bench," wishing "herself away on a desert island"—inside her "dirty ivory tower." (111)

Roshni, however, is not the only character in the novel who suffers from alienation. As she herself reminds us, "her confusions were but a quintessential version of the chaos outside." (57) Rustom, the go-lucky, bohemian sensualist, faces the same problem. As soon as she enters his house, she becomes conscious of his rootlessness. Rustom, like so many members of his community, has failed to have a sense of belonging here. He asks Roshni: "Did you not feel how rootless they [the Parsis] are? That they do not belong? What has this country to offer us? What kind of cultural life? We Parsis are aliens here." (18) He feels that he belongs, on account of his breeding, education and background, to England with its "rich life" and the "freedom, the dispassionate pursuit of knowledge, and the concern for the well-being of the individual." (18-19) Initially, Roshni notices a marked similarity between her and Rustom's plight. "He is like me," says she, "in that he feels he does not belong here. But while I feel like mere driftwood caught up in the swirl of these past two years, he stupidly believes he can come to shore *there*; and I belong nowhere." (19) Rustom's rootlessness is a natural consequence of his unbridled sensualism, satiety and the accompanying withdrawal. His ruthless egotism prevented him from developing intimate, natural relations even with his wife.

Two more cases may also be considered briefly. There is a reference to Zoroastrianism (and some other religions) in Farrukh Dhondy's *Bombay Duck*. An informal chat between Xerxes Xavaxa and Lyla goes on as follows:

> "What do you feel, Mr. Xavaxa, or Xerxes? As a Parsee."
>
> "Parsees. We don't feel threatened, I don't. . . . Sikhs do and Muslims do and there's been slaughter these last forty years."[6]

Despite their bravado, most of these characters suffer from a kind of cultural neurasthenia. A similar case is that of Daryus Kotwal (called 'Brittle' or 'Brit' because of his brittle bones) in Firdaus Kanga's *Trying to Grow*. He is gnawed by social alienation because he is "Educated, speaking [English] so well"[7] and belongs to a community which owes its allegiance to the British Empire. Like other members of his community, he lives in the past and psychologically assigns himself to the King Emperor. Everything Indian is looked down upon including the Hindu religion and the Indian way of life. The adoration of the British royal family reaches ridiculous heights. The protagonist himself says, "We are reluctant Indians." It is a different matter though that finally he comes to terms with himself. "I like the way I looked," he affirms. (235)

Literature, being a sub-system of a given culture, offers an illustration or exemplification of some general pattern or syndrome. Minority discourse is characterized not only by an urge to adapt and assimilate but also by a culture of protest and resistance. Culture is not merely an organizational principle holding together the members of a community; it is also a means of establishing its separateness from and resistance to other communities. Writing about the Muslims, M.J. Akbar maintained in his book *Riot after Riot* (1988) that they have developed "a siege mentality." The consequences of cultural colonization or subordination are too well known to be recounted here. It creates two conflicting tendencies, i.e. of imitation of the 'colonizer,' and revival of the past (e.g. the building of the Tower of Silence in *The Crow Eaters*). As Kenneth Frampton suggests, modern art forms may have "the capacity to cultivate [a] resistant, identity-giving culture."[8] The Resistance Theory advanced during the recent decades has more insistently emphasized the value of the rediscovery and repatriation of what has been suppressed in a minority's past. The Resistance Theory advises re-charting of "the place reserved for subordination" and regards cultural colonization not only as a form of enslavement and a loss of cultural independence but also as a form of historical denaturing and cultural deracination. 'Imperialism' is thought of today "not as a hierarchically structured system of global capitalism but as a relation."[9] In his Reith lectures, *Representations of the Intellectual* (1994), Edward Said has asked resistance to be content with marginality and self-exile. Earlier he adumbrated three choices to a minority community:

> One choice is to do as Ariel does, that is . . . when he gains his freedom he returns to his native element, a sort of bourgeois native untroubled by his collaboration with Prospero. A second choice is to do like Caliban, aware of and accepting his mongrel past but not disabled for future development. A third choice is to be a Caliban who sheds his current servitude and physical disfigurements in the process of discovering his essential, pre-colonial self.[10]

This is high time that relation between the centre and the periphery—the majority and minority communities—were recognised properly and serious efforts were made to invent more heterogeneous forms of unity that might be commensurate with the complexity of our subcontinent.

NOTES

1. Dorothy Spencer, *Indian Fiction in English* (Philadelphia: University of Pennsylvania Press, 1960), p. 11.
2. Bapsi Sidhwa, Author's Note to *The Crow Eaters* (New Delhi: Penguin India, 1990), p. 7.
3. Dina Mehta, *And Some Take a Lover* (Calcutta: Rupa, 1992), p. 136.
4. Bapsi Sidhwa, *Ice-Candy-Man* (London: Heinemann, 1988), p. 37.
5. Rohinton Mistry, *Such a Long Journey* (Calcutta: Rupa, 1991), pp. 9, 11.

6. Farrukh Dhondy, *Bombay Duck* (Calcutta: Rupa, 1991), p. 199.
7. Firdaus Kanga, *Trying to Grow* (Delhi: Ravi Dayal, 1990), p. 1.
8. Kenneth Frampton, "Towards a Critical Regionalism: Six Points for an Architectute of Resistance," quoted in Joseph Natoli, ed., *Literary Theory's Future(s)* (Urbana/Chicago: University of Illinois Press, 1989), p. 311.
9. Aijaz Ahmad, *In Theory: Classes, Nations, Literatures* (Bombay: Oxford University Press, 1993), p. 41.
10. Edward W. Said, *Culture and Imperialism* (London: Chatto and Windus, 1993), p. 258.

The Theme of Marriage in Parsi Fiction

NOVY KAPADIA

The Parsis have always been in the forefront of creative writing in English by Indians. The trend of Parsi authors in English started over a century ago. The poet Behram Malbari was one of the earliest Indians to write in English. His work, *The Indian Muse in English Garb*,[1] was first published way back in 1877. His later publications include a collection of twenty-six sketches *Gujerat and Gujeratis*[2] and *The Indian Eye on English Life*[3] which are both pseudo-fictional in nature. In the early decades of the twentieth century, another eminent Parsi writer was Cornelia Sorabji. She published three volumes of short stories, *Love and Life behind the Purdah* (1901), *Sun Babies* and *Between the Twilights*[4] and two autobiographical works. Another early Parsi novelist was the renowned journalist, D.F. Karaka Jr. who wrote some novels during the 1940s and the 1950s. Nergis Dalal wrote four novels in the 1960s and the 1970s and Perin Bharucha had her only work *The Fire Worshippers* published in 1968.

In this initial phase of Parsi writing in English, there was little stress on identity or the problems faced by India's smallest ethno-religious minority community. The assertion of ethnic identity commenced in Parsi fiction in the 1980s in the works of Bapsi Sidhwa, Farrukh Dhondy, Rohinton Mistry, Firdaus Kanga, Dina Mehta and Boman Desai. This group of Parsi writers can be classified as the second generation of Indian-English novelists, who mostly began their careers in the 1980s. The texts of these Parsi writers have given them and their small community an identity within the dominant culture of the Indian context. In such a task, the Parsi writers fulfilled an essential role namely that of "the writer as a preserver of collective tradition, a folk historian and myth maker."[5]

Nilufer Bharucha in her scholarly essay, "Why all this Parsiness? An Assertion of Ethno-Religious Identity in Recent Novels written by Parsis" says that Parsi identity is in conflict with Indian identity. She says, "The common historical background—persecution in Iran, flight to India, the Indian experience gives the Parsis a common historical identity. In addition, the Parsis share a collective elite consciousness, which has grown from the colonial times when the Parsis were closely associated with the British rulers of India. This Parsi identity, composed of religious exclusivity, common history and elitism has brought Parsis into conflict with Indian identity."[6]

The current fiction being written by Parsi authors tackles various aspects of Parsi identity as well as social problems being faced by the community. One of the major problems is the declining population. The Parsis are a minuscule minority in India. Madhavankutty Pillai in an investigative article in the *Asian Age* on 13 May, 1997 revealed that prosperity, extreme individualism, urbanisation, late marriages, low birth rates and antique laws about not accepting the children of Parsi women married outside the community into the fold is taking their toll on the Parsi community in India. Statistics show that Parsis are the most urbanised community in India. Ninety four per cent of the Parsi population is urbanised as compared to 16.4 per cent of Hindus. Also the Parsi population in India has declined from about 1,14,890 in 1941 to about 70-80,000 in 1997. Parsi scholars feel that late marriages and marriages outside the Parsi community by females, whose children are not accepted into the faith, and a low birth rate have resulted in a situation where the laws oı statistics dictate that the race could get extinct in the years to come. This can be seen by the measure worked out by the Swedish statistician Carl Sundburg,[7] which if applied to the age composition of a population, indicates whether it is growing, stationary or declining. For a regressive population, 20 per cent of the population should be under 15 years, 50 per cent between 15 and 49 years of age and 30 per cent over 50 years old. By this measure, the Parsis fall in the regressive category.

Paul Axelrod,[8] an American anthropologist of the University of California, in a comparative study of the Parsis, Jains and Saraswat Brahmins (as examples of enterprising communities) has made a significant observation about marital patterns. He has stated that among the two non-Parsi communities, only those with a higher education marry at a late age. In contrast, many Parsis who had not even completed secondary school married at an age later than college graduates of other communities did. Explaining the causes of this celibacy, Delhi-based sociologist, Ava Khullar has explained that complete lack of societal censure or shock at the unmarried state within the community is the crucial factor for the declining growth rate and late marriages.[9] The average age for Parsi marriages is one of the highest in the world, 28 years for females and 31 years for males. For generations, the Parsis also tried to maintain racial purity by the practice of endogamy. Marriages outside the community were strictly discouraged. Thus not surprisingly, the problem of inter-faith marriage and attitudes to marriage are major issues, which are tackled by several Parsi novelists in a very distinctive manner.

The dilemma of inter-faith marriages was first tackled by Perin Bharucha in her novel *The Fire Worshippers* (1968). Bharucha's novel, using the fictional discourse, provides details of the class based structure of Parsi society in Bombay. It also shows certain mental fixations in the community. At one level, it deals with the story of the idealistic Nari who startles his middle class parents Pestonji and Jerbanoo Kanchwalla by stating that he wants to marry an Anglo-Indian girl, Portia. The father Pestonji's reactions reflect the Parsi concerns about inter-faith marriage in the 1960s. During that phase, it was ethnic pride which led to Pestonji's objections to his son Nari's marriage to Portia Roy. She is described as being "intelligent, educated and not the least bit bigoted."[10] One of the reasons for Pestonji's objections to the marriage is that such mixed marriages will herald the disintegration of the community. The objections of the father reflect the author's views. Perin Bharucha was quite clairvoyant. In the 1960s, the trend of mixed marriages amongst the Parsis was a trickle but as the author subtly hints, it could become a deluge. Within the space of three decades, the trend of inter-faith marriages has increased rapidly amongst the Parsi community. So in the novel, we find Pestonji objecting to his son's marriage because he felt it would become a trend-setter.

Thus there is a difference in attitude to inter-faith marriages amongst the Parsi community in the 1960s and three decades later. This is aptly reflected in fiction also. The contrast emerges if we compare the novels of the 1990s, like Firdaus Kanga's *Trying to Grow* (1990) and Bapsi Sidhwa's *An American Brat* (1994) with *The Fire Worshippers* written in 1968. Pestonji Kanchwalla, the Parsi patriarch of the 1960s, has a different attitude towards inter-faith marriage than say Zareen Ginwalla in Bapsi Sidhwa's novel and the Kotwal family in Kanga's autobiographical novel. Pestonji's concern, as seen in the above paragraph, is that marriages like that of his son Nari and Portia are like harbingers of doom for the Parsi community. In contrast, in the 1990s, mixed marriages are seen as inevitable in the Parsi community. Hence the different reactions of Mrs. Zareen Ginwalla and Mrs. Sera Kotwal when their daughters wish to marry outside their community. Both the mothers are apprehensive that their daughters will be ostracised by the community, due to the contemplated inter-faith marriages. Their other concern is individualistic. Sera Kotwal is worried that her daughter Dolly's intended husband Salim may have more than one wife. Mrs. Ginwalla is worried about the family name and how her daughter Feroza would be cut off from her culture if she married the Jew, David Press.

Dina Mehta's novel *And Some Take a Lover* (1992) also presents another intended inter-faith marriage between the stylish Parsi girl Roshni Wadia and the austere Gandhian Mahipal Sudhir who puts the demands of public duty above personal desires. Roshni, an idealist and romantic, hopes that the love affair would give meaning to her life. The author cleverly shows the duality in Roshni's nature. She realises that she is a cultural hybrid and marriage would mean a choice between two contrasting worlds, the middle class comforts of Bombay or the squalor of Indian villages. Roshni's college boyfriend, the 25 year old Sudhir Mahipal, is a committed 'satyagrahi' who works in the villages in response to Mahatma Gandhi's call to eradicate untouchability.

Roshni's desire to marry Sudhir does not lead to crises in the family. Her family is mostly unaware of her deep feelings for the committed Gandhian, her former college-mate. The desire to marry Sudhir leads to personal crises. Roshni's essential honesty makes her realize the difficulty in reconciling the contradictory themes of love and politics. She changes from the impulsive, "All I know is that I love you," to a realization that in wishing to share Sudhir's life she was intent on a personal salvation. Conversation with the committed Sudhir made her realise that she would struggle to follow the obedience, restraint and new patterns demanded by Sudhir's austere vocation in the villages. Doubts assailed her. She understands that "between these people and her was a chasm which was as wide as it was deep and she did not have a common language with which to bridge it."[11] In trying to resolve her personal dilemma, Roshni subconsciously reflects the minority community's identity crises problem. It is the dilemma of an anglicized community trying to identify themselves with other communities.

Dina Mehta's novel does not directly deal with an inter-faith marriage but it shows problems, which occur in such an intended alliance. Sudhir dies of malarial fever whilst serving the people at Noakhali. Roshni grieves at her boyfriend's death but doubts assail her mind about the validity of such commitment. Earlier in the novel, she was a devout follower of Mahatma Gandhi. She wore khadi as a means of protest, a symbol of her Indianness and sympathy for the Nationalist movement. Now, after Sudhir's death, she questions such commitment and raises pertinent queries about why he had died. "To spread Gandhi's message of universal charity. But was it right to pursue people with so much expectation? Would the meek now inherit the earth?" (316)

Also when Roshni realises that she cannot reconcile love and politics in her affair with Sudhir, she seeks solace in a clandestine love affair with the archetypal enterprising, rich and successful Parsi executive Rustom. Yet she cannot play the role of a seductress for long. When their liaison ceased, she had no regrets, as she was not temperamentally a flirt. She tries to extricate herself from her net of wants, to live without hope, to learn how to love. Dina Mehta's modernist novel provides various points of view and offers a psychologically convincing presentation of reality. The ending of the novel is ambivalent. Roshni realises that sacrifices are not easy and the other option, the title of the novel, "And some take a lover" is not her way of life.

Particularly interesting are the attitudes towards marriage of the girl-child in Parsi fiction. Demographer Ketayun Gould has suggested that the emancipation of Parsi women is a major factor in late marriages or marriages outside the community.[12] This concept is reflected in the novels of Parsi writers. Significantly Nergis Dalal's *The Sister* (1973), Firdaus Kanga's *Trying to Grow* (1990) and Rohinton Mistry's short story "Exercisers" in his collection of short stories *Tales from Firozsha Baag* (1987), show ambivalent attitudes to marriage among the girl-children depicted in their work. The socialising processes of the girls, their attitutes to marriage as presented in these works are representative of the Parsi community.

Nergis Dalal in *The Sisters* reveals the values and attitudes towards marriage and human relationship of the twin sisters Rita and Nina. Written from a feminine perspective, the attitudes unfurl through the changing perspectives of Rita, the ugly twin with an unhappy childhood. The delineation of the twins reveals a characteristic paradox in the Parsi milieu. Many Parsis are cultural hybrids, living and sharing intimately in the cultural life, traditions, languages, moral codes of both the west and India, which never completely interpenetrate or get fused. Typically, the twins in the novel are products of the cultural hybrid; their father Firoze Patel is a Parsi and their mother Sophie an English woman. The identity dilemma and the attitude towards marriage and love are aptly revealed in the growth to maturity of both girls, living with their family in Hyderabad, in pre-Independence India.

The author uses the flashback technique to grasp reality

through the perceptions of Rita. Even as a mature woman, when Rita reflects on the past, her memories of childhood are full of unhappiness. Merely thinking about childhood makes her "stomach muscles tighten and shrink." Why does this happen? It was not a case of financial hardships. The father Firoze was employed by the Nizam in the Mint. The twins stay in a sprawling mansion with their parents and their rich maternal grandmother. But Rita was always slighted because of her ordinary appearance. With rough curly hair, dark skin and plump figure, Rita was always contrasted unfavourably with her slim, fair and attractive sister Nina. As they grew up, Nina, effortlessly charming, graceful and beautiful, was the centre of attraction at their birthday party, social gatherings, and school pantomime and dance parties. The social circle of Firoze and Sophie doted on Nina and neglected Rita because of their contrasting looks and pigmentation. The fundamental colour prejudices of the Parsis and of many other Indians get reflected in this unequal treatment of the twin sisters.

Consequently, the neglected Rita builds up defence mechanisms. Initially, it is childish revolt—destroying the roses her mother had nurtured, drowning her party dress or frightening her beautiful twin sister. Later, as awareness of her unhappiness increases, she builds "buffers to ease the ache, quilted padding against which I might recline." As a teenager, it is food: "When I was particularly unhappy I stuffed myself with food."

As a growing adolescent, she starts reading voraciously—another defence mechanism against neglect. In her formative years, Rita's role model is her maternal grandmother. She spends a lot of time with her rich grandmother who lives upstairs, cooks her own meals and preserves Parsi customs. Consequently, Rita's upbringing and attitudes to life become traditional. She learns about pickles and how to cook tasty chicken curry and manage the house. When Rita inherits her grandmother's wealth, she tells her astonished father and Mr. Sharma, a lawyer: "I have been doing her accounts for her since I was thirteen and going to the bank with her at least once a month. She had started my first account when I was only eight."[13]

Constant interaction with her Grandmother makes Rita's

views on marriage conservative: "The idea of love—romantic love that is—was conceived and born in the European mind. An Oriental, an Indian, does not necessarily expect marriage and love to go together." (47) Though brilliant in academics, Rita does not think of an independent career. She is enamoured with the idea of marriage. Both Rita and Nina consider marriage as the most important wish fulfilment in their lives. Such an ambition makes them representative of traditional Indian teenaged girls. However their approach to marriage greatly differs.

Conditioned by her traditional upbringing, Rita believes that money power is all-important. As a child, Rita is told by her grandmother, "In the end, the most important thing is, to have money. Money and reasonably good health." (55)

As Rita resembles her grandmother in temperament, attitudes and looks, she inherits her considerable wealth, jewelery and property. As a teenager, her ideas have crystallised and she has realised that she can get a husband with money power. Marriage without illusions is her ideal. She rejects her family upbringing, which assumes that beauty is the most important attribute amongst women. As a teenager, she also understands that marriage to a Parsi boy will cause her unhappiness. Her identity crises as a child, the constant rebukes and neglect by her family had intensified Rita's deep sense of despair about her community. She had grown up with a complex about her dark complexion. Rita has a nagging fear that her dark complexion and average looks would result in an unhappy marriage in a Parsi family, where people are judged in terms of skin colour and beauty. Rita's awareness of the prevalent Parsi prejudice against people of a dark complexion motivates her to marry outside her community.

The prettier of the twins, Nina, has starry-eyed illusions about marriage, "sharing everything, loving each other for ever, or belonging one to the other in a surrender so complete that nothing was held back, nothing restrained." (47) Nina has all the wish fantasies of a teenaged girl, the desire to marry a rich and handsome man, a 'prince charming.' Her attitude to marriage is, as the author says, distinctly Western. Hence, as a teenager, the role of a coquette, always effortlessly graceful, charming and using subtle flattery and glances to attract men even as a young girl. Thus, she is absorbed in her image as a successful romantic lover with thoughts only of beauty, passion and love. Nina represents the characteristic Parsi paradox—culturally alienated from traditional beliefs and ways of life due to her predominantly western consciousness. Her westernised upbringing gives her a distorted perception of boy-girl relationships and marital expectations.

Firdaus Kanga's candid novel, *Trying to Grow*, is set in a middle, upper middle class Bombay Parsi milieu. The attitudes to sex and marriage are described through the lifestyles of four Parsi girls, Dolly, Tina, Ruby and Amy. The emancipation of the girls, the lack of societal censure at the unmarried state, confused ideas about love and marriage and sheer eccentricity get reflected in the behaviour, motivations, relationships and views of the girls.

The author aptly shows that certain mental fixations about sex and marriage in the Parsi milieu leave a deep imprint on the growing girl child. The most eccentric case is that of the deaf Tina, fiercely protected by her mother Jeroo who has a morbid fear of the sexual appetite of all men. Jeroo feels that when a man is with a woman he only wants sex. Thus she prevents Tina from mixing with boys of her age and developing a healthy attitude towards them. Tina is allowed to go out only with the crippled narrator of the novel, Daryus Kotwal known as 'Brit' because of his brittle bones, perhaps because he is considered "safe." Jeroo is "terrified Tina would end up in a molester's arms."[14] Jeroo's attempts at protecting her daughter are farcical, absurd and laughable. However, it is also a subtle parody on the paranoid mentality of the widow Jeroo. "Jeroo tried to accompany Tina to every movie so that she could clap a hand on her eyes each time someone kissed. Furthermore, Tina wasn't allowed to read perverted writers, which meant Oscar Wilde, Thomas Hardy and E.M. Forster but excluded Harold Robbins, since Jeroo hadn't heard of him." (35)

Jeroo had a siege mentality about men and sex. So, as a mother, Jeroo tried to ensure that her daughter, Tina, like good Parsi girls, "didn't discover the facts of life till they got married." (34) Sadly for Jeroo, her eccentric treatment of her daughter does not work. "She [doesn't] know that Tina could have beat Masters and Johnson at a sex quiz." (35) The author cleverly shows that as Tina was not permitted a normal and healthy adolescent life, she develops fantasies about love, romance and charming boyfriends. Before her eighteenth birthday, she elopes with a Hindu boy, Rohit, who "lives in a boarding-house across the street from her window," and was "handsome as a Hindi filmstar, white-toothed and curly-haired." (87) Jeroo's eccentric behaviour and mental paranoia about sex ends in disaster as she is completely estranged from her daughter. Tina is not heard of in the novel again.

Dolly, the elder sister of the osteo child narrator 'Brit,' also grows up. But she is sent to a very "propah Parsi school which specialised in producing goody-goody girls." (230) So Dolly grows up with confused ideas. She does not imbibe the self-righteous morality of her 'propah' school. The constant references to love marriages and romance at home fire Dolly's erotic teenage imagination. She reads *Playgirl*, talk about enjoying sex and has a crush on the baby-faced Pervez Modi in her first year at college. Yet such a lifestyle and freedom of choice are only illusory. The Kotwal families are quite traditional and have many inhibitions. They prevent Dolly from becoming an airhostess. Later in life, Dolly faces the paradox of many a Parsi girl. Opportunities for socialising within the community are limited and Dolly has an aversion to meeting boys arranged by her parents. The attempted arranged marriage with Dinsu is a fiasco. It also parodies the typical Bombay Parsi situation, of the protected and pampered son being unable to interact with the more sophisticated Parsi girl of his age. So, Dolly as a growing girl, represents the typical Parsi girl's dilemma: should she be westernized or traditional? Her value system, life-style and cultural life are typically Western but the Parsi moral code curtails total freedom. Inevitably, she has hazy ideas about romantic love and the freedom of choice in selecting a life partner. Kanga stresses that this dilemma has stemmed from her upbringing in the schizophrenic Parsi milieu. Later in the novel, Dolly as an eligible young woman is unable to find a partner within the Parsi community. Finally she marries Salim, a Muslim doctor, and settles in New York. The fate of Dolly is that of the emancipated Parsi girl, compelled to marry outside the community, due to the near absence of emancipated Parsi young men.

The search for a suitable bridegroom for Dolly reveals all the contradictions and divisions within the contemporary Parsi society as regards mating and compatibility. It is the old-fashioned and conventional Defarge, a neighbour of the Kotwal family, who initiates the idea of searching for a suitable bridegroom within the community. Whilst knitting a "chunky red cardigan" (64) Defarge chides Sera (Mrs. Kotwal) for not making all-out efforts to get Dolly married. Defarge considers it a shame and says, "Your daughter is twenty-four, five feet-six, graduate, earning, and you are not getting her married." (64) Sera instead of being aroused, indignant or piqued, replies complacently. She says, "She [Dolly] refuses to let me arrange any boys for her to see. Anyway it doesn't worry me. Love marriages are a tradition in our family. Like in all *good* Parsee families." (64) This difference in perception to marriage represents a major contradiction within the Parsi society. Sera is depicted as a typical Parsi hybrid conditioned by her Westernised upbringing, reading *Woman's Own* magazines and watching Hollywood movies. Sera's indifference that her grown up daughter is unmarried vindicates Delhi-based sociologist Ava Khullar's analysis that complete lack of societal censure or shock at the unmarried state within the community is the crucial factor for the declining growth rate and late marriages. The dependence on the Westernised value system of love marriage which Sera propounds as an integral aspect of a 'good' Parsi family explains why the average age for Parsi marriages is one of the highest in the world, 28 years for females and 31 years for males. Defarge belongs to the old order, still basking in the euphoria of past glories and proud of her ethnic Parsi identity. Hence her hankering to arrange a suitable match for Dolly to ensure that the latter does not remain a spinster. Ketayun Gould, demographer and Professor at the University of Illinois, in her research on the declining Parsi population has noted that

20 percent of the community never married.

The other two girls in the novel remain unmarried. Both Amy and Ruby have a 'crush' and raging love affairs with Cyrus, a tall, handsome Parsi boy who opts for a career in a law firm in Delhi, rather than settling in Bombay. Again, the upbringing and socialising of both these girls has been very Western. Their value systems and desires are based on their image of being romantic lovers. Towards the end of the novel, Ruby when asked by the unsophisticated Jerry "to go out with him" hopes for a romantic relationship. Amy's hopes also fluctuate from wanting an intense love relationship with Cyrus to an ambivalent relationship with the osteo 'Brit.' It is this trend of generational drift and defiance of prescribed attitudes towards marriage and boy-girl relationships that is aptly reflected in Firdaus Kanga's *Trying to Grow*. The theme of marriage though occurring only as a 'sub-text' is a major topic of discussion in the novel.

Rohinton Mistry's perceptive short story "Exercisers" adds a new dimension to the portrait of the Parsi girl. It shows how Parsi parents mistrust the emancipated Parsi girl chosen by their son for a friend. Jehangir Bulsara, a teenaged Parsi boy from lower middle class residential quarters, is dating Parsi girl Behroze of a similar background. Here is a situation which should have been encouraged by Jehangir's parents. However, the overprotective and conservative attitude of the Bulsaras thwart the fledgling love affair. The frenzied parents perceive Behroze as a seductress, luring their son into a tempestuous affair. Written in sharp, pointed prose, Mistry's story contains many insights into the idiosyncrasies of the Parsis in Bombay. His characters are understressed emotionally but the effect is very telling.

After Jehangir brings Behroze home and introduces her to his parents, the tension begins to grow. Every night, he undergoes the dinner-table routine of debilitating sarcasm and barbed denunciation. There is no trace of generosity for his feelings. Initially, Behroze is criticized for talking without much respect. Later her sartorial habits are criticized: "Saw what she was wearing? Such a short skirt. And too much make-up. Why must a girl wear so much make-up unless she is hiding something underneath?"'[15]

Mr. Bulsara is occasionally conciliatory but his wife remains adamant in her dislike for Behroze, suggesting thereby that it is often women who are opposed to emancipated girls. After a few visits, the sensitive Behroze begins to notice the antagonism "that silently burgeoned on her arrival," (206) and she stops coming to the house: "There was no outward sign of it, on the surface all was decorum and grace welcome to kindness. But to sense what lay underneath did not take much." (206)

Jehangir is beleaguered, torn between filial duty and the stirring of love. The author cleverly shows that the Bulsaras' suspicion about Behroze is a manifestation of the conservative distrust of girls playing a lead role in seeking intimacy with boys of their age group. Mr. and Mrs. Bulsara distort a normal teenage infatuation with their middle class morality and strictures on the expected behaviour of the girl child. The irony is that Behroze is not a seductive *femme fatale.* However, even her harmless gestures at intimacy get misconstrued. When she gives her photograph to Jehangir, his parents describe her as a seductress and villain using black magic to trap their son into marriage. "People have been made to go crazy by a photo with a magic spell on it. Maybe her parents are involved in this, trying to snare my son for their daughter." (207)

Initially there is suspicion about Behroze's motives and the son, Jehangir, is seen as a helpless victim. Later, when Jehangir refuses to stop meeting his girl friend, the parents become unreasonable. They impose the "eight o'clock ultimatum" for him to return home: "Remember the door will never open for you after eight o'clock." (207) Then they take him to a self-proclaimed mystic and holyman, Bhagwan Baba, on the outside of Bombay to decide his future. Predictably, the self-styled mystic is ambivalent about the future of the relationship. Mr. Bulsara tries to interpret the mutterings of Bhagwan Baba as a warning that life is a trap, "full of webs" and that "Jehangir should stay away from that girl." (213) Distrust had made the parents paranoid and they now stop referring to the girlfriend by her name. The author, Rohinton Mistry, cleverly parodies the idiosyncratic behaviour, obsessive protection and traditional views of the conservative Bulsara parents. Their supercilious morality at times makes them act absurdly. When Jehangir returns home and changes his clothes, the mother would sniff and scrutinise his trousers under the light. Why? "To find smells of illicit sex? Stains to corroborate her suspicions of the girl's sluggishness? Evidence that her boy had been ravished by a flesh-and-blood succubus?" (213)

The constant harassment and mental pressure augments Jehangir's dilemma. Like Haemon in Sophocles's play *Antigone*, Jehangir encounters a loyalty problem. It is either a commitment to his beloved Behroze or to his objecting parents. Sensing his dilemma, Behroze tries to chide and later cajole him to ignore the rigid and obscurantist views of his parents. However, Jehangir in search of "place and serenity," attempts a compromise. He regularly meets Behroze but returns home to Firozsha Baag by 8 p.m. One evening after an intimate and romantic session with Behroze at her house, Jehangir forgets the time. In pouring rain, soaked to the skin, he rushes back home. Yet his attempt at compromise is a failure. As he reaches home late, his obstinate mother does not open the door. Drenched to the skin, he shuffles into the narrow corridor, sheltered by the staircase. The story ends with Jehangir overcome by a sense of failure. Behroze is piqued at her boyfriend behaving like a cowering child, still apprehensive of his parents. The author implies that the Bulsara's traditional, rigid middle class views about the behaviour of girls thwart the Behroze-Jehangir relationship. No marriage results from their relationship. Instead the parents's orthodox views about "good" Parsi girl are a barrier to what should have been an ideal relationship culminating in marriage.

Thus do Dalal, Kanga and Mistry focus on the attitudes of the girls, their feelings, thinking, behaviour and their actions of the elders who subtly try to control the sexuality of the girls in the kind of expectations of traditional behaviour they have of them. The girls themselves grow up confused, not knowing whether to become traditional like their mother or to be emancipated. The authors quietly suggest the connection between the attitudes and behaviour of the Parsi girl child and the marital problems/ patterns of the community.

Bapsi Sidhwa locates the theme of inter-community marriage in a non-Parsi context in her novel, *The Pakistani Bride* (1983). The two inter-community marriages depicted are between the white American woman Carol and the Pakistani Muslim Farukh and between the girl from the plains Zaitoon and the tribal from the hills, Sakhi. Both marriages are failures. Both Carol and Zaitoon are victimized and the marriages cause them intense agony and unhappiness. So in this novel, Bapsi Sidhwa shows that marriage outside the community can be self-damaging, thereby seemingly endorsing the traditional Parsi construct of prohibition of inter-community marriages.

In her third novel, *Ice-Candy-Man* (1988), an attempted inter-community marriage between the Hindu Ayah and her Muslim admirer Ice-Candy-Man becomes a victim of the communal passions of Partition. Initially the Ice-Candy-Man is part of the frenzied mob, which abdicates Ayah and keeps her in the brothels of Hira Mandi. Later he repents and attempts to make amends. He forcibly marries Ayah, changes her name to Mumtaz, and recites love poetry to her. But love is shown as powerless. Ayah has revulsion for her newly acquired Muslim identity. With the help of the girl-child narrator Lenny's Godmother, she is taken to a Recovered Women's camp and then sent to her family in Amritsar. The Ice-Candy-Man, now a "deflated poet, a collapsed peddler," follows her to Amritsar in vain. Their relationship is serrated forever, another victim of communal frenzy and the chaos of Partition. In this novel, Bapsi Sidhwa implies that love does not conquer when communal and obscurantist passions are aroused.

In *An American Brat* (1994) the marriage theme is examined in detail and in Parsi context. Feroza's horizons widen when she joins a larger university in the more cosmopolitan city of Denver. She moves into an apartment with two American girls and sheds many of her social inhibitions in their company. Her newly acquired confidence and sense of freedom culminate in her falling in love with a Jewish boy, David Press, at Denver. When Feroza announces that she wants to marry David, her family in Pakistan is both agitated and shell shocked. The mother Zareen flies to Denver to dissuade Feroza from taking a step that would lead to her being ex-communicated and expelled from the faith. The parents are also concerned that such a marriage would bring shame to the family honour. The family's opposition to Feroza's impending marriage represents the predominant traditionalist view of the Parsi community to such inter-community marriages. However, the author also cleverly depicts the growing discontent with such ancient traditions amongst the younger generation of Parsis. Whilst the family is discussing Feroza's predicament, fifteen-year-old Bunny implicitly expresses her revulsion at the rigid code by stating. "For God's sake! You're carrying on as if Feroza's dead! She's only getting married, for God's sake!"[16] Other adolescents in the room concur with Bunny's sentiments. However, they do not express them, as the dominating majority of elders quell such rebellious sentiments. This seemingly minor incident is used by Sidhwa to focalize the dissent amongst the younger generation of the community and hints at the demand of some re-thinking of the rigid tradition.

Ironically, Zareen, when she sees David and finds him a suitable match, has doubts about the rigid code. She expresses the author's owned unease with the ancient tradition. Zareen begins to understand the logic of the younger Parsis' opposition to the prohibition. "Perhaps the teenagers in Lahore were right. The Zoroastrian Anjumans in Karachi and Bombay should move with the times that were sending them to the New World.. The various Anjumans would have to introduce minor reforms if they wished their tiny community to survive." (288)

Zareen is now trapped in a paradox. She finds David admirable and appealing. Yet she is also aware that such a marriage would deprive her daughter of her faith, heritage, family and community. Zareen recalls the warning from the Athoran Mandal and the Notice from the Bombay Zoroastrian Jashan Committee. As a mother, she fears that marriage would cut Feroza off from her culture and her surroundings and her "child would eventually shrivel up." (289) Her dread for Feroza alters her opinion of David. She uses the tactics of "if you can't knock him out with sugar, slug him with honey," (272) to thwart the marriage. She pretends to agree to the marriage but insists on the rituals and ceremonies which, she knows, will frighten David, a very private and reserved person. The relationship disintegrates and Zareen's ploy partially triumphs. As a Parsi writer, Bapsi Sidhwa does not take a rebellious stance against the dominating ideology of her community. However, Sidhwa is no conformist. She does not endorse the traditional Parsi code on inter-community marriage. Instead, through Zareen and Feroza's reactions, she hints at the need for change. Zareen ironically realizes that by denying her daughter freedom of choice in marriage, she and the educated custodians of the Zoroastrian doctrine "were no less rigid and ignorant than the Fundos in Pakistan." (305) Similarly, Feroza is heart-broken after David's departure. However, she does not compromise and remains firm in her resolve to not to submit to the dictates of Parsi laws against inter-community marriages. She expresses her convictions towards the end of the novel thus:

> There would never be another David, but there would be other men, and who knew, perhaps someday she might like someone enough to marry him. It wouldn't matter if he was a Parsi or of another faith. She would be surer of herself and wouldn't let anyone interfere. As for her religion, no one could take it away from her; she carried its fire in her heart. (317)

So Bapsi Sidhwa cleverly highlights the sensitive issue of inter-community marriages amongst the Parsis. On the theme of marriage, she maintains a clever balance, implicitly opposing the rigid code but not appearing overtly rebellious.

Bapsi Sidhwa's handling of the theme of inter-community marriages is very relevant and contemporary. The issue of inter-faith marriages still arouses acrimonious debates amongst the Parsi community. Orthodox priests and reformists delve into the scriptures to argue over what it takes to be a Parsi. By the traditional rules of the community, a Parsi could be one only by birth. In the wake of a spate of mixed marriages, a number of children were thus deemed 'lost' to the community as were the erring parents. As the Parsis are a patriarchal society, there is a strong masculine bias. The rules tend to favour the Parsi men who marry outside the community and their children. The same does not apply to Parsi women. As an article by Lyla Bavadam reveals, the reformists are trying that the community is not depleted. They advocate:

(a) That a Parsi woman, either married or divorced from a non-Parsi (if such a condition is accepted by the orthodox section of the Parsi community, Zareen would have had no fears about the warnings from the Athoran Mandal and Bombay Zoroastrian Jashan Committee).
(b) That a child born of a marriage between a Parsi mother and non-Parsi father be treated as one of the community.
(c) That a person desiring conversion to Zoroastrianism be accepted into the fold.[17]

The orthodoxy considers such changes sacrilegious. Ervad Dastur (High Priest) Dr. Firoze Kotwal of Bombay is in favour of preserving the purity of the community at all costs. Hardliners like Ervad Dastur Peshotan Peer candidly and brusquely say that "Parsis who marry out of the community are living in adultery. The reformists rebut the argument of preserving the purity of the community as 'a phobia.'" Meher Amersey, married to a Gujarati business tycoon, heads the Association of Inter-Married Zoroastrians. She contends that if a non-Parsi spouse is agreeable to the children's navjotes (initiation or thread ceremony), there is no reason why anyone should object. Renowned jurist Nani Palkhivala supports this view. He observes, "one of the wonders of Zoroastrianism is that it places great emphasis on the freedom to choose."

Ultimately, this acrimonious controversy of whether a Parsi Zoroastrian ceases to be either a Parsi or a Zoroastrian because of an inter-faith marriage, hinges on the definition of the two terms, 'Parsi' and 'Zoroastrianism.' The two terms have been defined in the judgement of the Bombay High Court delivered by Honorable Justice Daver and Honorable Justice Beaman in Suit 689 of 1906. The background to the case is interesting and an important landmark in Parsi history. In 1903, Mr. Ratan Tata married a French lady (JRD Tata's mother). A very religious person, Ratan Tata consulted the Bombay High Priests about his wife's navjote (initiation ceremony to choose the Zoroastrian faith). The idea was welcomed and one of the High Priests, Dastur Kaikooshroo Jamaspji performed the Navjote ceremony, thereby investing the French lady with 'Sudra' and 'Kusti,' the sacred shirt and girdle which are the outward symbols worn by those who profess the Zoroastrian religion. He then got married to her, according to the rites of the Parsis. Ratan Tata next claimed that his wife had become a Parsi professing the Zoroastrian faith and was entitled, among other things, to enter all Fire Temples. The priests objected to this saying that each Fire Temple had its own Trust, which decided on rights of admission. This led to the case in the Bombay High Court. The contention of the Parsi Panchyat was that the community had never converted anybody since it came to India over a thousand years ago. The much-quoted reason for this was the promise of not coverting that the early Parsi settlers had given to the Hindu ruler who had granted them refuge in India in their flight from Islamic persecution in Persia.

Justices Daver and Beaman traced the history of the Parsis and came to the conclusion that the decision not to convert had been merely a demand of the times and not a restriction that the religion imposed. Justice Daver also categorically stated in his judgement: "The word Zoroastrian simply denotes the religion of the individual and the word Parsi denotes his nationality or community and has no religious significance whatever attached to it."[18] He also stated: "A Parsi born must always be a Parsi, no matter what other religion he or she subsequently adopts and professes." So, according to the 1906 legal definition, there is no doubt that a Parsi continues to remain a Parsi even after he or she marries a non-Parsi.[19]

However, the orthodox do not accept even the court's ruling, hence the controversy which Bapsi Sidhwa aptly delineates when Feroza wants to marry David Press. The ambivalent ending conveys a lot. Ostensibly, the ending of the novel upholds the orthodox views, as Feroza does not marry the Jewish boy

David. However, another view can be taken, that the novel ends with some repudiation of an empty and rigid tradition. Bapsi Sidhwa hints at such repudiation, implicitly, through her mouthpieces Zareen and Feroza.

Thus Bapsi Sidhwa's fourth novel, *An American Brat*, has two distinctive movements. Initially, there is the movement towards self-actualization in the life of Feroza Ginwalla made possible by acculturation to the American way of thinking and life-styles. Later as Feroza achieves a synthesis between tradition and modernity, the theme of marriage is elaborately examined with reference to the Parsis's attempt to maintain the status quo as regards the sanctity of their religion and continuity of their inherited cultural traditions. By providing insights and detailed information about the Parsis and their culture, Sidhwa attempts to foster a better understanding of her community and curbs possible prejudicial misconceptions of the Parsis. In this task, she fulfills the essential role of "the writer as a preserver of collective tradition, a folk historian and myth maker."

NOTES

1. Behramji M. Malbari, *The Indian Muse in English Garb* (Bombay: The Reporters Press, 1876).
2. Behramji M. Malbari, *Gujerat and Gujeratis* (Bombay: Education Society Press, 1882).
3. Behramji M. Malbari, *The Indian Eye on English Life* (Bombay: Apollo Printing Works, 1895).
4. Cornelia Sorabji, *Sun Babies* (New York: Harper, 1904). *Between the Twilights* (London: Nesbit, 1908).
5. M.G. Vassanji, "The Postcolonial Writer: Myth Maker and Folk Historian," cited in *A Meeting of Streams: South Asian Canadian Literature*, ed. M.G. Vassanji (Toronto: TSAR Publications, 1985), p. 63.
6. Nilufer Bharucha, "Why all this Parsiness? An Assertion of Ethno-Religious Identity in Recent Novels written by Parsis" cited in *Mapping Spaces: Postcolonial Indian Literature in English*, ed. Nilufer Bharucha and Vrinda Nabar (New Delhi: Vision Books, 1998), pp. 253-54.

7. Carl Sundburg, cited in a monogram, "The Parsis—A Socio-Economic and Demographic Survey" by Ava Khullar and Shanker Bose, for the Centre for the Study of Developing Societies, New Delhi, 1978. Also quoted in Ava Khullar, "Profile of a Forward looking Community—The Parsis of Delhi," Delhi Parsi Anjuman, Kaikhushru Pallonji Katrak Dar-E-Meher, Silver Jubilee Celebrations Journal, 1961-1986, ed. Novy Kapadia, Delhi, December 1986, p. 32.
8. Paul Axelrod, cited in a monogram, "The Parsis—A Socio Economic and Demographic Survey" by Ava Khullar and Shanker Bose.
9. Ava Khullar, "Let the boundaries give way," cited in *Parsiana*, November 1994, pp. 26-28.
10. Perin Bharucha, *The Fire Worshippers* (Bombay: Strand Books, 1968), p. 194.
11. Dina Mehta, *And Some Take a Lover* (Delhi: Rupa, 1992), p. 192.
12. Ketayun Gould, quoted in Roxanne Kavarana's research paper, "The Parsis in India: A Community Under Stress," *The Times of India Research Foundation Journal*, April 1989, p. 4.
13. Nergis Dalal, *The Sisters* (Delhi: Hind, 1973), pp. 58-59.
14. Firdaus Kanga, *Trying To Grow* (New Delhi: Ravi Dayal Publishers, 1990), p. 33.
15. Rohinton Mistry, "Exercisers," *Tales from Firozsha Baag* (Ontario, Canada: Penguin, 1987), p. 205.
16. Bapsi Sidhwa, *An American Brat* (Delhi: Penguin, 1994), p. 268.
17. Lyla Bavadam, "Thus Spake Zarathustra," Sunday magazine of the *Ananda Bazar Patrika Group*, 7-13, May 1995, p. 40.
18. Keki J. Gandhi, ed., "Fed Newsletter No. 138," of the Federation of Parsi Zoroastrian Anjumans of India, April 1995, pp. 1-2.
19. "Marriages of Parsis with women of other communities are only given a limited recognition in the community. The children of such marriages are accepted conditionally, but not however, the mothers, who remain foreign to the community. Parsi women who marry outside of the community however are categorically excluded and are therefore—along with other children—lost to the community. Also the average age for Parsi marriages is one of the highest in the world, 28 years for females and 31 years for males." Cited in Eckehard Kulke, *The Parsis in India: A Minority as Agent of Social Change* (Delhi: Bell Books), p. 78.
20. Novy Kapadia and A.G. Khan, ed., *The Parsis: Madyan to Sanjan: An Appraisal of Ethnic Anxieties Reflected in Literature* (New Delhi: Creative, 1997).

From Behind a Fine Veil: A Feminist Reading of Three Parsi Novels

NILUFER E. BHARUCHA

Parsi women have not been rigorously subjected to the regimen of the Purdah, but they share the limited and reductive world of their Hindu and Muslim sisters in India. Parsi traditions are rooted in the patriarchal society of ancient Iran and these patriarchal moorings have been reinforced by a 1300 year long residence in India.[1] Association with the British during the Raj coated some Parsis with a thin patina of westernization and emancipation,[2] but for the majority of Parsi women the fine veil remained, from behind which they looked at the world. As Sherry B. Ortner has put it: 'the secondary status of woman in society is one of the true universals, a pan-cultural fact.'[3]

Child marriages, truncated schooling and multiple childbirths were till recently the lot of most Parsi women. Bapaiji, in Boman Desai's *The Memory of Elephants*,[4] belongs to this group of repressed women. She is hemmed in by an oppressive world which she determinedly pushes aside to create her own female space, but is not quite successful.

Lenny, the girl-child narrator of Bapsi Sidhwa's *Ice-Candy Man*,[5] inhabits a more sophisticated cityscape, as compared to the rural universe of Bapaiji. However, she too is subject to the limitations of her gender. In fact she is a doubly marginalized figure—female and physically handicapped. Lenny, from behind this veil of marginality, offers a uniquely subaltern view of the bloody birthing of Pakistan. This view is as strong an indictment of patriarchy, as it is of colonialism.

Soul-destroying, mindless drudgery is the destiny of Dilnawaz in Rohinton Mistry's first novel, *Such A Long Journey.*[6] Dilnawaz hovers at the periphery of the novel as her domestic crisis assumes national importance. Her husband—the man—is an active participant in this crisis but she is the hapless spectator. She can only take recourse to superstition and prayers, as her beloved eldest son drifts away from the family and her husband's life is endangered by sinister elements outside her control.

This paper examines the world view provided by these Parsi women from behind the veil of patriarchy, marginality and haplessness and attempts a feminist reading of the three novels under study.

Two of these novels, *The Memory of Elephants* and *Such A Long Journey* are written by men, while the author of *Ice-Candy Man* is a woman. The paper also explores the difference this has made to the presentation of women characters in these books.

Desai's *The Memory of Elephants* begins with a section entitled 'Bapaiji.' Bapaiji is the Gujarati word for grandmother. The portrait of Bapaiji reveals the many female stereotypes, most writers harbour about their women characters. This is in spite of the fact that Desai's Bapaiji is apparently a 'strong' woman and Desai's male protagonist Homi, grudgingly admires her for this. The strength and admirable qualities, however, are related to Bapaiji's 'man-like' nature and behaviour—she is almost an honorary man. This tendency of attributing male, and hence superior, characteristics to a female character, happens when in the "creation of fictions, writers call upon the same signifying codes that pervade social intersections, representing in fiction the rituals and symbols that make up that social practice."[7]

What is, therefore, required is a reading of the novel which will go beneath the surface of the man-like Bapaiji and seek what Adrienne Rich has called "the true knowledge of women" which comes from "uncovering the hidden, making ourselves present . . . [and defining] a reality which resonates to *us*, which affirms *our* being."

In *The Memory of Elephants*, the male protagonist, Homi,

lives in a disoriented world upon which the Memo-Scan he has invented, imposes its own order. This Memo-Scan gives him the 'memory of elephants, the memory of whales, the equation of the universe.' It is an instrument which activates the collective unconscious of the Parsis, what Bapaiji calls the 'memory of the soul.' Bapaiji is Homi's guide through the intricate maze of racial memory. She is not just Homi's past, she is also the Parsis' link with rural India. She is a symbol of those first Parsis who had made a pact with Jadhav Rana, the king of Sanjan, who had given them refuge in Gujarat. The pact had included among other things, a promise to embrace the local language,[9] customs and clothes. So Bapaiji speaks only in Gujarati to Homi, whom she calls her 'American grandson.'

When the novel opens, Bapaiji is already dead, but 'speaks' to Homi from 'the Kingdom of God.' However, Bapaiji's voice is that of a man. In the magical realism of Desai's novel, Bapaiji is, in the 'hereafter,' a man. Bapaiji has shed what the male world considers a 'restrictive' female body: 'I am a man here; I wear pants, I walk more quickly, upright, directly forward without that ridiculous waddle with which so many women are afflicted, without those huge breasts like a cow elephant's which always got in my way; I even have a deeper voice—you will doubtless find this comical, but it is what I had always wanted, to be a man, to do things men did.' This is a classic example of what Kate Millett[10] has termed the "expected traits of minority status: group self-hatred and self-rejection." In a man-dominated world, women, irrespective of their class/caste, are minority figures, who believe in the male-version of the inferior attributes of women and as a result hate themselves.

Bapaiji's definitive statement also opens up various avenues of investigation, the most important of which are the questions of gender-identity and male taboos/disgust connected with the female body.

A flashback to Bapaiji's childhood in Navsari, a small town in Southern Gujarat, reveals an early dissatisfaction with her feminine identity. As Millett says, the fact of being female is a biological reality, the matter of feminine identity is a matter of sociological conditioning. Bapaiji, from early girlhood, waged a battle against the constriction of a feminine identity. She is what Heilbrun has called a "male-identified" girl.[11]

Bapaiji plays tag and 'Hu-tu-tu' with the boys and is unembarrassed when her skirt rides to her thighs. She defies social expectations and refuses to identify with her mother. She takes to wearing her brother's pants in an effort to rid herself of the restrictions of her sex. By putting on male clothes, she also indirectly seeks to put on the power that goes with being a man.[12]

With approaching adolescence, Bapaiji finds it increasingly difficult to ignore her female body and begins to consider it an encumbrance to her fantasy of being a boy. She soon finds herself married off to the staid Hormusji Seervai. Hormusji had been married earlier to a girl who had a baby by someone else. The marriage had been annulled and 'the baby made to drink milk.' Here we are in a social milieu where child marriages and infanticide were a reality.

This marriage 'made a woman out of Bapaiji' and she hated it. The reductive existence of the youngest daughter-in-law in a patriarchal family jars on Bapaiji. She is subjected to all the taboos patriarchy imposes on female sexuality—isolation during menstruation, segregation from unrelated males, etc. Bapaiji nearly revolts against these sanctions but cannot subvert her husband's deep-rooted faith in the patriarchal system. And since Bapaiji cannot imagine a revolt outside the matrix of male approval, she is unwillingly subdued.

However, the most restrictive bondage is imposed on her by motherhood: 'She had hated pregnancy and she hated motherhood; it was just one more way, perhaps the most diabolical, of tying down a woman.' Chodorow says that societies 'ensure an adequate supply of child-tenders by encouraging all women to be empathic and nurturant.'[13] Bapaiji resists being the nurturant female.

With the arrival of middle-age, Bapaiji involves herself with the local affairs of Navsari, attends meetings and makes speeches. Yet she turns down the invitation to be on the governing board of an institution,[13] 'Fifteen years of domesticity had tamed Bapaiji to the point of questioning a woman's role outside the home.'

In her later years Bapaiji is given the title of Rajya Ratna by the Maharaja of Baroda, for the services rendered to Navsari. In spite of these successes, achieved as a woman, Bapaiji wishes herself into becoming a man after her death. The restrictions she had faced as a girl and woman, the fights she had to wage against a suffocating patriarchy, make her turn against herself—against her identity as a woman. It is only by becoming a man that she can finally shed the restrictive veil which had impeded her existence as a woman.

Bapsi Sidhwa's girl-child Lenny in *Ice-Candy Man* is rather different from Bapaiji. She is the creation of a woman writer. Gubar has remarked: "If artistic creativity is likened to biological creativity, the terror of inspiration for women is experienced quite literally as the terror of being entered, deflowered, possessed, taken, had, broken, ravished—all words which illustrate the pain of the passive self whose boundaries are being violated."[14] The woman writer is like Charlotte Bronte, who suffers a 'secret, inward wound.'

These are rather perceptive remarks in the context of Sidhwa's novel and her protagonist. Here Lenny experiences through the surrogate character of her Ayah, the terror and trauma of rape, as her world is shattered and the boundaries of her universe violated.

Sidhwa's novel, like Desai's is technically sophisticated. It was post-modernist characteristics of fantasy and the fragmentation of time. It also employs the device of allegory. As Mihai Spariousu says: 'Allegory appears whenever there is an overload felt so overwhelming that it can only be dealt with in a multiplicity of dimensions.' As allegory, the novel operates at a different level from that of a pure narrative.

Ice-Candy Man is set in the partition period when the colonizing power, presented her erstwhile Empire with the parting gift of a yet-to-heal wound, i.e. the partition of India into the two nations of India and Pakistan. Lenny, the girl-child is herself a wounded creature. She is maimed by polio. Thus to the biological disadvantage of being female in a male world, are added the handicaps of a physical deformity and a colonial milieu. The novel could thus be interpreted as a political allegory.

However, it also operates as a feminist allegory. Through the character of Lenny, Sidhwa explores a female universe hemmed in by the restricting and reductive forces of patriarchy and colonialism.

The novel begins on this note of restriction and reduction, 'My world is compressed. . . . My child's mind is blocked by the gloom emanating from the wire-mesh screening the oblong ventilation slits [of the Salvation Army wall]. I feel such sadness for the dumb creature I imagine lurking behind the wall. I know it is dumb because I have listened to its silence, my ear to the wall.' This capacity to 'listen to silence,' to create text from a negation, is the special gift of women writers who are denied articulation in a man's world. It is also significant that this silence is experienced in relation to the Salvation Army wall—the Salvation Army bringing the civilizing message of a colonizing power to the dumb Calibans of this earth.

Sidhwa's opening pages also stress other woman-related issues. Lenny, unlike Bapaiji is not male-identified. She has strong female models with whom she has a woman-to-woman bonding. This is in keeping with current psychological theories of a girl-child's positive bond with her mother. Lenny identifies with her Godmother: 'The bond that ties her strength to my weakness, my fierce demands to her nurturing, my trust to her capacity to contain that trust—my loneliness to her compassion—is stronger, than the bond of motherhood. More satisfying than the ties between men and women.'

Lenny also shares a strong bond with her mother and her Ayah. Both these women also possess the strong female qualities of Godmother—strength, a capacity to trust and be trusted, nurturant natures and compassion. These two women also share with all other women the pressures and pains inflicted by a male world.

The mother blames herself for Lenny's polio: 'I'm to blame.' she says, 'I left her to the ayahs.' Here she is a victim of social expectations *vis-a-vis* the female as a nurturer. The Ayah become a victim to the politics of rape and is violated and humiliated like countless other women in that apocalyptical year of 1947, caught in the crossfire between rampant patriarchy and callous colonialism.

Lenny's world is also populated by other deprived female characters. Papoo is the daughter of Muccho, the sweeper woman, who considers her to be a nuisance and a curse. The maltreatment of Papoo by Muccho runs through the novel like a malevolent strand. Muccho is a victim of a patriarchal society which has engendered a fierce self-hatred in her, which manifests itself in violence against her daughter whom she sees as an extension of herself. She finally marries Papoo off to a middle-aged dwarf. This is the ultimate wound she inflicts not just on her daughter, but also on herself.

The question of education and the female-child, is also touched upon in this novel. Lenny's handicaps are piled one on top of the other and her lameness is allied to her femaleness, to deprive her of a proper education. The doctor tells her parents, 'she'll marry—have children—lead a carefree, happy life. No need to strain her with studies and exams, he advises: thereby sealing my fate.'

Thus deprived of schooling, Lenny is thrust more and more into the company of her Ayah with whom she explores the multi-faceted world of Lahore. It is this association which forms the core of *Ice-Candy Man*.

Through the agency of the Ayah, Lenny is awakened to a frank appreciation of female sexuality. The Ayah is assiduously courted by a cross-section of men in Lahore. The favoured suitor is the Masseur whose clever fingers 'massage Ayah under her sari' till 'she moans, a fragile, piteous sound of pleasure.' From these moments of vicariously shared excitements Lenny discovers the 'secret rhythm of creation and mortality.' It is through the Ayah and her many admirers that Lenny also learns of betrayal, pain and violation.

The idyll which Lenny and Ayah share with the Masseur, the Afghan knife-sharpner and the Ice-Candy Man is abruptly shattered as India is torn apart into two bleeding nations. The fantasy of romantic love is shattered and Ayah, the chivalrously-courted beloved, becomes the victim of a male conflict.

Overnight the secular landscape of Lahore is fragmented into religious enclaves. 'One day everybody is themselves—and the next day they are Hindu, Muslim, Sikh, Christian. People shrink, dwindling into symbols. Ayah is no longer just my all-encompassing-Ayah—she is also a token—a Hindu.' As a token[15] Ayah is raped by her erstwhile Muslim admirers and friends. She is abused in retaliation for the trainloads of dead Muslims and bags full of the breasts of Muslim women cut off by Hindu men. As Millett has put it rape is an offence 'one male commits upon another—a matter of abusing "his woman." The Ayah becomes a victim of these sexual politics allied to the carnage set off by a departing colonial power.

The most tragic aspect of the abuse of Ayah is that it is set off by Lenny's 'truth-infected tongue.' It is Lenny who betrays Ayah to the mob which had come looking for her at Lenny's house. Taken in by the blandishments of the Ice-Candy Man, 'Don't be scared Lenny Baby. . . . I'll protect Ayah with my life!' Lenny gives away her hiding place and sees the Ice-Candy Man change before her eyes and knows that 'I have betrayed Ayah.' Here Lenny is like Muccho who betrays her own daughter into male bondage. A betrayal, the result of centuries of patriarchal conditioning, a misplaced faith in the integrity of men and a searing lack of confidence in and hatred for the female self.

The much-loved Ayah now becomes what Lenny's boy-cousin calls 'the opposite of Virgin Mary'—a whore. As a whore she is outside the pale of 'respectable' society. Lenny is kept away from her as her mother and Godmother strive to 'rehabilitate' Ayah and thousands of other violated women like her. Women, who like Hamida, Lenny's new Ayah, have become untouchables because their husbands 'do not like other men to touch their women.'

Ayah is by the end of the novel married to the Ice-Candy Man, now professes to be desperately in love with her. But having been betrayed by him Ayah prefers to go back to her family in Amritsar—which is now in India. In a final, sinister sentence Sidhwa tells us that the 'Ice-Candy Man too, disappears across the Wagah border into India,' thereby underlining the ever-present nature of the betrayer.

Rohinton Mistry's *Such a Long Journey* tells the tale of Gustad Noble who is unwittingly caught up in the world of Indian politics and mired in the quicksands of high finance and warmongering that accompanied the Indo-Pak conflict of 1971. The book is based on the real-life scandal involving Sohrab Nagarwala, the State Bank cashier, who was at the center of the 60 lakh rupees scam which had rocked the Indira Gandhi government.

In this novel the domestic life of Gustad Noble clashes with the forces of money—capitalism. Trapped in this crossfire is Dilnavaz, Gustad's wife and their children. This is very obviously a novel written from the male point of view. It opens with Gustad Noble saying his early morning prayers and closes with Noble's belated action of tearing off the black-out papers from his ventilators and windows—thereby symbolically letting in light and reality. It is the male characters in the novel who 'act,' who 'do' things—Gustad, his sons, Major Billimoria—a thinly-disguised Nagarwala, the sinister underworld figures of Ghulam Mohammed, the Christian friend Malcolm and the Bank cashier Dinshawji. Even the retarded and lame Tehmul initiates some action.

The female characters are the passive recipients of the results of these actions. Dilnavaz, her daughter Roshan and their neighbour Miss Kutpitia are female stereotypes much beloved of male writers around the world. Like the secondary status of women, female stereotypes are also a pan-cultural phenomenon. Dilnavaz is the perfect foil to Gustad—soft and pretty, where he is big and muscular. As a couple they exhibit the typical features of male aggressiveness and female passivity. As Millett has sarcastically noted: 'If aggressiveness is the trait of the master class, docility must be the corresponding trait of a subject group.'

The child Roshan is a doll-like creature, sickly and fragile. She is in direct contrast to the sons Sohrab and Darius. She has neither the mental prowess of Sohrab nor the physical robustness of Darius. As is the wont of female children, she cries, gets scared and is petted and cosseted by Daddy.

Miss Kutpitia (her name in Gujarati means the 'quarrelsome one') is the archetypal spinster, much reviled by the neighbourhood. She is 'the ubiquitous witch of fairy stories come to life,' Mistry informs us. Miss Kutpitia could have been a strong character, privy to ancient wisdom of women, living a life of independence. However, all we get is a caricature of a silly, superstitious woman. Miss Kutpitia's spells and magic, her being a 'witch,' is not at all in a positive feminist sense.

Instead her magic spells are reduced to being a mere manifestation of women's irrational nature. Mistry pokes fun at this 'inferior' female behaviour. Miss Kutpitia, being a spinster and a little batty is to be allowed her superstitions. However, Dilnavaz, the happily-married woman, a 'fulfilled' mother's belief in Miss Kutpitia's 'jadu-mantar,' is indirectly attributed to her concern and love for her husband and children. So, whenever she is not cooking, filling water or settling quarrels between her husband and their son Sohrab, she is found conspiring with Miss Kutpitia in creating spells for the well-being of her family. Sohrab's intractability is sought to be removed by a spell involving a lizard's tail. Limes, chillies, alum and even poor Tehmul are pressed into service to cure Roshan's illness.

Gustad, the rational male, is never party to this 'mumbo-jumbo.' His mind is occupied with more important matters of national importance—how to legalize the large sums of money sent by Major Billimoria. He is not house-bound like Dilnavaz. He ranges as far as Delhi.

Dilnavaz's universe is on the other hand the restricted world of her home and she ranges only as far as Miss Kutpitia's flat. Her role is that of wife, mother and home-maker; she cooks, serves and withdraws discreetly while the men discuss politics. Unlike Lenny, she is not even aware of them. Nor does Mistry attempt to probe beneath the surface of the reductive lives of Dilnavaz and Miss Kutpitia. He does not attempt to seek the reasons for their belief in spells, instead there is an exploitation of their 'stupidity' for comic effect. The pathos underlying Miss Kutpitia's lonely life, or Dilnavaz's drudgery is not explored. Indeed the pathos and sympathy in the book is reserved for the eponymously named Gustad as he nobly strives for the welfare of his family. There is even empathy for the retarded Tehmul as he copulates with Roshan's stolen doll but not a sliver of sympathy is thrown the way of Miss Kutpitia. Maybe her stridency and apparently unbalanced behaviour too were caused by repressed sexuality. Mistry, however, is not willing to concede sexuality to his female characters. Dilnavaz interacts only in a Romantic way with her husband, not sensually, or even worse, sexually! Miss Kutpitia is celibate in the cause of an orphaned nephew, who eventually dies and little Roshan, unlike Lenny, is neither troubled nor curious about her body.

In the novel entitled *Such a Long Journey*, the female characters in it do not journey at all. They remain stationary while the world around them moves and changes. Theirs is a static universe where they are even denied the knowledge of their own stultification and repression by their creator. This novel which is a fictional account of recent history is in the genre of what Greene and Kahn have called history as 'written by men, from a male perspective. What has been designated historically significant has been deemed so according to a valuation of power and activity in the public world.'

Such writing disregards the 'histories' of the Dilnavazs, Miss Kutpitias and Roshans. These women have to emerge from behind the veil, to speak, to fill in the blank pages of their stories. It is feminist, woman-centered readings which will help in tearing this veil to shreds so that a Bapaiji may exist proudly as a woman, instead of aspiring to be a man and a Lenny's universe is not subjected to the brutality of repeated violence.

NOTES

1. The present-day Parsis are descendants of the Zoroastrians who fled Iran around 800 A.D., after its invasion by the Arabs. They fled to avoid forcible conversion to Islam and took refuge in Gujarat, on the Western coast of India. Here they were given refuge by the King of Sanjan, Jadav Rana, on the condition that they neither prose-

lytize nor wage wars. These Zoroastrians were called Parsis in India, after their language, Farsi. The name Parsi could also be traced to the Persian province of Pars, from where these people were presumed to have come.

2. In British India, unhampered by the taboos of the Hindu caste system and the isolationism of the Muslims, the Parsis surged ahead and became the most westernized of all Indian communities. However, this westernization was mainly confined to men. Even though some rich Parsis educated their daughters, who became doctors, lawyers and teachers, the majority of Parsi women received little education and were subjected to the taboos and repressions of a strict patriarchy.
3. Sherry B. Ortner, "Is Female to Male as Nature is to Culture?," Rosaldo and Lamphere, eds., *Woman, Culture and Society* (Stanford, Cal.: Stanford University Press, 1974).
4. Boman Desai, *The Memory of Elephants* (London: Andre Deutsch, 1988).
5. Bapsi Sidhwa, *Ice-Candy Man* (UK: Penguin Books, 1988).
6. Rohinton Mistry, *Such a Long Journey* (London: Faber and Faber, 1991).
7. G. Greene and Kahn C., *Making a Difference: Feminist Literary Criticism* (New York: Methuen, 1985)
8. Adrienne Rich, 'Taking Women Students Seriously,' in *On Lies, Secrets and Silences: Selected Prose 1966-1978* (New York: Norton, 1979).
9. The language spoken in Gujarat is called Gujarati. It belongs to the Indo-Aryan group of languages. However, this modern day Gujarati developed only around the 15th century A.D. At the time the Parsis made a pact with Jadhav Rana, the local language was Apabhransh Bhasha or what Grierson (quoted in Rawal Anantrai, *Gujarati Sahitya*, 3rd ed., Macmillan, Bombay, 1968) called Old Gujarati. It was from Old Gujarati that Nagar/Gujar was derived between 10th and 12th century A.D.; modern Gujarati developed from this Nagar/Gujar language.
10. Kate Millett, *Sexual Politics* (New York: Doubleday, 1969).
11. Carolyn Heilbrun, *Reinventing Womanhood* (New York, 1979).
12. Sandra Gilbert, "Costumes of the Mind: Transvestitism as Metaphor in Modern Literature," in E. Abel, ed., *Writing and Sexual Difference* (Sussex: Harvester, 1982).
13. Nancy Chodorow, *The Reproduction of Mothering* (Berkley, 1978).
14. Susan Gubar, "The Blank Page and the Issue of Female Creativity," in E. Abel.

15. The Ayah's character can also be interpreted as a symbol of the Indian earth and that of the titular Ice-Candy Man as the ravisher—the conqueror(s) of India. (For details see N.E. Bharucha, "The Parsi Voice in Recent Indian English Fiction: An Assertion of Ethnic Identity," in V. Sarang and N. Bharucha, eds., *Indian English Fiction 1980-1990: An Assessment*, B.R., Delhi).

Power, Politics and Politicians in the Parsi Novels

R.S. PATHAK

Literature and politics may appear to be two irreconcilable aspects of human experience. While literature is regarded as the product of the highest form of development of aesthetic sensibility, politics is generally considered to be something mundane and gross. A piece of literature, however, cannot afford to peevishly shy away from social reality. As a social discourse, it is written by a social being for some other members of the society to read and comprehend what is written and conveyed. A serious work of literature, created as it is within the framework of existing social relations, is not only a living document of the contemporary happening but also of the historical processes underlying them. This is particularly true of the novel. Novelists have on several occasions revealed more political and socio-cultural truths than all the professional politicians put together.

The relationship between art and society therefore cannot be ignored. A work of literature contributes to the reaffirmation or devaluation of people's ideas, goals and values; it moves or shakes people. As Ngugi wa Thiong'o puts it,

> literature cannot escape from the class power structures that shape our everyday life. Here a writer has no choice. Whether or not he is aware of it, his works reflect one or more aspects of the intense economic, political, cultural and ideological struggles in a society. What he can choose is one or the other side in the battlefield. . . . What he or she cannot do is to remain neutral. Every writer is a

> writer in politics. The only question is what and whose politics.[1]

It would be interesting to evaluate the Parsis' response to great national events and political movements and their attitude to some well-known politicians, on the basis of a close study of the Parsi fiction. The present paper aims at highlighting the Parsis's dilemma and ambivalence as reflected in some representative works by the Parsis.

II

The Parsis constitute a minuscule minority community in India. They are the descendants of the Iranians who had sought refuge here in the eighth century A.D. when Iran was invaded and conquered by Arab invaders. Using Toynbee's terminology, the Indian Parsis may be called one of the important "creative minorities."[2] They are the "fossil"[3] of an extinct culture, and yet have gone through a remarkable process of internal change in some respects and have influenced, in turn, as active participants, the process of transformation in Indian society. Despite their latent ethnocentrism, religious exclusivity and identity crisis, they have been able to make a niche for themselves in India on account of their close contacts with Europeans, inner dynamics, social orientation, willingness to learn and a high level of education.

On the whole, the Parsis limited themselves to non-political professions. Notwithstanding some notable exceptions, they generally practised political abstinence and neutrality. They were advised by their social leaders not to involve in politics. For example, Sir Jamsetjee Jeejeebhoy, the President of the Parsi Central Association, advised the Parsis in 1930 "to keep aloof from politics at the present juncture."[4] The decision to keep away from politics was prompted by common sense and instinct for preservation. They knew that they stood to gain little from the controversy between the British rulers and Indians and, later, from the dissensions between the Hindus and the Muslims, for it was thought that "When the elephants fight, the forest suffers, and you [Parsis] have no business to be there; you have nothing to do in that battle."[5] There are nevertheless stray references to major political events affecting the subcontinent and major political players in the political drama, which give us a fair idea of the Parsis' attitudes to them. It will be worthwhile to collate these views and see if they constitute a body of opinion expressive of the mindset of the Parsi populace in general and the Parsi novelists in particular.

In the pre-Independence India, the Parsis were known for their loyalty to the British rulers. They considered themselves to be really lucky for having been "placed under the enlightened British rule."[6] Loyalty to the rulers was a deeply ingrained virtue with them. According to the Parsee Ghamat, "A disloyal Parsee is as rare as a black turnip."[7] Through private and semi-official channels the Parsis conveyed their gratitude to the rulers. At times this expression of solidarity with the Britishers crossed Indian borders. In 1869, for example, a monument was built in London's Regent Park with Sir Cowasjee Jehangir's donation with the inscription "as token of gratitude to the people of England for the protection enjoyed by him and his Parsee Fellow Countrymen under the British Rule in India."[8] Approximately 6,000 Parsis gathered in Bombay on the occasion of the Crimean War in order to offer public prayers for the victory of the British.[9] The Parsi press of the time unequivocally conveys their pro-English sentiments. "To serve the British flag in the different parts of the east," wrote *The Parsi*, summing up the state of affairs, "is now the earnest desire of a large number of the younger generation of educated and well-to-do Parsis, which are daily getting dissatisfied with their surroundings in India."[10]

The Parsis' ethnocentrism went in hand with a widespread anglophilia based on a high degree of anglicization. According to *The Parsi*, "The closer union of the Europeans and Parsis is the finest thing that can happen to our race. . . . The complete Europeanization of the Parsis is now a mere matter of time."[11] Characters in the Parsi novels almost invariably adopt European values and relate themselves to their Rulers' way of life. Roshni, the main character in Dina Mehta's novel *And Some Take a Lover*, for example, observes: "The Parsee way of life was the most Westernized in India. More than the Anglo-Indians they could afford the tastes, the standards, the luxuries introduced by the alien rulers." In this respect, Roshni was not different from other affluent modern young people of her community:

> She spoke English better than her adopted mother-tongue, Gujarati. She even thought in English. . . . She read no Gujarati books or papers. She did not know Persian, the language of her ancestors. . . . She did not know a word of Avesta, in which her prayers were written. She knew more about Christianity than of her own religion. . . . She was more familiar with the Bible than with the *Gathas*, with the Acts of Apostles than with the life of Zarathustra.[12]

The Parsis' anglophilia, as said earlier, was the direct result of pragmatic considerations. Faredoon Junglewalla in Bapsi Sidhwa's *The Crow Eaters* spells out the advantages of being close to the English. "Where do you think we'd be," he asks, "if we did not curry favours?" and adds: "Next to the nawabs, rajas and princelings, we are the greatest toadies of the British Empire! . . . Otherwise, where would we Parsis be? Cleaning our gutters with the untouchables—a dispersed pinch of snuff sneezed from the heterogeneous nostrils of India!"[13] These considerations obliged the Parsis to be loyal and respectful to the British during the Raj.

There were also in some circles of the Parsi community apprehensions about the two more numerous communities and feelings of insecurity in the days to come. Their real struggle for existence and the survival of their community, they feared, would begin on the day of the departure of the British. The Parsis had no autonomous political organization of their own and a large group of them attempted to find a political base in the westernized, secular ideology. Some of the Parsi Associations offered radical solutions to this problem including the founding of a colony outside of India and the raising of Parsi Pioneer Battalion for the military defence of the community. In

1943 they even demanded an autonomous Parsi state, 'Parsistan,' within the Indian Union of about 1,000 square miles around Nausari, where the Parsis would not have to fear being degraded to a socially and politically inferior position.[14] Moreover, in 1950, after the Independence, the Parsi Central Association passed a resolution demanding reservation of seats for members of 'political minorities.'

In *And Some Take a Lover*, which presents the conflicting loyalties of a Parsi family enmeshed in the political and personal turmoil, Roshni's mother, who represents the mature, elderly persons of her community, feels that once the British leave, the country would go to dogs. "See what a country we'll end up as," she would say, "once the British leave the country, scoundrels of the first water will line their pockets from unclean sources, judges will be bribed, juries fixed and you Uttamchands and Mulchandanis will become multi-multies while honest folk like us will starve." (37) Similar apprehensions are expressed by Col. Bharucha, the leader of the Parsis in Lahore, in Bapsi Sidhwa's *Ice-Candy-Man*, on the eve of the Independence:

> No one knows which way the wind will blow. . . . There may be not one but two—or even three—nations! And the Parsees might find themselves championing the wrong side if they don't look before they leap! . . . If we're stuck with the Hindus they'll convert us by the sword! And God help us if we're stuck with the Sikhs![15]

In the event of the Partition of the country, therefore, they resolve to "run with the hounds and hunt with the hare." To most of the Parsis, the going away of the British would bring miseries of many kinds. "Parsis were the kings of banking in those days" and earned a lot of respect, but now they would be reduced to "second class citizens."[16] To some others, "Johnie Walker scotch [was] freely available under the British," which was to become rare.[17] The only consolation that the Parsis can derive is from the inexpensive supply of beef; let the majority community "eat pulses and grams and beans spiced with their stinky asafoetida . . . keep down the price of beef. And it is healthier because it is holier."[18] Because of their numerical superiority it is the members of the majority community that are vehemently criticized. Even Roshni's great-aunt Piroja, supposedly a "liberal" otherwise, would come out with her "flaming denunciations" when it came to talk about them and she had her own reasons for it:

> the Hindu wore *dhotis;* he turned his world into a vast spittoon by ejecting streams of betel juice on walls, staircases, roads, pavements; his bathrooms stank of urine and kitchens of *heeng*; [and] he was dishonest in his business practices and mean with his money.[19]

This approach was bound to beget problems of a deep psychological nature. This would culminate in many cases into elitism, craze for power and alienation.[20]

III

During the Raj, the Parsis acted very often as mediators between the British and Indians. Because of this significance and also because of the fairness of their skin and a better access to and mastery over English education, the Parsis developed in due course what Kulke calls "elite consciousness." (262) Some of them regarded themselves as a "purely white race"[21] and consciously remained aloof from the 'backward' Indian society. Some others took pride in consciously copying English manners, declaring that "We want the English language, English manners, and English behaviour for our wives and daughters, and until these are supplied, it is but just clear that the present gulf between the Englishman and the Indian should remain as wide as ever."[22] The deliberate anglicisation at times resulted in ambivalence and created serious problems in the process of acculturation, and the Parsis continued to live with the co-existence of orthodoxy and progressive attitudes. Consequently, as Masani puts it "The Parsees . . . [were] a puzzle to their neighbours. Their virtues lie very close to their weaknesses. The same sterling qualities that contribute towards their intellectual progress drag them down to the abyss of unreasoning orthodoxy."[23] If they found things not moving according to their wishes, they would occasionally resort to self-deprecation. More recently, diagnosing their problem, Luhrmann feels that some of their self-criticism may be an "epiphenomena of a rapidly changing culture." He also ascribes their problems, to some extent, to a losing "power play":

> Parsis seem to be caught by this power play, and by a slow lag [of] tome in adjusting their semiotics to the changing political order. At least some Parsis seem now more likely to describe Hindus—who have won the battle for political and economic domination—as aggressive and progressing; many Parsis seem to condemn themselves as effeminate, irrational, and backward . . . this phenomenon is not unique to Parsis but is shared in some respect by other elite, sophisticated people whose grandparents defined themselves through the values of the western colonizing culture and who now, as postcolonial subjects in a very different world, must reconstruct and reorient a quite complex sensibility.[24]

This would explain adjustment problems and irritations in facing the complex reality of the present postmodern social set-up. It is also for this reason that disenchantment for the present and nostalgia for the past are writ large in the Parsi novels.

It is interesting to note that words like 'power' recur in some Parsi novels meaningfully. Roshni, in *And Some Take a Lover*, for example, who had never met Gandhi, was "aghast when she thought of the strange, awesome power he wielded over other people's lives." (219) After her failure to marry Sudhir, an indignant Roshni begins to see Gandhi as a despot. "What manner of man was this Gandhi," she asks "who could command such terrible obedience from his people? A despot, a tyrant more implacable than any feudal lord who ever reigned over the serfs." (200) The influence of Gandhi is viewed here in terms of 'power play.' *Ice-Candy-Man* contains a still better example of this kind of relationship. Commenting upon political prisoners and their "short cut to fame and fortune," (36) Col. Bharucha remarks: "It is no longer just a struggle for Home Rule. It is a struggle for power. Who's going to rule once we get *Swaraj?* . . . Hindus, Muslims and even the Sikhs are going to jockey for power." (40) The banker Mr. Bankwalla advises his people not to "try to prosper immoderately" and never to "try to exercise real power." Through Lenny, the narrator, the novelist seems to convey her view on the relationship of others' needs with one's power: "when you want something very much it gives people power over you." (72) The Godmother with her "network of espionage" represents the real centre of power. "It is in her nature to know things" so much so that "No baby—not even a kitten—is delivered within the sphere of her influence without her becoming instantly aware of its existence." (211) The wisdom arising out of knowledge is the ultimate source of her strength:

> And this is the source of her immense power: this reservoir of random knowledge, and her knowledge of ancient lore and wisdom and herbal remedy. You cannot be near her without feeling her uncanny strength. People bring to her their joys and woes. Show her their sores and swollen joints. Distilling the right herbs adroitly instilling the right word in the right ear, she secures wishes, smooths relationships, cures illnesses, battles wrongs, solaces grief and prevents mistakes. She has access to many ears. No one knows how many. (221-22)

Pitted against the Godmother, ordinary human beings would look helpless—"Weak, susceptible and fickle." (238) According to her, "there's some things best left alone." Her "canny and uncanny resources" and "the naked power and fury of her attack" (249) would make others twitch and cower. The narrator can feel "a potent sense of her presence" and "can smell the formidable power of her attack." (250) The novel's politics is effectively juxtaposed against day-to-day happenings and through imaginative insights, abstractions of politics and religion are made to interplay.

Yet another kind of power relation is depicted in Rohinton Mistry's *A Fine Balance*. Power in this novel is mainly of five types—exploitative, manipulative, competitive, nutrient, and integrative,[25] although these categories overlap and interpenetrate at times. Exploitative power can be successful when power-wielders take effective decisions regarding choices and means. An epistemic power[26] thus precedes the manifestation of the exploitative power. This power play originates from the sufferer's "own desperation and anxiety."[27] The 'nutrient power' is "for" the other, accruing from a certain care and responsibility. Integrative power, however, makes opposites come together forging proper links to attain "power with the other."[28] The power play, as Mistry shows, is responsible for tension and violence in the society. Self-assertion by the marginalised invites aggression and violence. And the powers that be always side with the perpetuators of aggression and exploitation. We may even have in the name of public good "violence from above."[29] We have in *A Fine Balance* illustrations of these various kinds of power and their effects. In the present scenario, politics is destiny, which changes only in form and not in essence. Integrity without power is poignantly weak. In our world "good and bad" are interlinked, and what one is advised to do is to maintain "a fine balance between hope and despair."[30] The recurrence of the idea of balance is ironic as in *Measure for Measure*, for "With the Emergency, everything is upside-down. Black can be made white, day turned into night." (362) The political and the normal are interlinked in the novel. As John Ball points out, "what galvanizes this novel is not only the urgency behind its rogues' gallery of moral grotesques, but also the way the intersection of the political and the personal is given such compelling moral resonance."[31] Dina Dalal in the novel regards the Emergency as "Government problems—games played by people in power" and in her naivety thinks that "It doesn't affect ordinary people like us." (75) Later on, however, she comes to the conclusion that "the road had turned bumpy." (78) But, as Isvar Darji tells his nephew, "this is the way the world works. Some people are in the middle, some are on the border." (82)

The relationship between the centre and the margin is one of the significant themes in the novel.

A Fine Balance is a postmodernist novel in more ways than one. It highlights the emergence of the less privileged classes in a big way on the political firmament of the country. It powerfully delineates the rise of the Dalits, their assertion, the social tension in the rural areas, the changing aspirations of the lower castes and caste-based violence. When Isvar goes to the police chowki about his nephew's castration, the constable on duty "wondered if this meant a fresh outbreak of inter-caste disturbances." (539) Marx conceptualized a classless society, which is yet to happen in India. Postmodernists like Derrida and Lyotard seem to endorse an anti-politics rejecting both dominant institutions and oppositional social movements. Some other postmoderns have expressed their disdain of the political in terms of James Dean's nonchalance or Stephen Stills's contention that "politics is bullshit." Postmodernists like Foucault,[32] who have rethought the nature of power in a disciplinary society, seem to shun large-scale social movements that seek to shift power. This line of enquiry, feels Ben Agger, only reflects political ambivalence of postmodernist problematic simply because power would take new forms not imagined earlier. "We can find [power] politics today," says Agger, "everywhere but in the traditionally defined political arena."[33] In overcoming the duality of oppressor and the oppressed, he would eliminate all hierarching differences.[34] Difference, he adds, is eternal, and history has not transcended as yet into a frictionless, fractionless, classless, raceless and genderless epoch. Agger finds support to his position in the postulates of the Frankfurt School of theorists, especially Marcuse, who insist that politics is found in culture as well as in desire.[35] This analysis also holds good to power play in the Parsi novels.

IV

In *Midnight's Children*, the Parsis are said to be only good for "soo che? saru che!/ Danda le ke maru che![36] which literally translated means: 'What's the matter? Everything is well!

Take a stick and beat them." This is what Rushdie precisely does to the Parsis if the treatment accorded to Pimple Billimoria and Zeeny Vakil in *The Satanic Verses* is any proof. In his narrative it is Salman, the farsi, who is blamed for the 'Satanic Verses.' But as Salman himself bitterly protests, "The closer you are to a conjurer . . . the easier to spot the trick."[37] It would be unfair to set aside the Parsis's role in Indian politics. As Nani A. Palkhiwala observes, "History affords no parallel to the role of Parsis in India. There is no record of any other community so infinitesimally small as Parsis, playing such a significant role in the life of a country so large."[38] It would not be improper to remember the significant contribution of some leading Parsi politicians and take a cognizance of the Parsis's perception of the Indian leaders as found in their fiction.

The Parsis, as said earlier, looked at politics with disfavour and misgivings. But there were some of them who became prominent in politics. Dadabhai Naoroji, Behramji Malabari, J.N. Tata, K.N. Kabraji, and Jamestji Jeejeebhoy were the pioneers in this respect. Among exponents of the first attempts at political participation, the names of Naoroji Furdoonjee, Sohrabjee Shapurjee Bengalee, Khurshetjee Rustomjee Cama, Maneckjee Cursetjee and Dosabhoy Framjee Karaka may also be mentioned. The three top Parsi politicians Dadabhai Naoroji (1825-1917), Sir Pherozeshah M. Mehta (1845-1915) and Sir Dinshaw Edulji Wacha (1844-1936)—particularly the first two—can be put on the same level with the great politicians of the country. However, "Following the death or withdrawal of these three politicians, no Parsee ever again had a comparable influence on Indian politics."[39] In the first twenty-one years of the Congress movement, these three Parsis held the presidential office for five times (Naoroji in 1886, 1893 and 1906; Mehta in 1890; and Wacha in 1901). Wacha worked as the General Secretary of the Congress together with A.O. Hume from 1896 to 1903, with Gokhale in 1904-1908 and with D.A. Khare from 1909 to 1913. B.M. Malabari, though not associated with any specific political party, was a great social reformer. Only three Indians were elected to the British Parliament—Naoroji, Mancherji Bhavnagari and Shapurjee Saklatvala—before 1880 and all of them were Parsis. Bhikaji Cama, the first Parsi woman to participate in the National Movement and a reputed orator, published revolutionary papers *Vande Mataram* and *Talwar* from Geneva. The flag she hoisted in Germany on 18 August 1905 was the true precursor of our national flag. Feroz Gandhi and Taleyarkhan were great parliamentarians. Among later politicians also, some Parsis emerged as important leaders. When the All India Congress Socialist Party was initiated (though still within the Indian National Congress) in Bombay in 1943, the inner circle of its founders included, in addition to Jayaprakash Narayan, E.M.S. Namboodiripad, Ashok Mehta, Ram Manohar Lohia and S.M. Joshi, two Parsis—Minoo R. Masani and S.S. Batlivala. Batlivala soon changed over to the Communist Party of India, but Masani became the General Secretary of the Congress Socialist Party in 1936. He played a leading role in the founding of the Swatantra party in 1959 and served as its General Secretary for years. Morris-Jones judged him "India's most modernistic politician."[40] Like his father, Sir H.P. Mody, Piloo Mody played a significant role in the growth of the Swatantra Party. Finally, Naushir C. Bharucha represented the Praja Socialist Party in Parliament from 1957 to 1962, and Homi Daji was elected into Parliament in 1962 for the CPI from Indore.

This necessarily brief and sketchy account of the Parsis' role in Indian politics is sufficient to make us inquisitive about the Parsis' views on Indian politics and politicians as found in their novels. The Parsis' decisive influence through their chosen leaders was confined to the period 1885-1915. The community developed later apprehensions and distrust towards the Congress politics. Those Parsis "who became especially active in the national movement, were opposed by the majority of the community."[41] Right from the day of their settlement in India, the Parsis were strictly loyal to every ruling authority, keeping themselves generally out of tensions and conflicts between various groups and powers in the state. It is for this reason that even Naoroji when he vehemently advocated secular nationalism, was called "hypocrite" and his loyalty was questioned in

Raft Goftar—the paper he himself had started in 1852. The Congress cause, it was thought, was "chiefly advocated by the Deccan Brahmins and Bengalee Baboos and a handful of mischievous Parsees."[42] Most of the Parsis thought that if the government and the country were in the hands of the Hindus, the Parsis would be pushed to the wall: their rights would not be respected and their monopoly in business would crumble: "Mr. Dadabhai . . . may rest assured that . . . he will be the first to be elbowed and hustled out and that the first Viceroy or president will be Jabberji from Bengal and the first Commander-in-chief a Bajirao from Poona until the stalwart Pathan or Punjabi makes short of the both and establishes a despotism of his own."[43]

The Parsis were particularly disturbed by increasing radicalism of the national movement strongly influenced by the neo-Hindu renaissance. They felt that they had very limited access to the socio-religious nationalism of the Congress movement under Tilak and Gandhi. These fears encouraged the Parsis to oppose even the concept of the Home Rule in India. Rustom Rustomjee, for example, wrote voicing the feelings of his community that the establishment of the dominion-form of self-government "in the present state of the people . . . will mean the restoration of Brahmanical autocracy, with all its attendant evils."[44] This approach hurt leaders like Naoroji and Wacha like anything. "Nothing could be more suicidal," thought Naoroji[45] and Wacha would prefer to let them "cry in wilderness" and "become so many donkeys."[46] Nevertheless, as *Raft Goftaar* would put it, the "Parsee community stands alone and by itself," the code of its political behaviour being: "loyal to the British, friendly to the Indians."[47]

Even Dadabhai Naoroji, the Grand Old man of India, was not spared. A product of the Elphinstone College, he was appointed as Professor of Mathematics in it—in fact, the first Indian to be chosen for the college—in 1852. Through his writings, especially *Poverty* and *Un-British Rule in India* (1901), he exposed the exploitation of India by the British and propounded the 'drain theory.' He struggled for the 'Indianization' of administrative services. He also served as the Prime Minister of the State of Baroda in 1873. In the historic session of the Congress held in 1906, in which he was elected the President of the party, he demanded Swaraj for India, his being the first demand of its kind. He was a staunch nationalist who declared: "Whether I am a Hindu, a Mohammedan, a Parsi, a Christian, or of any other creed, I am above all an Indian. Our country is India; our nationality is Indian."[48] This attitude of Naoroji was not liked by some Parsis, his affiliation with the Congress and secular nationalism along with his criticism of the British being the greatest irritants.

In Bapsi Sidhwa's *The Crow Eaters*, Freddie has a deep-rooted distrust of the national movement. He exhorts his children to be loyal to the British. If anyone goes against the wishes of the British, he would be worthy of denunciation. Dadabhai Naoroji is to him nothing but "that misguided Parsee from Bombay" who has had temerity to launch "something called Congress and keeps shouting off his mouth like a lunatic, 'Quit India! Quit India!'" Freddie is obviously "perturbed by the trend of events in India"; he is "stirred by [the] talk of rebellion, self-rule, and Independence from the British—and most of all by the role of a few Parsis [like Naoroji] in all this." (282) Such people, he believes, are "making a monkey of themselves." While other communities will benefit by breaking the country, he feels, the Parsis will be wanted nowhere. Asked where then the Parsis will go in the event of the Independence, he says: "Nowhere. . . . We will stay where we are . . . let Hindus, Muslims, Sikhs, or whoever, rule. What does it matter? The sun will continue to rise—and the sun continue to set—in their arses!" (283) Freddie's thinking is in line with that of most other members of his community.

The references to Mahatma Gandhi, the Father of the Nation, are even more derogatory in *And Some Take a Lover*. To Roshni's mother and people like her, he is merely a "scoundrel and vagrant . . . the arch-traitor, the unmentionable, except with abuse." (38) Roshni's cousin Framrose regards Gandhi's fasting as "political blackmail," and to Aunt Piroja he is pro-Japanese and a fifth-columnist. After failure in her love, Roshni comes to the conclusion that on account of his vicious influence on young people, Gandhi is nothing less than a despot and an implacable tyrant. (200) The underground Congress worker Fazil Baig, though not unimpressed by Gandhi's message of universal charity, mutual forbearance and love, has his own reasons to choose a path different from the one shown by him simply because his approach is too idealistic:

> if these are his expectations, the Mahatma is courting disappointment, he is courting humiliation, he is courting failure. . . . Yes, we have in Gandhi an example of heroic failure, in spite of all he has achieved. His great spiritual aims are doomed to failure. They will be blurred, obscured, not so much by his enemies, but by his followers. For a prophet's wisest measures must necessarily be executed by the unwise. His purest aims are tarnished, in the course of fulfilment, by human passion. (150)

Baig's appraisal of Gandhi and his way of life contains significant grains of truth. Roshni only says: "All this will be for posterity to determine"; with this "spiritual adventure story" she, like most other Parsis, is "blasphemously out of tune."

In Bapsi Sidhwa's *Ice-Candy-Man*, Lenny, the child narrator, goes to meet Gandhi when he comes to Lahore. He is already a "mythic figure" and "ahead of his times." Lenny's mother, despite her "consternation," glances at him with a "rapt and reverent interest." Lenny, however, is at a loss to explain an "improbable toss-up between a clown and a demon" in Gandhi. She is also puzzled by "the hypnotic and dynamic femininity of Gandhi's non-violent exterior." She cannot nevertheless but be impressed by his humour, compassion, tolerance and understanding. (86-88) Some of his practices appear to the Parsis merely fads. His insistence on enema—"An enema a day keeps the doctor away"—looks obsessive and ghoulish. Another character says: "That wily Banya is an expert on fasting unto death without dying." (62) Yet another one refers to him as "that non-violent violence monger—your precious Gandhijee." (91) There is also a mention of Gandhi's Salt March, and the reactions of two Parsi characters, the Bankwalla and Col.

Bharucha, are significant. The banker reminds the Parsi audience: "Gandhi says, we must stop buying salt. We should only eat salt manufactured from the Indian Ocean!" To this Col. Bharucha retorts: "Who does this Gandhi think he is? . . . Is it his grandfather's ocean?" (35) The Salt March was a symbolic act, and the two responses to it represent the gamut of the Parsi response to it.

Commenting upon the Gandhian movement, the distinguished historian Sumit Sarkar writes: "varied sections of the Indian people seem to have fashioned their own images of Gandhi, particularly in the early days when he was still to most people a distant, vaguely-glimpsed or heard-of tale of a holy man with miracle working powers. . . . Peasants were giving vague rumours about Gandhi a radical, anti-zamindar twist."[49]

The Parsis, however, generally lived in urban settings and were not swayed by these rumours. Gandhi, they thought, "was fool enough to think he could save India with his milk-and-water non-violence."[50] At times the sense of insecurity made them reject Gandhi and his approach as humbug: "What is this spinach-chewing rascal going to do if the British are not here to protect us."[51] For common people, the Gandhian ideology in abstraction has no meaning. The narrator remarks in *Ice-Candy-Man:* "Mother, Father and their friends are always saying: Gandhi said this, Nehru said that. Gandhi did this, Jinnah did that, What's the point of talking so much about people we don't know." (29) Most Parsis, happy in their own small world, would not think differently. It may however, be remembered that while in South Africa, Gandhi had very good relation with some Parsi.. One of the books that he had read carefully was called *The Sayings of Zarathustra.* Parsi Rustomji was one of his close associates. When he went to meet Sir Pherozeshah Mehta, the latter met him "as a loving father would his grown up son." Gandhi found him to be "unscalable" like the Himalaya but was helped by him generously. Sir Dinshaw Wacha, the right hand of Sir Pherozeshah Mehta, who was the President of the Congress in 1901 when Gandhi met him in Calcutta, also gave him advice and help.[52] Gandhi's love of honesty, truth and charity was in keeping with the Parsis's cherished ideals in life and would have ordinarily evoked a favourable response from them. But because of his associations with the Congress politics ["He's a politician," says a character in *Ice-Candy-Man*, "It is his business to suit his tongue to the moment," (91)] his excessive insistence on simple living and his principle of trusteeship, he is treated in the Parsi novels as the villain of the piece. Even otherwise, Gandhi has evoked different responses from different persons. Malgonkar, for example, found in Gandhi, "the enemy of India's national aspirations."[53] According to Naipaul, India "undid" him by making a Mahatma out of him and today he "remains a tragic paradox." "The revolutionary Gandhi," he adds, "became a god and his message was thereby lost. He failed to communicate to India his way of direct looking."[54] If the Parsis, who had a different worldview, failed to recognize the true Gandhi, it is not surprising at all.

For their supposedly ungenerous treatment of Feroze Gandhi, Nehru and Indira Gandhi have always remained an eyesore with the Parsis. Another contributory case to their animosity was their economic policies which were bound to affect the Parsis's business adversely. Nehruvian socialism and the Parsis's free enterprise were irreconcilables. In *Such a Long Journey*, for example, Nehru is taken to task for the country's "humiliating defeat" at the hands of the Chinese in 1962. The novel also exposes *en route* his frustration, ill temper, political intrigues prospering under his nose and his "monomaniacal fixation" with "his darling daughter." (9) "Suave, Cambridge-polished, he carries about him an aura of power and a presence that flatters anyone he compliments tenfold. He doles out promises, smiles, kisses-on-cheeks." (11) This is how the narrator describes Nehru in *Ice-Candy-Man.* He is "presumed to be" Edwina Mountbatten's "lover." Nehru and Mountbatten are like "two entwined fingers." To some other people, Nehru is a "sly" person who has "got Mountbatten eating out of his one hand and the English's wife out of his other what-not." (131) Indira Gandhi has been run down because most Parsis thought she did not treat Feroze with the respect he deserved and also because she destroyed the Parsis's hegemony over the banking system by nationalizing banks in 1969. Dinshawji, in *Such a Long Journey*, ruminates: "What days those were, *Yaar*. What fun we used to have. . . . Parsees were the kings of banking in those days. Such respect we used to get. Now the whole atmosphere only has been spoiled, ever since that Indira nationalized the banks." (38) Gustad adds: "Nowhere in the world has nationalization worked. What can you say to idiots?" (38) Moreover, she is said to have encouraged the communal politics in Maharashtra: "And today we have that bloody Shiv Sena, wanting to make the rest of us into second class citizens. . . . Don't forget, she started it all by supporting the racist buggers." (39) The Congress Party which they led is alleged to comprise "crooks," (68) being reduced to "a rogues' gallery" while the country is no better than "a patient with gangrene at an advanced stage." (313) As compared to Nehru and Indira Gandhi, Lal Bahadur Shastri has been given unqualified praise because under his stewardship "the stagnant waters of government would at last be freshened and vitalized." (114) "The big little man" gave a "pucca purgative" to Pakistanis and saved India's honour in 1965. (130)

The Parsis' assessment of Indian leaders is on the whole tinged with preferences and prejudices. The community's interests were uppermost in their rating of them. Even Jaya Prakash Narayan, who played a crucial role during the Emergency, has not remained unscathed. In *A Fine Balance*, his action is said to have encouraged unionism responsible for strikes and lack of production: "Who wants to deal with union goondas if it can be avoided? Especially these days, with so much trouble in the country. And leaders like that Jaya Prakash Narayan encouraging civil disobedience. Simply at all creating problems. Thinks he is Mahatma Gandhi the second." (65) What the Parsis liked most was an excellent law and order condition so essential for good business. On this count they would commend even Indira Gandhi as "a very strong woman . . . very intelligent woman" for providing a successful leadership in the 1971 war. But they would not approve of any tall talking in business matters. For example, in *Such a Long Journey*, the plans of Sanjay Gandhi and his car manufacturing company are thought to be hardly better than "idiotic lunatic talk" or "just a way of talking." (60) This consideration seems to have worked in their de-mythicizing leaders like Nehru and Indira Gandhi also, whose, "I Witness accounts" would not take the country very far. Lastly, the Parsis seem to have an in-built revulsion for politics and politicians, and particularly hate those countries and politicians whose actions would go against their interests in any way. "The wicked China" of the 1962 Sino-Indian war is described as "the number one bogeyman," (9) and for their covert role in the 1965 and 1971 wars, Nixon becomes "the scowling one with rat's eyes" and Kissinger is attributed to have "the face of a constipated ox." (298) Politicians have thus been generally deflated, for they are held responsible for the myriad problems of the country in general and of Parsis in particular.

In Bapsi Sidhwa's *Ice-Candy-Man*, however, Jinnah is treated with understandable consideration. In an interview, the novelist claims to have set the record straight regarding Zinnah's personality and political stature:

> I do regard Gandhi partially to blame for the Partition. . . . I think that the Partition was a mistake. . . . I blame Mountbatten a lot. He has left us with so many problems. . . . Naturally the Indians have brought out their own perspective, to deify Gandhi and Nehru. Well, the world had deified them. No doubt, these are men of great stature, but in the interim the Muslim role has been vilified altogether. Jinnah has been made out to be a villain.[55]

Zinnah is remembered in *Ice-Candy-Man* as a reserved person, preeminently rational and practical, discreet and dispassionate, who believes that "Statesmen cannot eat their words." (59-60) He is also "incapable of compliments. Austere, driven, pukka-sahib accented" but "deathly ill." "A first-rate lawyer" he "knows how to attack the British with their own laws." (131) Jinnah was undoubtedly endowed with some enviable qualities of head and heart but can he be absolved of the overzealous advocacy of Pakistan? His vision of a secular Pakistan, in which minorities will have the same opportunity to prosper and equal rights, floundered, and this 'Ambassador of Hindu-Muslim Unity,' as the novelist says, died "of a broken heart." (160) At the fag end of his life, he is said to have repented over his role in the creation of Pakistan. Sidhwa has had one more reason to be partial to Jinnah, and is less than fair to Gandhi. Gandhi was always soft with Muslims and he cannot be held directly responsible for the cracking of India. Jinnah's wife was a Parsi. Sidhwa waxes eloquent when she talks about the qualities of Jinnah's "astonishingly beautiful" wife: "Large eyes, liquid-brown, radiating youth, promising intelligence, declaring innocence, shining from an oval marble-firm face. Full-lipped, delighting in the knowledge of her own loveliness: confident in the knowledge of her generous impulses." (160) Giving—like Ayah. Daring like Mother of Lenny. Thus barring Jinnah at the hands of Sidhwa and Shastri at Mistry's, very few politicians have escaped criticism and even downright denunciation from the Parsi novelists. The views cited here may not always be the novelists' but they do represent the opinion of a cross section of the Parsi society. The reasons for this negative attitude have already been suggested earlier.

The Parsis's attitude to momentous movements and events affecting the entire subcontinent such as the Quit India Movement, the Naval Ratings Mutiny of 1946, the Partition, the Independence, Pakistani wars and the creation of the Bangladesh, appears to be ambivalent. Some insiders have testified to this dilemma of their community members. "This ambivalence and alienation," writes Nilufer Bharucha, "became exacerbated during the colonial period. . . . [And] Most Parsis . . . felt bereft at the end of Empire and the resultant loss of the special elite status they had enjoyed during the colonial period."[56] Kapadia also talks about what he calls the 'Parsi paradox' projected in Nergis Dalal's novels *The Sisters* and *Minari*. According to him, "Most of them are cultural hybrids, living and sharing intimately in the cultural life, traditions, languages, moral codes and value systems of two distinct peoples, which never completely penetrate or get fused.[57] Bapsi Sidhwa's *Ice-Candy-Man* is a fine illustration of this ambivalence. "The novel is at once about provisionality and the need to transcend that ambivalence."[58]

Set in the pre-Partition Lahore, *Ice-Candy-Man* highlights the Parsis's response to the danger of the imminent cracking of the country along with the vulnerability of human relationships. The Parsis find it difficult to decide whether to support the Swaraj or to continue their loyalty to the British. At a special meeting organised at the temple hall, an acrimonious debate on the political situation takes place. Col. Bharucha advises the Parsis to keep away from the nationalist agitation. Dr. Mody, however, pleads for involvement in the freedom struggle for the simple reason that "our neighbours will think we are betraying them and siding with the English." (37) Finally, on the initiative of the banker Bankwalla, they resolve to follow their time-tested path of compromise and adaptability—"to run with the hounds and hunt with the hare." In the event of the partition, they would side with the community that rules: "let whoever wishes rule! Hindu, Muslim, Sikh, Christian! We will abide by the rules of their land!" and "As long as we conduct our lives quietly, as long as we present no threat to anybody, we will prosper right here." (37) Dina Mehta's *And Some Take a Lover* also delineates the Parsis's apprehensions and political crises in the wake of the Quit India movement and the Naval Ratings Mutiny. Happy in their orbits and left to themselves, most Parsis, we are told again, would prefer not to remember "the strings and freedom-agitations in the country." (136)

However, in some Parsi novels, political events of national significance serve as background or backdrop. In *And Some Take a Lover*, for example, the mutiny in the Royal India Navy and its consequences occupy a sizable space. "The ratings," we are told, "were not fighting for food, they demanded freedom for their country. It was a secret, personal revolution within the orbit of the general one, part of the national quickening." (226-27) The novel also makes a pointed reference to Gandhi's action in Noakhali, ravaged by a fury, where dreadful things were happening. Sidhwa's *Ice-Candy-Man* depicts the rise of obscurantism, jingoism, mindless violence and communal tension perpetrated during and after the Partition. The atmosphere is charged with panic and misgivings: "Blue envy: green avidity: the grey and black stirrings of predators and the incipient distillation of fear in their prey." (131-32) People were never prepared for this unfortunate turn, but now "Things have become topsy-turvy." Consequently, "Within three months seven million Muslims and five million Hindus and Sikhs are uprooted in the largest and most terrible exchange of population known to history." (147) For several years people in the affected areas had lived peacefully and "felt secure, inviolate." (159) "And to uproot themselves from the soil of their ancestors had seemed to them akin to tearing themselves, like ancient trees, from the earth." (198) The pervasive impact of the Partition on common men's life has been powerfully evoked in the novel. It is Rohinton Mistry's novels that deal with major political strifes and also advance a significant debate. *Such a Long Journey* revolves around the Bangladesh war of 1971 and the Nagarwalla episode of cheating a bank by imitating the voice of the former Prime Minister. *A Fine Balance*, the latest novel by Mistry, brings to the fore the excesses committed during the Internal Emergency of 1975-76 and voices concern for the underprivileged in the wake of forcible eviction from their hutments, forced labour and indiscriminate sterilization.

> Women and children sat amid the debris, dazed and weeping. . . . Whole families [of Sikhs were] burnt to death in their homes. . . . Some ministers are even helping the gangs, providing official lists of Sikh homes and businesses.
>
> Of course, for the ordinary people nothing has changed. Government still keeps breaking poor people's home and jhopadpattis. In villages they say they will dig well only if so many sterilizations are done. They tell farmers they will get fertilisers only after nussbandi is performed. Living each day is to face one emergency or another. (581-82)

Criminalisation of politics, upward mobility and rising expectations of the backward classes along with upper-class callousness and misuse of administrative powers have also been projected in the novel.

On the basis of their themes and contents, some of these novels, especially Mistry's, may be regarded as political novels. In a political novel, as Irving Howe points out, "political ideas play a dominant role" or "the political milieu is the dominant setting."[59] There may not be much ideological interplay in some of these novels but most of them have a political setting. They represent the contemporary scenario seen through the eyes of the narrator or the character concerned. This mode of "witness" narration is the method used in *Midnight's Children.* In many cases, the interplay between the individual and the political forces is undeniable. In his article entitled "The Empire Writes Back," Rushdie remarks: "Those who were made powerful then [i.e. during the Raj] remain, for the most part, powerful now." He adds that the texts of the non-White writers today are about "politics," unlike those in the West which "exclude politics from fiction" and "treat public affairs as peripheral."[60] In an interview also, Rushdie tells us that ordinary people in India know a lot more about history and politics than their counterparts in the West.[61] Politics, because of historical reasons, has occupied such a central position in Indian thinking and subsumes the ways in which power is manipulated in various transactions in day-to-day life. In the presentation of reality, memory, nostalgia and fantasy play significant roles. As Rushdie puts it, memory "creates its own reality" and "Reality is a question of perspective, the further you get from the past, the more concrete and plausible it seems."[62] Some problems are bound to surface when one comes face to face with the political reality. Orwell would advise us to solve them by "robbing reality of its terrors by simply submitting to it"—by getting "inside the whale."[63] Rushdie, however, would prefer remaining outside the whale, i.e. withdrawal and spirited action:

> Outside the whale is the unceasing storm, the continual quarrel, the dialectic of history. Outside whale there is a genuine need for political fiction. . . . Outside the whale we see that we are all irradiated by history, we are radio-

active with history and politics.[64]

The Parsi novelists have perceived and interpreted Indian political reality in their own distinct way, making it suit their convenience. Generally happy to be inside the whale, they have yet raised occasionally significant issues with a view to facing it boldly. They have not always emerged successfully but the courage they have evinced—especially in the writings of novelists like Rohinton Mistry—is commendable.

NOTES

1. Ngugi wa Thiong'o, Preface to *Writers in Politics* (London: Heinemann, 1981). According to Kate Millett, 'politics' refers to "power-structured relationship, arrangements whereby one group of persons is controlled by another." There is a host of poststructurist writing, including that of Foucault, Lacan, Gramsci and Edward Said, which has discussed the ways in which power works.
2. A.J. Toynbee, *A Study of History* (London: OUP, 1948), V, p. 29.
3. *Ibid.*, II, p. 234.
4. Sir J. Jeejeebhoy's statement in the Parsi Central Association's Political Subcommittee, dated 2 October 1930. Quoted in Eckehard Kulke, *The Parsees in India: A Minority as Agent of Social Change* (New Delhi: Vikas, 1978), p. 213.
5. *The Parsi*, 19 August 1906.
6. *Raft Goftar*, 16 November 1862.
7. Khusrau E. Ghamat, *The Present State of India* (Bombay, 1907), p. 1.
8. See Kulke, p. 135.
9. *Ibid.*, p. 136.
10. *The Parsi*, I, No. 6, p. 213.
11. *Ibid.*
12. Dina Mehta, *And Some Take a Lover* (Calcutta: Rupa, 1992), p. 188.
13. Bapsi Sidhwa, *The Crow Eaters* (New Delhi: Penguin India, 1990), p. 12.
14. Kulke, p. 199.
15. Bapsi Sidhwa, *Ice-Candy-Man* (New Delhi: Penguin India, 1988), p. 37.

16. Rohinton Mistry, *Such a Long Journey* (Calcutta: Rupa, 1991), pp. 23, 39.
17. Rohinton Mistry, *Tales from Firozsha Baag* (Calcutta: Rupa, 1993), p. 15.
18. *Such a Long Journey*, p. 23.
19. *And Some Take a Lover*, p. 38.
20. See R.S. Pathak, "Problematising the Minority Discourse: Inlets to the Parsi Sensibility," *Points of View*, 5/2 (Winter 1998), pp. 85-95.
21. *The Parsi*, I, No. 11, p. 533.
22. 'Shereen,' "How to Learn European Manners," *Journal of the National Indian Association*, No. 117 (September 1880), pp. 534-35.
23. R.P. Masani, *Dadabhai Naoroji, The Grand Old Man of India* (London, 1939), p. 48.
24. T.M. Luhrmann, *The Good Parsi: The Fate of a Colonial Elite in a Postcolonial Society* (Delhi: OUP, 1996), pp. viii, ix.
25. Rollo May, *Power and Innocence: A Search for the Sources of Violence* (New York: Norton, 1972).
26. Peter Morris, *Power: A Philosophical Analysis* (Manchester: Manchester University Press, 1972).
27. May, pp. 107-8.
28. *Ibid.*, p. 110.
29. *Ibid.*, pp. 186-87.
30. Rohinton Mistry, *A Fine Balance* (London: Faber & Faber, 1995), pp. 378, 279.
31. John Ball, "Taking the Measure of India's Emergency" (Review of *A Fine Balance*), *The Toronto Review* (Winter 1996), p. 85.
32. Michele Foucault, *Power/ Knowledge* (New York: Pantheon, 1980).
33. Ben Agger, *The Discourse of Domination* (Evanston, Illinois: Northwestern University Press, 1992), p. 296.
34. B. Agger, "Critical Theory, Poststructuralism: Their Sociological Relevance," *Annual Review of Sociology*, 17 (1991), pp. 105-31.
35. H. Marcuse, *Negations* (Boston: Beacon, 1968).
36. Salman Rushdie, *Midnight's Children* (London: Picador, 1982), p. 188.
37. Salman Rushdie. *The Satanic Verses*, Quoted in Feroza Jussawalla, "Post-Joycean Sub-Joycean: The Reverses of Mr. Rushdie's Tricks in *The Satanic Verses*," *The New Indian Novel in English*, ed. Viney Kirpal (New Delhi: Allied, 1990), p. 227.
38. Nani A Palkhiwala, *We the Nation: The Lost Decades* (New Delhi: UBSPD, 1994), p. 317.
39. Kulke, p. 173.
40. W.H. Morris-Jones, *Government and Politics in India* (London, 1964), p. 156.

41. Kulke, p. 146.
42. *Raft Goftar*, 2 June 1989.
43. *Ibid.*, 2 May 1897.
44. *The Times*, 23 October 1924.
45. Naoroji's letter to Wacha dated 20 December 1888, quoted in Kulke, p. 169
46. Wacha's letter to Naoroji dated 15 November 1889, quoted in Kulke, p. 188.
47. *Raft Goftar*, 19 May 1889 and 31 January 1997.
48. Presidential Address in the Indian National Congress (1893), rpt. in *Speeches and Writings of Dadabhai Naoroji* (Madras: Natesan, 1910), p. 61.
49. Sumit Sarkar, *Modern India, 1885-1947* (Madras: Macmillan India, 1983), p. 181.
50. *Such a Long Journey*, p. 72.
51. *And Some Take a Lover*, p. 39.
52. M.K. Gandhi, *The Story of My Experiments with Truth* (Ahmedabad: Navajivan Publishing House, 1927), pp. 133, 144, 148, 186.
53. Manohar Malgonkar, *A Bend in the Ganges* (Delhi: Orient Paperbacks), p. 17.
54. V.S. Naipaul, *An Area of Darkness* (London: Andre Deusch, 1964), ch. 3.
55. Chelva Kanaganayakam, ed., *Configurations of Exile: South Asian Writers and Their World* (Toronto: TSAR, 1995), pp. 87-88.
56. Nilufer Bharucha, "The Charting of Cultural Territory," quoted in Novy Kapadia and A.G. Khan, ed., *The Parsis: Madyan to Sanjan* (New Delhi: Creative, 1997), p. xiii.
57. Novy Kapadia, "The Dilemma of Marriage in Nergis Dalal's *The Sisters*," in R.K. Dhawan, ed., *Indian Women Novelists* (New Delhi: Prestige, 1995), V, pp. 79-80.
58. Kanaganayakam, p. 85.
59. Irving Howe, *The Idea of the Political Novel* (New York: Horizon Press, 1957), pp. 22-24.
60. Salman Rushdie, "The Empire Writes Back with a Vengeance," *The Times* (London), 3 July 1982.
61. Sunil Sethi, "After Midnight: An Interview," *India Today*, 15 April 1983, pp. 76-77.
62. *Midnight's Children*, pp. 211, 165.
63. George Orwell, *Collected Essays* (London: Secker & Warburg,

1961), p. 158.

64. Salman Rushdie, "Outside the Whale," *Imaginary Homelands* (London: Granta Books/ New Delhi: Penguin India, 1991), p. 100.

Firdaus Kanga's *Trying to Grow*: A Tale of Parsi Life

K.V. SURENDRAN

Trying to Grow (1990) is a brilliant novel of Firdaus Kanga which easily establishes him to be a writer who cannot be easily ignored. Being a Parsi writer, his major concern in the novel is to delineate the life style of the community which is considered by many as an endangered community. This perception is shared by the eminent solicitor Palkhivala too. According to him, it is entirely upto the present generation of Parsis to decide whether "they will become a decadent community with a glorious past, a perilous present, and a dim future."[1] The novel centres round the Osteo child narrator Daryus Brit Kotwal who is born handicapped. It is with remarkable candour, sympathy and honesty that Kanga unveils the several paradoxes in his life.

Apart from being a story about the crippled Brit, *Trying to Grow* can be said to be about several other things. In the initial pages of the novel, Wagh Baba's mysterious behaviour arouses some curiosity in the reader. The Parsi way of life is unveiled somewhat poignantly almost throughout the novel. The city of Bombay which is known for the hybrid existence of Parsis is very effectively depicted in the novel. Kanga's novel is sometimes described as a treatise on sex where the protagonist himself is referred to as a 'sex maniac.' The abundant use of humour is another characteristic of the novel which will not escape the attention of the readers. This article is an attempt to have a close look at the novel and show how it depicts Parsi life and traditions which ultimately contribute to make the novel a unique literary creation.

Trying to Grow is set in a characteristic Bombay middle class milieu. The opening sentence of the novel itself shows that there is an inescapable 'Parsi touch' about Kanga's maiden work: "'His teeth are like windows,' said Father to the Old Parsi with the droopy, white moustache, sitting next to us on the bus."[2]

The Parsis are known for their superstitious beliefs and we get a reference to this on the same page of the novel. The old man is found warding off the Evil Spirit that's always ready to pounce on Parsis when they are not looking. This is in reaction to Brit's father's remark that his child is being taken to a witch doctor. The old man was one who believed in prayers and he wanted to know from the child's father whether there was no Parsi prayer for children like the one he was carrying with him.

The Parsis, it is reported, were fond of the number 'a hundred and one.' Brit's grandfather was one who was known for his chivalrous nature and having slained one hundred tigers in the service of his princeling, he was given the Diwan's only daughter, a Parsi lady, in marriage:

> On their wedding night he boasted he would give her a hundred sons, one for each tiger. Since his bride was almost forty, it's obvious he was ignorant of the menopause. But it doesn't really matter, because the morning after the nuptial night, the Tiger's Nemesis decided to go hunting in order to give his new wife a gift of his hundred and first trophy, a hundred and one being a number much loved by the Parsees whose wedding gifts always consist of white envelopes with a hundred and one rupees inside. (13)

Parsis celebrate their New Year's Day with traditional gaiety and enthusiasm. Everyone would celebrate it with parents, brothers, sisters and other kinds of relatives. The local fire temple would be crowded with the worshippers of stylish clothes so that they would be seen in the 'Right Place.' In this context Brit's remarks appear to be interesting: "We Parsis don't take our religion too seriously; those who do are considered downright dangerous and a little mad." (14)

In naming their children Parsis had their own likes and dislikes. The novel has all kinds of names which are short and easy like Brit, Sera, Sam, Dolly, Tina and so on.

> We delight in stretching, snipping and squashing given names out of all recognition, with a view to making them roll off the tongue easily and, perhaps, even sound English. So boys who are named Fardoon become Freddy, Nowroji become Neville, Adi become Eddy, and everyone is delighted with his new name and what he hopes is his new image. (22)

In fact Brit's parents went about it a bit differently when their first girl child was born. They decided they would call her Dolly. Then they hunted about for a suitable Parsi name to put on the birth certificate. They discovered 'Daulat,' which they thought was auspicious because it meant wealth.

Parsis have peculiar food habits. According to Brit, the Parsis were reluctant Indians who had their own way:

> Parsees have this nauseating habit of slumming when they went to eat *Indian* food which means non-Parsee food, since we are reluctant Indians. My family happily spent four hundred rupees at the Taj Mahal Hotel on an English meal, bland as ulcer diet, but when it came to trying out some tongue-scorching, tasty food they made a bee-line for the cheapest joint they could sniff out. (27)

The argument given by Sera is that the Indians are a poor people and so the best place for genuine Indian cuisine has got to be cheap. Of course, there is the general rule that the dirty food is always dirtier!

There was a time when Parsi girls did not discover the facts of life till they got married. There is an interesting anecdote in the novel which emphasizes this point. When Jeroo was eighteen one morning she woke to find her elder brother sleeping with his arm on her stomach. He was fully clothed in a striped pyjama suit:

> When Jeroo saw that hairy arm, heavy on her stomach, she screamed so loud her brother has been slightly deaf in one year ever since. 'I'm pregnant!' She howled. 'By my own brother! What will I do? Oh God! I'll jump off the Rajabai Tower!' (34)

The nurse who was called said that it was a criminal offence and the police should be informed. Then came the most interesting of the questions. Sera asked the nurse whether an arm could make one pregnant. Jeroo did not forget to add that she was not guilty as she had been sleeping!

Brit was of the view that the Parsi community abounded with eccentrics. Meheroo Manekshaw was such a one and she was as Parsi as any other Parsi woman: "Dinshaw lived for his stamps which occupied the top floor of his two-storeyed villa on Warden Road. The stamp collection was worth a million rupees which represented a tenth part of his wealth." (39)

The question remains whether it was Meheroo or Dinshaw who eclipsed the other in eccentricity. When Dinshaw proposed to her she said 'yes' before he could finish his question, although he was fifty-one and she was just seventeen! After that a lot of envious people called her 'Seventeen Threes Are'—but she never gave a damn. She was busy with other things. She finished a Bachelor's degree in French and grabbed a Master's in English and then took one more degree. Degrees became the substitute for all the toys she never had as a kid. Maybe such strange behaviour has to do with the existential crisis the Parsis are facing: "They would live and get lost in it rather than leave it. They are facing a grim 'to be or not to be' crises of existence."[3] Interesting enough, Meheroo's face is said to bear an astonishing resemblance to Indira Gandhi's who was not a Parsi although she was the widow of one.

It was Madame Manekshaw, the formidable figure who was to teach Brit, the seven-year-old child. She began with the question whether the child did not have a proper teacher before. Sera replied that her husband and she had taught him conscientiously every day. She immediately rejected the tall claims made by the child's mother for two reasons. To begin with, there was nothing in that house that she coveted. Secondly, she did not care how much her son knew. Being a typical Parsi, she believed that parents were not meant to be teachers, especially when they were Parsi parents and the pupil was their only son. Thus Meheroo proves herself to be a typical Parsi in every sense!

The Parsis, according to Madame Manekshaw, had a craze for foreigners. She spoke as if she were an English woman and this irked Sera considerably. This made her ask whether she was an English woman from London. The whole question came up when Sera requested Madame to make an attempt to get Brit admitted to Campion School. In fact she was against this proposal: "Such poor taste, Mrs. Kotwal," sniffed Madame Manekshaw. "That Catholic School with its shuffling priests and cruel discipline. And no girls, just boys—most unhealthy for Brit's budding sexuality."

Sera made it clear that the priests at Campion were all foreigners, Spanish or Irish. Finally Madame had to say that she would see that Brit was in.

Madame Manekshaw believed that Parsis did not have the guts to make money: "all they want is a nine to five job and their trifling three thousand a month." (41) According to Sera, there was nothing communal about the Sindhis and Gujaratis paying five thousand rupees as donations for getting admissions to schools. Parsis also were not an exception to this rule and even they would do the same if they could afford it.

Parsis had their own ways when it came to marriage. Everyone in Bombay retired at the age of fifty-eight to take a new job with some private firm that paid half the salary. Sam was forty-five years old when Brit was born.

> Young Parsee men have this inbuilt resistance to get married, when they're about thirty-five they suddenly panic at the thought of a lonely old age (the Parsee Old People's home being a cross between a loony house and the Lubyanka) and get married. (60)

Sam had fallen in love at this age. He was also good at tricks of smuggling out money: "One night, he returned from a tryst with the black money-changer, his pockets pregnant with dollar notes. We had to hide them in our luggage." (61) He had his own tricks to hide them. Brit was capable of keeping a note in his powder box. The young Parsi plucked out the plastic cap on the powder box, rolled up ten-dollar notes and buried the bundle deep in the white stuff.

Love marriages, we find, were the tradition in all good Parsi families. Sam's family also was not averse to such an arrangement. When Defarge remarked that Sera's daughter was twenty-four, graduate, and earning and still not married, Sera expressed her helplessness.

> 'What do I do?' said Sera complacently.
>
> 'She refuses to let me arrange any boys for her to see. Anyway, it doesn't worry me. Love marriages are a tradition in our family.' (64)

But Defarge had a different explanation to offer her for Dolly not getting married. According to her, the real reason was that she wanted her to stay and look after Brit, the handicapped boy. When she said that everyone was talking about this issue, Sera regretted that her neighbours were such shameless gossips.

The Parsis wear special dress for funerals. Madame Manekshaw slit her throat and invited death which was a sequel to the killing of her husband. Sam was called home from his office to help take Brit to the funeral. Then he remembered that he didn't have the knee-length white muslin coat with bows down the front that Parsis were supposed to wear at funerals and weddings. Brit who was never found wanting sense of humour believed that the best way to show respect to Madame was to wear his uniform for the funeral. This was because he thought that without her he wouldn't have had that uniform at all. The Parsis took the dead body to the vultures and Brit stood a mute witness to the event.

Adoption was forbidden to the Parsis and this issue is also discussed in the novel. Sam was almost sure that life would be tough for Brit and that he would not be able to go out and compete with young men bursting with energy. But he thought that it would not be difficult for Brit to find a rich wife. Sera wanted him to be a bachelor. Of course, Brit was not very happy with this statement:

> I wanted to shoot back, certainly not. I mean, what guy of fourteen is a confirmed bachelor, unless, of course, he is still stuck in that all-girls-are-asses phase. I answered nonchalantly. 'I guess so.' (79)

Sam did not want to confine Brit to a 'loveless future.' In other words, he wanted to ensure that romantic love was not out for him. But Sera's worry was that Osteo could be inherited. Then came the question of adoption. When Sam said that Brit could adopt children, Sera shot back that Parsis were not allowed to adopt children. Naturally the saddest man was none other than Brit. He kept quiet and could only hear the swish of the taxi on the road.

The Parsis have a unique way of celebrating their birthday. They have their *roj* birthday to be followed by the actual birthday five days later. In the novel it was Sera who made this statement when it was pointed out that Tina was going to have her birthday: "All of us had two birthdays: there was one that we celebrated on the date we were born, and the other, which stepped back one day every leap year, was by the calendar we'd carried across from Persia." (90)

Smoking was a taboo at least for good Parsis. Brit had the first experience of smoking in the company of his friend Cyrus. When a cigarette was offered to him, he was not sure as to which end he should set on fire.

> How flimsy the little white stick felt in my fingers. I put it in my mouth and sucked like I imagined I would on Raquel Welch's nipple. Suddenly there was a gas chamber in my chest and the taste of burnt chicken in my mouth. For the first time in my life I saw stars. (108)

He had literally to struggle with the cigarette which made him realize that there was some reason why good Parsis did not smoke.

Dolly happened to fall in love with Salim, a Muslim which made Sam and Sera talk about the attitude of the Parsis to the Muslims: "The Muslims are the traditional, nay, the historical enemies of the Parsis. And to give yourself to one of them is a shameful act of Betrayal, nay, High Treason." (139)

Sam's view was that even though the British had conquered India, people like Sera were worshipping them. But she had her own argument. The British never had pushed them out of their homes. According to her, it was the Muslims who made them 'pitiful refugees.' Dolly was extremely angry to listen to the way the arguments went:

> "Oh, cut it out!" said Dolly, leaping out of bed, her hair like the mad wife's in *Jane Eyre*. "You know you're talking shit, the height of stinking shit. What the hell does Salim have to do with the Arab tribesmen who beat the hell out of the milksop Persians more than a thousand years ago?" (139)

Sera couldn't put up with the idea of Dolly marrying 'a filthy Mussalman.' She was sure that if Dolly married him she would have the same fate of Tina, that is ending up in a bawdy house in Brooklyn.

The Parsis are crazy about their children and mostly the father and mother adopted a child each when they had two children:

> We thought it was absolutely right for Dolly to take Sam along instead of her mother because she was always his daughter like I was Sera's son. That is how it is with almost every family I know. Both parents are crazy about both kids but in some tiny way each adopts one—a kind of division of labour. I don't know how it works for people who have more than two kids because Parsees almost never do. They feel it's some sort of extravagance, like

> having a television in the bedroom. (142)

The whole discussion was the result of Salim's inability to come to Bombay. The plan was for Dolly to fly out to New York with Sam, on her free tickets, and get married there.

According to Cyrus, the Parsis suffered from a strange 'disease' called Anglophilia:

> As for this creature who was sitting between us, to her I wanted to be nasty as a Nazi. 'I say, is your name really Amy? Or is it short for Aimai? Which is one of the stupidest Parsee names and went out with Queen Victoria. (161)

Amy clarified that her real name was 'Amy' itself and it was all because her parents were of the 'Raj kind.' She wanted to know whether Brit's name was really so when Cyrus remarked that it was Anglophilia, the Parsi disease. Brit told her that his name was Daryus and he was called Brit because he had little bones.

In most of the works by Parsi writers, we find reference to Fire temples and in this novel also we get such references:

> The next day, we had the *uthamna* in the hall of the squat-domed fire-temple that guarded the Parsee colony across the street like a white Buddha, which was sad because most of Sam's colleagues from the bank had to stand outside. They weren't Parsee. Their presence would have defiled the fire temple. (166)

Thus Sam's colleagues had to wait listening to the prayers that wafted through the arched doors.

To sum up, the novel turns out to be one reflecting the ethos of the middle, upper-middle class of Bombay Parsis in every sense: "The hybrid existence of the Parsis, subsidiary theme of the novel, often adds to the humour. Sera's 'oath to the country,' her faith in the value of British guineas, pictures of the British Royal family on all the glass fronted cupboards and the constant references to English films and Hollywood moviestars add a quaint humour to the narrative and reveal the Parsis as cultural hybrids."[4]

The theme of marriage is a major concern in the novel where we have four Parsi girls—Tina, Dolly, Ruby and Amy. Tina eloped with the Hindu boy next door and Dolly was married to Salim, a Muslim doctor in New York. Ruby and Amy were frustrated in their love affairs with Cyrus, the tall, handsome Parsi boy who opted for a legal career in Delhi instead of settling in Bombay. Interfaith marriage continues to be a problem in the Parsi community and Kanga effectively discusses this issue in the novel. The only attempt to 'arrange' a marriage became a failure. The Parsi community has within it contradictions and this is brought out well by the novelist where he discusses the search for a bridegroom for Dolly. Sera, a typical Parsi hybrid, was conditioned by her western upbringing and Defarge belonged to the old order living in the euphoria of past glories. She was proud of her ethnic Parsi identity. The determination of the younger generation of Parsis to go ahead with their plans is something that will not be missed in the novel. Dolly's decision to marry a Muslim is to be seen in this light. In a sense one might say that Kanga's concept of a mixed marriage is that of tolerance and acceptance. Undoubtedly one can say that *Trying to Grow* is a brilliant novel which will specially be remembered for the depiction of Parsi life and the essential Parsi spirit.

NOTES

1. A. Nani Palkhivala, *We, the Nation: The Lost Decades* (New Delhi: UBS, 1994), p. 320.
2. Firdaus Kanga, *Trying to Grow* (New Delhi: Ravi Dayal Publisher, 1990), p. 4.
3. N.P. Sharma, "Parsi Culture and Vision in Rohinton Mistry's *Such a Long Journey* and Firdaus Kanga's *Trying to Grow*: A Comparative Study," *The Fiction of Rohinton Mistry: Critical Studies*, ed. Jay-

dipsinh K. Dodiya (New Delhi: Prestige, 1997), p. 36.

4. Novy Kapadia, "The Handicapped as Survivor in Firdaus Kanga's *Trying to Grow,*" *The Postmodern Indian English Novel: Interrogating the 1980s and 1990s*, ed. Viney Kirpal (Bombay: Allied, 1996), p. 239.

Of Brittleness and Growth: The Quest for Self in Firdaus Kanga's Fictional Autobiography *Trying to Grow*

PALLAVI GUPTA

Trying to Grow[1], Firdaus Kanga's first foray into the field of writing as a novelist, is a thinly disguised autobiographical piece of work. The pointers within and without the autobiography which indicate this are, among others, the dedication to his parents "For Valour," the work itself which is referred to as "an expose called *The Cruel Kotwals*" (150) in chapter 17, and most significantly the mode of narration in the first person, with its intimacy and identification with the author. The interesting thing about *Trying to Grow* is that it functions on a plane which is not only unusual, but perhaps, also unique: while it is supposedly Brit Kotwal's Autobiography, it is also Firdaus Kanga's autobiography. So explicit is the identification that one is tempted to conjecture that Brit Kotwal, the subject of narration, is the Kanga of the past, an objectification of all that Kanga has loved, despaired about, enjoyed, secretly desired, and suffered in trying to grow. The suggestion is that Brit Kotwal functions as a persona which enables Kanga to maintain an aesthetic distance from his past self, thereby enabling him to voice emotions and recall events which would, perhaps, overflow the work if the author would make a direct claim for his work as his autobiography.

Kanga's concern in writing *Trying to Grow* appears to be what John Pilling calls a study in "self scrutiny," a concern "with the formulation of an image . . . that is not contaminated by subjectivity." (3-4) What is intriguing in *Trying to Grow* is the manner in which the author of the autobiographical fiction relates to the subject. The conflation of the author and the "I" which is writing produces an impression akin to a frame-within-a-frame. While on one level, it is the "I" of Brit Kotwal which is writing and putting his memories of the "I" in the past together, on another level, surrounding this is the larger authorial consciousness of Firdaus Kanga, which is "co-conscious,"[2] with the "I" which is writing the autobiography.

This leads to a discussion regarding the truth-claims of autobiography and autobiographical fiction, and it is wise to take P.J. Eakin's observation into account: "Autobiographical truth is not a fixed but an evolving content in an intricate process of self- discovery and self-creation, and, further, that the self that is the center of all autobiographical narrative is necessarily a fictive structure."[3] This statement seems to suggest that the truth lies not in the facts but in the way they are viewed by the person who has experienced them. A good example to cite, in this regard, would be Vladimir Nabokov whose two autobiographical novels are considered—by the author himself—as more truthful than his autobiography *Speak, Memory* (1947). It appears that the truth-claims refer not so much to the author—who might be telling the truth in fiction and lying in his autobiography—but to the reader who sets up certain specific modes of acceptance with regard to autobiographies and fictional works.

Coming back to Kanga, the point in question is not so much an occupation with the truth-claims of *Trying to Grow*, or even with the extent to which Kanga figures in it—biographically—but an investigation of how *Trying to Grow* is a quest of the discovery of the Self and also of the growth of an artist. The paradigms by which this journey is negotiated are, roughly, Marginality, Disability, Homosexuality, Search for a vocation, and Humour which makes the journey bearable not only for the Self but also for others. It would be helpful to regard this work as a fragment, or a part, of a larger attempt at autobiographisation, which is connected to Kanga's second novel *Heaven on Wheels* (1991), which comprises of Kanga's adventures in England.

The Self of Firdaus Kanga/ Brit Kotwal in *Trying to Grow* is caught up in a matrix of "difference" which ultimately leads to a situation of being doubly marginalised. Brit tells us in Chapter 3, "I liked being different from most people. It tickled me. Though it didn't tickle me when I came into life howling with pain." (24) While Brit is marginalised on account of his disability on a personal level, he is marginalisd on a socio-cultural level as he is born into a Parsi family. The reality of the latter permeates the work, as not only does Kanga attempt to recreate the life of the Parsis in Bombay, but Bombay as well. In addition to this, the insulated, cul-de-sac atmosphere of the setting, with no Parsis in sight seems to substantiate Eckhard Kulke's perceptive observation, "[t]he vast majority of Parsi literature is the expression of a latent ethnocentrism as well as of century-long uncertainty regarding their feelings of identity."[4] This uncertainty regarding feelings of identity may well be the reason for the absence of a single autobiography by a Parsi, though there have been instances of biographies of famous Parsi achievers. This added dimension complicates the scenario as it may well be the reason for Kanga's choice of the mode of autobiographical fiction rather than autobiography.

The temptation to regard *Trying to Grow* as a *Kunstlerroman*—somewhat like James Joyce's *A Portrait of the Artist as a Young Man* (1916)—is strong and seemingly justifiable. Brit Kotwal's search for a vocation comes full circle when he starts with the thought of writing a book "one day," (21) becoming a lawyer on coming to know Cyrus, and finally returning to write. Kanga takes great pains to establish the milieu, which gave rise to his writerly proclivities, including *Trying to Grow*. At times, Brit Kotwal and Firdaus Kanga are superimposed, especially when the "I" indulges in reflection or in commenting on a particular event, e.g., in Chapter 3 where Brit reconstructs the scene at the hospital, immediately after his birth, and Sam asks Sera if she is "just putting on a brave act?" (24) This is followed by a shift to the present where the mature, older Brit muses, "That's a question I've been trying to find an answer to ever since I could find answers." (24) And one is left with the distinct feeling that there are certainly more questions for which

Kanga is trying to find answers and perhaps *Trying to Grow* is one of the answers.

The autobiographical fiction is also unique in being, among other things, composed of dialogues and reflections on those dialogues. While, on the one hand, this profuse use of dialogues lends the work the air of fictionality, on the other hand, it conveys the sense of immediacy, which projects an impression of veracity. In addition to this, not only does it generate interest, as the events are enacted and not merely recollected, but also, the reaction "then" and the reflection on it "now" is a marker of the growth of the Self. Unlike Rousseau's *Confessions* (1782) which offers the reader readymade and judgmental vignettes of people, Kanga's work offers situations in which people are shown to be interacting. It is not surprising therefore, that we find ourselves smiling indulgently at Jeroo, or sympathising with Madame Manekshaw, or scoffing at Defarge. Moreover, in reporting from memory, conversations peppered with contemporary allusions and Parsi words, Kanga manages to retain the flavour of the times and of his own age. Brit, aged four, is very different from Brit at fourteen, and the meticulous manner in which the growth is observed and shown is remarkable. A four-year-old Brit, having returned from his visit to Wagh Baba questions his irate mother, 'Lust!,' I interrupted, 'Is that some kind of disease?'" (5), and at fourteen, to his mother's inquiry of his future as a bachelor boy, Brit casually remarks, "I guess so," while thinking, "I wanted to shoot back. Certainly not. I mean what guy of fourteen is a confirmed bachelor, unless of course, he is still stuck in that all-girls-are-asses phase." (79)

At one point in the work, Cyrus remarks, "If nothing else, your books will be remembered for their startling honesty," (117) a self-reflexive statement as *Trying to Grow* functions on the magic formula of "truth tempered with humour." Kanga is not unaware of the fabled "bitter pill of truth" though he certainly knows how to sugar-coat it just enough so that the pill tastes bitter-sweet. Success, as Kanga shows us, comes packed with the suspicion that it was undeserved. On winning a prize for academic excellence in school, Brit remarks,

> Around me the applause burst and swelled like some orchestral climax while I grew smaller and smaller in my seat wishing I wasn't there, wishing Father Ferra hadn't talked about me, wishing I hadn't got this prize for legs that didn't work. (48)

Kindness, Love, Relationships, are looked upon with suspicion as different forms of that abhorrable emotion—pity. And Brit's reaction to his self and to others is, to a large extent, governed by what the Other thinks of the Self and how it chooses to define it. Brit recognises this process rather late in the autobiography but early in life, when he confesses to Amy, "I guess a lot of my problems come from the way I think people look at me." (189) And not surprisingly Brit's self-estimate is severely damaged by what Others impose on him as the "truth" about himself, e.g., Jeroo vindicates Brit from the category of "men" when she apologizes: "So sorry. . . . I forgot about your son. You understand, when I say men, I mean—men. Not someone like you, Brit," and Brit remarks, "I wasn't male. Not to them. The magic mirrors of their minds had invented a formula: osteo = sexlessness." (33) Later Madame Manekshaw puts a damper on his philanthropic spirits, when she declares, "People are going to find it very difficult to trust you to solve their problems. . . . To a lot of people you seem stupid because you are so short and, I know it's absurd, because you can't walk." (57) Brit's reaction is characteristically enveloped in humour, "'That a blackmailer is a crook,' I said grinning like crazy because I was feeling all hot inside." (57) Brit also focuses on the counter-drive within his parents, vis-à-vis him, as while they try to make him independent, their supporting figures are never too far away. Brit tells us in Chapter 5, "I was perfectly capable of doing all this [getting dressed] myself. But you know how it is when you can't do some things people feel you can't do anything." (43) Elsewhere, Brit remarks, "If there was one thing about which Sera and Sam were firm and frank it was not letting me treat them like bonded labour." (53)

However, while focussing on what the other thought of him, Kanga/ Brit Kotwal also focuses on his own shortcomings.

The fact that he is dependent, helpless, in terms of the body is driven in with equal force as is his desire for independence; as in the incident with the binoculars (53), his escapades with Cyrus (110), and his dates with Amy go in to show.

It is pertinent to note that when it comes to the "Self," Brit's defining factor is the body, and as the work illustrates his self-realization, or discovery of the truth about himself is intricately linked with his coming to terms with his Body, as is his choosing the profession of a writer instead of a lawyer. Anima Sen, in her book entitled *Psycho-Social Integration of the Handicapped* (1988), observes: "Strong bodies, well-formed and socially approved statures predispose people to develop extroverted, realistic and social traits. Conversely, malformed or markedly a-typical physiques tend [in relation to social and environmental statures] to produce introverted, intellectual, or artistic personalities."[5]

In one sense *Trying to Grow* is also about trying to come to terms with and even transcend the body. Donald Moss in his essay "Brain, Body and the World: Perspectives on Body-Image" discusses the importance of the body in Existential-Phenomenology, where the body is regarded as forming "a unity with the mind or mental processes."[6] The concept of the "lived body," (74) propounded by Merleau-Ponty gives rise to two terms which are pertinent in the given context: Body-image and Body-schema. While body-image is generally understood as "the picture that the person has of the physical appearance of his body," (74) from mirrors and from the others' point-of-view; Body-schema refers to "the implicit knowledge about both the actual and possible positions of the body." (74) Using these terms, in a slightly loose manner, one may say that Brit's problems arise from the inability to accept the reality of his body-image, and exploit the possibilities of his body-schema. He undergoes a process, which begins with the disowning or "depersonalization" (87) of his body-image, and his self-realization takes place only when he learns to express identity or "mineness" (87) with his body. The growth is monitored beautifully in the work, as Chapter 16 records this bit of conversation with Cyrus, where Brit's discomfiture with regard to his body is expressed:

> 'You [Cyrus] look good and not all the cosmetic surgeons in America can make me like looking at myself.'
>
> 'Is any of that important?'
>
> 'Don't tell me beauty is bone deep and all that crap because it isn't true. I want to be straight and tall because I've one life and I'll go through it without anyone ever wanting me like I wanted you. It's like—'
>
> 'A sweeper watching a Brahmin?'
>
> 'Yes, you either hate that something you can never have, or you adore it.'
>
> 'Tell me more.'
>
> 'The desire of the moth for the star.'
>
> 'That doesn't explain lust.'
>
> 'It does. If I could have you, which meant you wanted me, that meant my body was as good as yours.' (145)

The book ends with Brit's appearance at the door of the elevator, which he has boarded minus the wheel-chair; "'Amy,' I called into the glass, 'd'you think I look a few inches taller?' There are some things we just can't believe. I liked the way I looked." (235)

Not surprisingly, Brit Kotwal's transformation is the result of Love—parental, homosexual, and finally heterosexual. Paradoxically, Brit Kotwal's discovery of love—for Amy—is the result of his acceptance of his body, and therefore the belief in the likeability of his self and of his body.

In Merleau-Ponty's analysis, "Love is very intimately related to sexuality; in fact sexuality is the most intimate expression of love."[7] And though Love is expressed as all types of communication are, through the body, yet it is "not merely a bodily instinct." It is this problematic relation between body and love which Firdaus Kanga explores in Brit Kotwal's relationships with Ruby, Cyrus and finally, Amy. This movement—from Ruby to Amy—can be read, on another level, as a movement from Infatuation to Lust and finally to Love. This is precisely what makes giving up Ruby easier than giving up Cyrus, and giving up Amy the most difficult.

An exploration of, what Madame Manekshaw calls, "Brit's budding sexuality" (40) entails a study of why Brit moves from an almost reciprocal homosexual relationship to one that is heterosexual. Brit's advent into "love" is heralded by Ruby's impetuous suggestion to French kiss in the absence of their parents. Brit's refusal is accompanied by regret—"I wanted to kick myself hard as a goat's hoof," (83) and reflection: "The fact was I just didn't want to kiss Ruby. But that was a bloody lie. . . . But the Truth was—and it was awful—I thought she didn't deserve a kiss from me." (83-84) The root of his refusal lies, as we readers might believe, not in homosexuality but in his low estimate of his body.

With Cyrus, the relationship is a combination of friendship, lust and envy. "This is love! Divine love," squawks Brit, but soon one realizes that this love is actually lust. And lust not for Cyrus, but for the body that Brit does not possess. In a telling statement, Brit remarks about Sera, "I wondered if she was thinking how grand it would be if he [Cyrus] were her son." (126) And later in his conversation with Cyrus, Brit remarks, "If I could have you, which meant you wanted me, that meant my body was as good as yours." (145) This is precisely why Cyrus's sexual advances fall flat with Brit's remark, "Somehow it felt all wrong as if I had clasped the wrong partner in the dark." (144) However, this homosexual relationship enables Brit to "connect" with the world at large. George Kovacs in his article "The Body and Sexuality" observes, "sexuality awakens the human person to relational living, to the realm of meaning, existence, and language."[8] Coincidentally, this may be applied *in toto* to what happens to Brit. Kovacs adds: "Thus sexual, erotic comprehension is not a thought, not an idea, it is the desire establishing the presence of the other person by linking one body to another body." (212)

Applied to Brit's situation, this homosexual episode in his life enables him to establish his presence and desirability in his own estimate and on his own terms. This provides the springboard for his relationship with Amy, which turns from rivalry over Cyrus to desire for each other. This is, however, not to say that forging a relationship with Amy is a cakewalk for Brit:

he has to first overcome the enemy within—*Osteogenesis imperfecta* and his complex regarding his body. Brit tells us in Chapter 22,

> I looked long and hard so that I would never forget. I saw my neck squat as a toad's and my hollow shoulders, one higher than the other like Richard the Third's, my rib cage thrust forward so that it bulged in the centre and sloped down the sides, and below that my legs thin as a famine child's, the shins bowed as if some kid had plastered on some clay as a joke, or an after-thought. To have thought, even for a moment, that Amy was charmed by this. (195)

The point is that Amy is charmed, so charmed that she is glad Brit has osteo. It is Amy who instills the sense of inherent beauty into Brit in the solitary bathroom conversation that they have in Amy's house, when she says:

> 'And you always will, till you realize how beautiful you are.'
>
> 'I'll never be beautiful.'
>
> 'You are—more sensual and adorable than Cyrus.' (205)

And it is their love-making which proves to be the final nail on the coffin of Brit's complex. A peculiar twist in the work, however, shows that Brit's exorcisation of the demon within is incomplete when he finds himself face-to-face with Amy's insecurity when she tells him about her reasons for breaking-off with Cyrus: "Oh, Brit it was awful never being able to trust him; but it's different with you, isn't it? I mean, I never ever have to worry." (225) For a moment it seems as if the demon had come alive again, and it is this which prevents the autobiography from becoming a fictional fairy tale. Brit Kotwal's life is not a tale of wish-fulfillment, and Kanga makes sure that it never seems to be one.

Trying to Grow functions as a metaphor for the autobiography, as every human being in it is striving for growth. And true growth, as Kanga will have it, comes with the knowledge of one's limitations, its acceptance and the accompanying pain. Love, as Kanga portrays it, is also a process of growth; a process which is based not on the formula of "I loved you because I needed you," (232) but as Brit puts it, "If I can do without Amy, why should I." (234)

NOTES

1. Firdaus Kanga, *Trying to Grow* (Delhi: Ravi Dayal, 1990).
2. Galya Diment, *The Autobiographical Novel of Co-consciousness: Goncharev, Woolf, Joyce* (Florida: Florida UP, 1994), p. 41.
3. Paul John Eakin, *Fictions in Autobiography: Studies in the Art of Self Invention* (Princeton: Princeton U.P., 1985), p. 3.
4. Eckhard Kulke, *The Parsis in India: A Minority as an Agent of Social Change* (Delhi: Vikas, 1974), p. 10.
5. Anima Sen, *Psycho-Social Integration of the Handicapped: A Challenge to Society* (Delhi: Mittal Publications, 1988), p. 162.
6. Donald Moss, "Brain, Body, and World: Perspectives on Body-Image," *Existential-Phenomenological Alternatives for Psychology*, ed. Ronald S. Valle and Mark King (New York: OUP, 1978), pp. 69-83.
7. Qtd. in Rose Mary Barral, "Self and Other: Communication and Love," in Keith Hoeller, ed. *Merleau-Ponty and Psychology. Studies in Existential Psychology and Psychiatry Series* (New Jersey: Humanities Press, 1993), p. 169.
8. George Kovacs, "The Personalistic Understanding of the Body and Sexuality in Merleau-Ponty," in Hoeller, p. 212.
9. John Pilling, *Autobiography and Imagination: Studies in Self-Scrutiny* (London: Routledge, 1981).

Anglomaniac Tendencies in Firdaus Kanga's *Trying to Grow*

FATIMA SUGARWALA

Firdaus Kanga's first novel *Trying to Grow* presents the peculiarities and pretensions of the Parsi culture and manners. The novel is an interesting study of the diasporic displacement experienced by the Parsis who came from Iran in the eighth century and made their home in India. The present article proposes to look into the anglomaniac tendencies of the Parsis in India and the crazy glamour of the West among this gradually declining community.

Kanga's novel *Trying to Grow* is full of vivid images of the life of a degenerating community, created in the mind's eye of an "Oesteogenesis Imperfecta."[1] Brit Kotwal, the protagonist, a handicapped born with "bones as brittle as glass . . . legs . . . delicate as test tubes," (24) the entire novel is Brit's valiant attempt at trying to grow mentally and become physically self-reliant. In this process of growing, he seems more clearly, feels more deeply, thinks more profoundly and reacts more prudently.

In *Trying to Grow*, Kanga lays open the ache and the anguish of a handicapped who tries his utmost to seek adjustment with people around him and his environment and live like a normal healthy man, but as he grows he realizes that all around him there is a poignant sense of alienation.

Brit Kotwal, the similitude of Kanga, projects mentally, their attitude and approach to life in postcolonial India. The Parsis came to India a thousand years ago, yet there is a feeling of insecurity and an air of detachment toward India and the Indians. When the Parsis came to India during the pre-colonial days, they were welcomed, immigration-friendliness was extended and they were permitted to practise their mono-theistic religion, but they could not proselytize and had to adopt the costumes, traditions and language of their Hindu hosts. They had to celebrate their festivals moderately and could not bear arms.[2] Such biased attitude of their benefactors provided them a conditional home but alienated them from India. When the British came to India, the Parsis were given a nonpartisan treatment, they became an intermediary link between the Indians and the Britishers. This state evoked the dichotomy between their loyalty and the British royalty.

The Parsis shifted their loyalty, they completely accepted subjugation to their colonial masters and became Westernized. Colonial writes like Behram Malbari and Cornelia Sorabji depict the Parsis' diasporic traces of nostalgia and the loss of their past Persian glory.[3] The Parsis established a rapport with the British in India. Glamorized by the West, they settled down in Bombay which was more Westernized as it was then a seat of British administration. Bombay provided them the right environment to flourish and adapt themselves as it was and still is a cosmopolitan town where they had more freedom to practise their religion and customs.

During the postcolonial period, when the British left India, the Parsis suffered a tremendous social and economic degradation directing them to the West, shedding off their Indian identity. But men like Dadabhai Naoroji emphatically declared, "Whether I am a Hindu, a Mohemadan, a Parsi, a Christian or any other creed, I am above all an Indian. Our country is India, our nationality is Indian."[4] Although the Parsis have accepted India as their home and have contributed in almost every sphere—Politics (Dadabhai Naoroji and Phirozeshah Mehta,) Industry (The Tatas), Science (Homi Bhabha), Law (Nani Palkhiwala) and Music (Zubin Mehta)—to the development of our country yet deep down there is a strong feeling of disorientation and deprecation.

Firdaus Kanga in his novel *Trying to Grow* reveals the Parsis's attempt to adapt to the realities of the postcolonial India, but most of them experience a social and psychological alienation. They cannot forget their Persian glory and their colonial privileges. They are too sophisticated and they think of themselves as too cultured to mingle with the down-to-earth Indians. Brit gives a vivid picture of Bombay. "wherever you go before you say urchin you are surrounded by fifty five grey kids—their clothes, their hair, even the look in their eyes is grey. . . . I couldn't stand them because I always thought I'd catch mumps or measles or may be (sweat of sweats) TB from them." (33) The Parsis belong more to the Western world of "Kraft Cheese. . . . Dior clothes. . . . Caviare and champagne—all imported of course. They don't enjoy anything Indian." (108) They despise the stinking heat of the day, the dirty and dusty streets of the red light area with its pathetic "whores" and the lusty men with "tongues hanging out," (109) loitering on the streets of Bombay.

Like Rohinton Mistry in *Tales from Firozshah Baag and Such a Long Journey*, Firdaus Kanga in *Trying to Grow* also depicts the ghetto-like world or the 'Coopmandup' Parsi clan which Kulke calls the forming elements of Parsiness—the Zoroastrian faith, a shared history, flight from Iran and refuge in India, a colonial elite consciousness and a feeling of unease in decolonized India.[5] All these traits are common among them. Their lives revolve round their religion, Parsi associates, Parsi food and Western valorizing. All the major characters in Kanga's novel are Parsis—except the Christian Priests of the Campion School, the breathing generator Rutty Regina and Wagh baba reflecting the murky side of India—they reflect the life and temperament of their community.

Kanga, through a number of Parsi characters and a series of events, manifests their diasporic fate which has given them a feeling of insecurity, developed their anglomaniac tendencies and led them to change their loyalties from time to time. The traces of these fluctuating loyalties is seen more strikingly in Brit's parents Sam and Sera. Their flat is decorated in the "late Victorian" (19) style. Brit vividly describes their home, "They were everywhere, the British Royal Family grinning at us from behind glass-fronted cupboards, looking out like dour prisoners from book case windows, splashed over my bedroom wall." Walking past the Gateway of India, Sera never forgets to read in sonorous tones the inscription high on the arch: "ERECTED TO COMMEMORATE THE LANDING IN INDIA OF THE IMPERIAL MAJESTIES KING GEORGE V AND QUEEN MARY." (10) It gives her a feeling of pleasure and pride to see the Gateway from which the British had entered India.

Everything about their life has a Western outlook, their anglomaniac tendency is so finely knitted with their ways of life that they are not even conscious of it. Sera is described as having Betty Gable legs and Sam Gregory Peck looks, Dolly has Shirley Temple curls and Brit has the "Casanova's" (29) sexy eyelashes. Sera is a staunch Anglophile, Cyrus describes "Anglophilia the Parsi disease." (161) Apart from her Parsiness, she is obsessed by the Western life-style. She prefers to call her daughter Daulatbanoo as Dolly and Daryus as Brit. She proudly claims "Brit with one 't' will sound rather English." (26) Traces of anglicized culture are present in most Parsis. Even while using names the "Parsi delights in stretching, snipping and squashing given names out of all recognition, with a view to making them roll off the tongue easily and perhaps even sound English. So the boys who are Faredoon become Freddy, Naoroji becomes Neville, Adi becomes Eddy" (26) or Zarthost becomes Jerry, "nice English name, no?" (154) Everyone is delighted by these new impressive British sounds, very musical and romantic.

Brit describes the Parsis as "reluctant Indians." (36) In his opinion, a Parsi prefers slumming to eating non-Parsi food. In unavoidable situations, they put up a brave act like the clown in the Hindi movie—"a smiling face and a weeping heart." (36) Sam and Sera do not hesitate spending extravagantly on an English meal at the Taj Mahal Hotel, though it tastes "bland as ulcer diet," (27) but for a scorching tasty Indian food they prefer the cheapest joint. Sera's logic has a trace of distaste, she says, "The Indians are a poor people so the best place for genuine Indian cuisine has to be cheap." (27) Sera's comment has a stink of aversion towards Indian food, though she has lived all her life in India.

Sam and Sera breathe Western culture in their children's lives. They send Brit to Campion School for the Catholic

Priests there, are "all foreigners, Spanish or Irish. . . . They are foreigners so they are good." (40) Like Brit, Madame Manekshaw is skeptical about the "Parsees and their craze for foreigners." (41) Their craze for Westernization has gone so deep that it neither disturbs nor ruffles their sentiments when a man at the Shell gas station in Los Angeles is surprised at Brit's fluent English and calls him a smart kid. Brit is confused whether it is an Indian speaking English that has surprised the man or his handicap, but Dolly nonchalantly replies, "To them, it is all the same." (62)

The entire novel has various expressions referring to English dignitaries and events such as—"as triumphant as Margaret Thatcher at the fall of Port Staley," (41) "barked in George Patton Style," (146) "Trying to look like Saint Joan and ending up like the Dauphine," (147) "Smiling like Hercule Poirot in the last chapter of Agatha Christie," (149) "And I was as sick as the Duke of Windsor on 11 December 1996," (171) "To my First English Man Brit, from your compatriot, Rati D. Davierwala" (176) written on the flyleaf of Housman's Last Poems gifted to Brit for his sophisticated English airs. These remarks reveal the characters's mental state and their deep-rooted obsession and admiration of the Western style.

Despite their anglomaniac tendencies and the Western glamour, there are certain aspects of life with which they cannot compromise. Even in their day-to-day life, the impact of their diasporic state and the tension built up by their anglophilic attitude is clearly experienced by them. Despite her modern Western outlook, Sera is highly skeptical about Dolly's wish to become an air-hostess. She tells her: "An air-hostess, that's what! . . . Can you imagine? . . . you might as well say glorified ayah!" (58)

Sam's reaction is also typical of an Indian male. Although he is crazy about planes, and on bank holidays he goes to the airport just to gaze at those sleek silver bodies from a distance, he does not permit Dolly to be an air-hostess. He tells her, "I know a lot about airlines, the kind of people who work with them. And it's not the kind of life a girl like you would want." (59) Both Sam and Sera are torn between the diverse cultural impact, the permissiveness of West and the conservativeness of the East. Dolly and Brit are brought up in the Western style. Dolly has the freedom to choose her friends, attend dinners or late night shows as any Western teenager, but "Sam would have died" (94) if she meets with the same fate as Tina who was seduced, raped and turned into a prostitute by her boyfriend. Again, Dolly's wish to marry a "filthy Musalman" (140) raises a great hue and cry in the house. Sera cannot accept a non-Parsi son-in-law, even Dolly's hunger strike like the Mahatma's, which had once shaken the solid British empire, has no effect on her. She proudly declares, "I'm no gentle fair-minded Britisher, I'm Persian pure Persian." (140) The only consolation she derives is that Salim comes from a "fine aristocratic family. So Westernized you would think they were from there, and he looks like a Parsi!" (141) While adopting the anglicized attitude, she does not want to relinquish her Parsiness, though she can conveniently forget her Indianness.

Sam suffers from a dichotomy between the reality of his Indianness and the illusion of his anglicized self. He is truly shocked when Sera not only condones but also repeats Brick's abusive slang "Oh, bloody rot and poppy cock!" very casually, saying that "Every English solder in Colaba used to say it. In the good old days when they were here." (6) Although he is critical about the conservativeness of the Indian marriage and man-woman relationship, his Indianness comes to the fore in reprimanding his wife. He says, "If I were a Hindu husband I would have thrashed you just now." (6) Kanga indirectly points at the male dominance and the conservative Indian marriage system in which the woman must follow the man's dictates.

Sam and Sera's relationship, judged by Indian standards, seems to be very different. There is a tremendous amount of sharing, patience and a healthy humour between them. They are a perfect foil to each other. Brit writes that when he was born Sam felt that it was very unnatural that Sera was not shattered by the doctor's declaration that he'll never walk, he'll be toothless and have brittle bones. (24) But Sera's stoic reply was:

> Sam that was awful. He's our son, he's a boy like any

> other, only his body has problems. He'll cope with them more easily than you think; they'll just be a way of life for him. (25)

Such courage in the face of tragedy is what is called the British cool. When she gets the news of Sam's death in America, she still retains her reserve, telling Brit, "Don't worry, we'll manage. I'm here to take care of you." With a brave smile, she declares "I'm prepared." (165) Her courage is commendable. A typical Indian woman would have broken down helplessly. Sera's composure seems to be the result of her Western upbringing and culture. Though Sera appears cold and unfeeling, there is a lot of warmth and understanding in her. She is the anchor of the family, protecting them whenever they need and giving them as much freedom. She is a glorious combination of the sensitive Indian and a practical level-headed Britisher.

The Parsi diaspora is visualized at a variance in the different characters of the novel. Madame Manekshaw distrusts anything Parsi, though at the age of seventeen she has married a shabby fifty-one-year-old Parsi millionaire, to escape from a life of squalor and struggle. Unlike Sera and Sam, she hates the Catholic schools with their "shuffling priests and cruel discipline" and pities the Parsis and their obsession of the West. Though an Indian patriot, she dresses in the latest Western style, a painstaking imitation of the "Vogue" with a lavish dubbing of the "French Perfume" (39)—like Kersi in Rohinton Mistry's "Lend Me Your Light," who lives in Canada, but becomes the member of the Parsi-club, keeps Parsi friends and cannot relinquish his Indianness. Mehroo Manekshaw, despite her Western airs, is not an anglophile. Sitting at the Taj Mahal Hotel, she proudly admires the "shores of mainland India." (46) She has accepted India as her homeland, hence she does not suffer from a divided identity. According to Nilufer Bharucha: "The Indian based Parsi, in spite of increasing tolerance of minorities and 'otherness' in India decides that for the time being at least the country of refuge is home."[6]

Brit, Mehroo Manekshaw and Cyrus echo this feeling. Although their allure of the West is as vibrant, yet they come to terms with their dichotomies and accept India and the city of Mumbai as their home. Cyrus dreams of being a successful solicitor, he believes his dream can come true only in Mumbai, the guiding and the guarding force of all who take refuge here. He prefers to stay only in Mumbai, as he says, "you can be anyone in Bombay, as long as you have brains and bluster, you've got it made." (110) Such an attitude proclaims a sense of acceptance and belonging.

Brit, the narrator-protagonist, does not miss any opportunity to comment critically though mildly and at time humorously at the Parsis's anglomaniac tendencies. Brit is the mouthpiece of the writer. The younger generation represented by Brit, Dolly, Tina, Cyrus, Amy and Jerry seem to have adapted to their present reality. They are daring, ready to take challenges and opportunities which the older generation Parsis could not. Madame Manekshaw points out that the Parsis "don't have the guts to make money, all they want is a nine to five job and their trifling three thousand a month." (41)

According to Kanga, the younger generation has undergone a sea change in their approach to life. They are prepared to break away from the cloying moribund shackles of a narrow-minded community to seek fresh pastures. They are very much different from their ancestors. According to Tindall: "Today every Parsi family in Bombay seems to have relatives usually younger relatives in London, New York or Toronto."[7]

Dolly marries a Mussalman doctor residing in New York and settles down there. She relishes life in America, enjoying freedom working in Brooklyn. She writes to Brit "The job's with Pan Am. Isn't that great?" (222) Like Sam she has always wished to escape India. So she takes up the job of an air-hostess. In Boman Desai's *The Memory of Elephants*, Rusi and Homi migrate to America for further studies. In Rohinton Mistry's "Lend Me your Light," Jamshed and Kersi migrate to America and Canada for material prosperity and career opportunities.

The older generation of Parsis migrated to India but always suffered from mental and emotional alienation. Now the younger generation answers the call of the West. According to Sulman Rushdie:

> A full migrant suffers, traditionally, a triple disruption, he loses his place, he enters into an alien language and he finds himself surrounded by beings whose social behaviour and codes are unlike and sometimes even offensive to his own. And this is what makes a migrant such a pathetic figure, because roots, languages and social norms have been three of the definition of what is to be a human being.[8]

Contrary to Rushdie's version, Dolly in *Trying to Grow* seems to be perfectly happy and comfortably settled in America. Even Jamshed, in Mistry's story "Lend Me Your Light" staying in America, in his letter describes India a "dismal place" where "Nothing ever improves, just too much corruption" which is all part of the "ghati mentality." (9) Sam, Sera, Defarge and Rati Deviare are, as Rushdie describes, dissatisfied migrants in India, but they have had little guts or opportunity to adopt a new identity as Dolly and Jamshed have.

Like Firdaus Kanga in *Trying to Grow* many Parsi novelists like Boman Desai in *The Memory of Elephants*, Dina Mehta in *And Some Take a Lover*, Bapsi Sidhwa in *An American Brat*, and Farrukh Dhondy in *Bombay Duck* deal with the diasporic fate and the conflicting interests and loyalties of the Parsis. Like Sera and Sam, Shaila Bhave in Bharati Mukherjee's "The Management of Grief" is torn between her Indian heritage and the Canadian identity.

The anglomaniac tendencies of the Parsis persist strongly. Their Parsiness is fast dying out as the young prefer mixed marriages and migrating to the West. The rootlessness is rapidly spreading like the poison is gradually destroying a once great Persian heritage. Their divided loyalties between India and the West have left them anchorless, but Jungian collective unconsciousness still prevails, whatever happens whether anglicized or Indianized their Parsiness will proclaim.

N O T E S

1. Firdaus Kanga, *Trying to Grow* (New Delhi: Ravi Dayal Publisher, 1990), p. 25.
2. Nilufer Bharucha, "When Old Tracks are Lost: Rohinton Mistry's Fiction as Diasporic Discourse," *The Fiction of Rohinton Mistry*, ed. Jaydipsinh Dodiya (New Delhi: Prestige, 1998), p. 24.
3. *Loc. cit.*
4. Nani A. Palkhiwala, *We the Nation: The Lost Decades* (New Delhi: UBS, 1994), p. 320.
5. See E. Kulke, *The Parsis in India: A Minority as Agent of Social Change* (Delhi: Vikas, 1978).
6. Nilufer Bharucha, "Reflexion in Broken Mirrors: Diverse Diaspora in Recent Parsi Fiction," Jaydipsinh Dodiya, ed., *The Fiction of Rohinton Mistry*, p. 33.
7. Gillian Tindall, *City of Gold* (New Delhi: Penguin, 1992), p. 80.
8. Salman Rushdie, *Imaginary Homelands* (New Delhi: Penguin, 1991).
9. Rohinton Mistry, *Tales from Firozshah Baag* (New Delhi: Rupa, 1993), p. 181.

Firdaus Kanga's *Trying to Grow*: A Tale of the Sensual and Adorable

K.V. SURENDRAN

Firdaus Kanga's *Trying to Grow* (1990) is a moving novel where the novelist recreates the struggle of Daryus Kotwal with extraordinary honesty and precision. The novel which has attracted great critical attention has been described as one which celebrates courage, faith, idealism, the vitality and resilience of Indian family life, the endearing idiosyncratic style of the Parsis of Bombay and the city of Bombay itself. The presentation of Bombay in the novel very often reminds one of a similar exercise by Rohinton Mistry, another Parsi novelist. His *Fine Balance* has several instances of Bombay seen in close up as the following description shows: "Eight, nine or ten people in a small room. Sleeping one over the other on big shelves, from floor to ceiling, like third class, railway berths. Or in cupboards, or in the bathroom. Surviving like goods in a war house."[1] The novel has been evaluated as a delightfully unexpected portrait of the writer as a young trapeze artist, flinging himself out energetically. There will be no two opinions if it is stated that the novel ultimately celebrates the pain and embarrassment of the protagonist who makes an all out effort to assert human dignity.

The novel is about Brit Kotwal and his effort to grow up in the most adverse circumstances. Brit was one who was not even able to guess what his mother really felt when she was destined to have a son like him. He saw that his father, a sophisticated public-school man, believed in miracle-cures. But it was increasingly becoming clear to him that Wagh Baba, the sex-crazed 'holy man,' couldn't make Brit grow taller, or walk, or stop his bones from breaking. For Brit it was a life where he was made to drink powdered pearls in his milk and had almond oil rubbed into his legs until it gleamed like 'Bangalore silk.' This article is an attempt to show how the novelist makes us experience the pathetic life of a handicapped boy who was born to fight in every possible way.

Brit makes his first appearance on the opening page of the novel as an eight-year-old boy who looked just four-year-old or even three. The novel is narrated in first person by the protagonist himself and in the beginning we find that he was being taken to 'a witch doctor' by his father. The doctor had forgotten to say that he was going to be a dwarf and he had forgotten to grow. In fact there was a view that Parsi prayers would help children recover from such physical problems and Sam, his father, had tried it for six months: "The priest told me to say them at three every morning. All they did was give me insomnia—listening for the stroke of three."[2] The old man who was told about it considered it shameful for educated English-speaking people going to a 'mumbo-jumbo Baba.' His apprehension was that some of them could be swindlers who were after money.

The Baba was known for his mysterious ways; women were his weakness: "True to his name, Wagh Baba was stretched out on a tiger skin. He was stark naked. A woman in white with heavy coils of black hair falling over her sari was rubbing a perfumed ointment into his right thigh." (4) Wagh Baba, the miracle man who had laid a spell on Bombay's citizens was one day arrested together with his beautiful accomplice Ma Shanti Devi on charges of fraud, cheating and indecent assault. Police raided his ashram in Chembur, after receiving complaints from the outraged parents of a seventeen-year-old girl who had been assaulted by him on the pretext of being treated:

> The Baba apparently claimed that he could diagnose women's diseases by feeling the shape of their breasts.
>
> The father of the girl, one Ramdas Patil, broke down as he told this reporter that his innocent daughter, who suffered from asthma, had allowed Wagh Baba to fondle

> her breasts. The Baba told her that her breasts were lemon-shaped and so she was to avoid all citrus fruits. (20)

There was no record of any miracle being performed by Wagh Baba, although every devotee claimed he had heard of many cures. It was more out of desperation than strong faith in his magical powers that prompted Sam to take Brit to him in the hope of an early cure. He always felt that it was not wrong of him to trust the heartless Wagh Baba who was fond of going around feeling "apple- and mango- and lemon-shaped boobs." A couple of years carlier, someone in his office had advised him to feed Brit powdered pearls: "A lot of people take them as medicine, and in some shops you see bottles of the gleaming white powder sitting below the glass counter, humble as aspirin. I was awfully proud to be the only kid in the building who drank pulverised pearls stirred into his milk. Unfortunately the month I started gazzling them I broke two ribs." (27)

In fact, breaking ribs was the major problem that the child was made to confront with ever since he was born. Brit who liked to be different from others came into life howling with pain. He suffered from *osteogenesis imperfecta* and when Sera, his mother, came out of her 'anaesthetic fog' she was received by the bad news which was going to make far-reaching consequences in the family. This was what the Saint Bernard-faced doctor told Sera:

> I'm afraid I have bad news for you, Sera, . . . Your boy is born with bones brittle as glass. The ones in his legs are delicate as test tubes; I doubt he'll ever walk. He'll probably be toothless, too; his teeth will break as soon as he bites into anything hard. (24)

Of course, there was the silver lining. The doctor did not forget to tell her that his disease would burn itself out by the time he was in his late teens. At the same time he was sure that Brit was never going to talk. The way Sera reacted to the doctor's remarks was almost a riddle for Brit. She put up a brave face and told Sam that the boy was like any other and only his body had problems was something incredible for Brit: "That Sera's behaviour was unnatural is undeniable. But are the responses we expect the only natural ones? Could it be that Sera really had the courage to meet the disaster that had slipped into her life? Or was it one of those blockades that we impose on our minds so that unpleasant facts are sunk like ships bringing sustenance to an enemy?" (24-25) Without knowing that she was describing the telling features of osteo, she told Sam that their son had a strong chin, sharp nose and a face that was a perfect triangle!

Obviously it was a terrible and painful life that was in store for Brit (Daryus, on certificate). Dolly who thought of making him cry by calling his name was told that he would have enough to cry without that. If he was lucky he would only fracture his bones a dozen times before he was five. He would feel pain about four times as much as normal people did. To add to this was the physical deformity. He was short, but his arms were long. At the same time he was a Casanova for the female neighbours. At least for sometime, he continued to be what the TV advertisement says: 'Owner's pride and neighbour's envy.' The almond oil rubbed into his legs made his skin the envy of his female neighbours.

> "Brit, let us feel your legs!" they pleaded, the teenagers who lived upstairs. "Ooh! Like Bangalore silk. Look! He's winking at us. Give me your eyelashes, Brit? you seven-year-old Casanova!" (27-28)

Brit was extraordinary in more ways than one. Even at a very young age of ten he was in the habit of reading the *Reader's Digest.* The bone-marrow of a goat which he was made to take made him sick and it was an article in *Reader's Digest* which had told him that bone-marrow had nothing to do with brittle bones and produced only blood cells. This forced his father to rub the marrow into his bones. As Novy Kapadia writes: "By portraying the resilience and precociousness of Brit Kotwal, the novelist highlights the handicapped's assertion of human dignity. However, a subordinate theme are the frequent callous reactions, masked in the cloak of sympathy by the normal people, to the handicapped."[3] One such 'callous reaction' flowed from Rutty, Regina the breathing Generator who came into Brit's life when he was twelve. She claimed that she could work wonders:

> 'I have the power to conduct electric currents from my body to my patients. It is a rare gift for which I have been called the Breathing Generator by none other than—' she named some Parsee top brass in the army. 'I have worked wonders with wounded soldiers.' (29)

For two months the Breathing Generator came and stripped Brit naked. She rubbed her hands until they were hot with the friction and laid them on his spine, his feet, his neck and his thighs. She was insufferable and Dolly's turning off the main switch helped to drive her away. She left the place remarking that Sera had the rudest children she had ever met.

Though Brit himself was a crippled child, he was scared of the other handicapped people: "I was scared of the way handicapped people looked. You know, the hesitant gait and robot-stiff movements of the blind, the lolling heads and strangulated speech of the spastics. Whenever I saw them I wondered if I seemed as ugly and pathetic. I'd shudder and turn my mind away." (32) The callous observations which others made very often turned out to be unbearable for him. Jeroo his cousin who was gentle, soft-spoken, beautiful and frigid once said that men wanted sex and only sex. She was immediately apologetic and told Sera that she did not have people like Brit in her mind:

> 'So sorry!' said Jeroo. 'I forgot about your son. You understand, when I say men, I mean—men. Not someone like you, Brit.' I wasn't male. Not to them. The magic mirrors of their minds had invented a formula: Osteo = sexlessness. (33)

Brit had the sexual lust and desire of any growing boy. At one point Dolly had openly declared that Brit was a sex maniac!

The protagonist himself had admitted that he was a sexual maniac: "After my final exams at Campion I had a half-year of holidays, because the college term didn't start till then. That's when I became a sex maniac, making Dolly's words come true." (81) He jerked off any time he felt like it—listening to the BBC news, while solving a bridge puzzle, in the middle of a scale he was practising and so on. Tina and Ruby were both budding before him and watching their growing feet and breasts and bottoms filled him with 'giddy delight.' Later Brit got enough opportunities to have sex with Amy, his girlfriend. Kanga's "obsession with sex can be easily understood, but in the context of the work, the sexual jousts between the narrator and Amy lack the psychological support."[4]

Brit put up a very brave face even when he was fighting a tough battle against adversities. He often told his father that he was quite happy and did not have any problems. If one weren't happy, it was like flunking examinations, he said. But Sam was not absolutely sure whether Brit was making an honest statement: "Or is it just your brave act? Smiling face, weeping heart. Y'know, like that movie we saw last week about the circus clown, how he was always putting on his comic act while he was really having a rotten time!" (36) But Sam knew pretty well that the pain he had been through should have been enough to put off his life for ever. It was certainly a mighty will that Brit possessed for days and nights were born only to terrorize him. For him the nights were the worst as sleeplessness drove his thoughts recklessly 'round the craziest bends.' In the morning he would think of the tough time ahead, starting everything from sitting in his wheelchair to having a bath as if he had never done them before. In spite of these problems, he never lagged behind when it came to acquiring knowledge. This made Sam tell Madame Manekshaw that she could test him if she wanted and see that he knew more than more children of his age did.

Brit was known for his sense of humour which is repeatedly made clear in the novel. He appeared before the Principal of Campion School with a copy of *Tales from Toyland* to create an impression that he was mad about reading. When the

Principal asked him whether he wanted to study in their school, the boy replied in the negative as he was horrified at the thought of leaving home! He frankly told him that he brought the book along only to show him that he loved reading:

> 'A child speaks weeth the tong of angels,' said Father Ferra, joining his hands and looking at Sam who was desperately groping for a handkerchief to wipe the sweat-beads off his face. (42-43)

The Father had to say that he liked his son and if he passed the tests he would admit him to the school without even charging fees. The day he was to take the entrance test appeared to be a horrible one for him. He looked like a goat at the butcher's. He was asked to write five crows in figures and he failed to respond properly: "I opened my mouth to say Pardon? but what came out was quite different. I can't forget the horror on Miss Pinto's skull of a face, the relief that left me crazily happy, the grey vomit held in her red lap like a grotesque bowl of soup." (45) The only thought that came to his mind at that time was that all good children would go to heaven and the gates of Paradise had swung open and he had wheeled himself in!

Brit enjoyed himself to be a master blackmailer. Once he threatened to tell Sam about the *Playgirl* if Dolly didn't tell him about his sexy desires. His argument was that he didn't have any other way of getting it out of her. In fact that was just the beginning of his role as a big-time blackmailer. On another occasion, he asked for his binoculars. Dolly who was busy painting her nails gave the excuse that she was not in a position to do it at that moment as her nails weren't dry. The next moment he decided to blackmail her: "If you don't give those binos to me before I count sixty I'm going straight to the phone to tell Parvez Mody you are crazy about him! Parvez, who looked like the matinee idol, Rishi Kapoor, all pink and baby-faced, only had to know and before the week was out he would have her." (53-54) Later whenever Brit wanted a glass of water in a hurry, he would just have to remind her about a band of lice which made their home in her hair! On another occasion, he blackmailed her into not going to her long-awaited college social because he wanted her to take him to a fair.

The handicap never stood in the way of Brit making an impression on others. Once in Los Angeles when they were going back to the hotel, they got lost. They stopped at one of the shell gas stations where he wanted to go. Brit interrupted and told them that they had to go about three blocks away from the Lankasheim-Burband junction: "The owner of the gas station, who looked like Bob Hope, exploded. 'You mean your kid knows English? Such good English? My! This kid is out-a-sight. A genius in a wheelchair—Oooff.'" (61-62) He also remarked that he was a smart kid. But Brit was not sure if he was astonished by his very ordinary remark because he was Indian or because he was handicapped. Dolly knew that for the Americans it did not really matter and all were the same.

The thought of leaving Dolly was more than a shock to Brit. The proposal for her marriage came from Dinsu Dinshaw who lived at the other end of town in Bandra. According to Defarge after the first talk, the happy couple could go for dinner to the Taj Mahal Hotel across the road:

> Hearing these words, I broke out in an icy sweat. It sort of made Dolly getting married and going away to live in far-off Bandra like a pair of hands on my throat. I was terrified of Dolly leaving me. I mean, she gave me those binos to watch the birds. And anyway I was too small for my twenty-foot-square bedroom. (66) .

The meeting between Dolly Kotwal and Dinsu Dinshaw at Apollo Bunder became farcical in every sense. Dinsu, handsome, sixfooter with body built like a Mr. Bombay and with 'big-big thighs and chest dark with hair' was 'interrogated' by Dolly rather mercilessly! A series of questions on philosophy, painting and science were asked and a bewildered Dinsu struggled hard to give proper replies. He was rejected by Dolly and thus the attempted arranged marriage ended in a fiasco much to the relief of Brit.

The news of Madame Manekshaw's death, which followed the killing of her husband by her, disturbed Brit considerably. The news was conveyed to him by Aloo Manekshaw, Mr. Manekshaw's sister, on telephone. Both the funerals were slated for the same time. His immediate instinct was to say "Thank you." But he did not stop there: "I knew I wanted to break open and get rid of the awful smush churning inside me. I knew I couldn't do that once I told Sera the news. I went into my bathroom locked the door and got ready to start. I waited and waited. Have you ever cried after you've had a cry? It's like trying to get an orgasm five minutes after you've just had one—all you get is dry heaves." (74)

He remembered his first meeting with her when she said it was the most unhealthy for a growing boy's budding sexuality. When he attended the funeral, Aloo Manekshaw recognized him and handed in a small envelope which Madame Manekshaw had left him. He was advised to open the letter only later. It contained a short message, 'Sorry I couldn't stay. Shall miss you up there, MM.'

It is nothing unusual that Brit wanted to feel what everyone else was feeling. Thus he wanted to love someone as any other person. The singers he heard were in love, the books Dolly read were love stories, and Tina and Ruby were in love. So he turned to Ruby who he thought was shamelessly sexy. "Her figure was a perfect hour-glass (how quickly she'd changed from the bony little thing of three years ago) and she revelled in it, wearing hotpants that clung to her as if they were wet, and brief little tops that were colourful glorified bras." (82)

In fact Ruby was in love with Alphonso Almeida, the English teacher at school, a dark and dashing Catholic, fresh out of B.Ed. class. That never stood in the way of her flirting outrageously with him. But strangely enough, he didn't want to kiss her when he got an opportunity as he thought that she did not deserve a kiss from him.

It would appear funny to see that Brit began to show faith in chanting mantras. It became a precious part of his life as jerking off. In fact they went together beautifully: "Jeroo's mantra became for me what a marrow transplant is to a leukaemia patient. And I took it up as eagerly, rolling the eight magic words off my tongue one hundred and eight times. Of course, that took up quite a bit of my time especially since I had to make sure no one, not even Dolly, knew what I was doing." (96) He said mantras, for a movie ticket was not easily available. When he wrote his first short story for the correspondence magazine and when he desperately wanted David Reuben's *Everything You Wanted to Know about Sex* but was afraid to ask for it, he said mantras. Sometimes the mantra worked, sometimes it didn't. The remark Defarge made about mantras finally dismayed him:

> "Swamiji told us today that all mantras said in the bathroom are as worthless as a botched up ballot paper. Those were his words." And, her voice broke, "and I always said my mantras in the loo, most of them, I mean!" (98)

Now he could shut his eyes and forget that such a thing as a mantra ever rolled on man's tongue.

Cyrus, Defarge's cousin-brother's son, 'the six-feet tall guy' made a tremendous influence on the life of Brit. A close friendship was established between them ever since they met. It was Cyrus who gave him the feeling that he was already grown up young man. Thus he had the first experience of smoking a cigarette in Cyrus's company: "How flimsy the little white stick felt in my fingers. I put it in my mouth and sucked like I imagined I would on Raquel Welch's nipple. Suddenly there was a gas chamber in my chest and the taste of brunt chicken in my mouth. For the first time in my life I saw stars." (108) The immediate feeling that he had was that good Parsis did not smoke because of the kind of suffocation that he had felt. Brit and Cyrus had long arguments on different topics and Brit was tired of being the smartest kid around, especially when he knew he was not a genius. It was Cyrus who enlightened him about the pathetic condition of the capital city of the country and the greatness of Bombay. "You know what New Delhi's like? It's monstrous. If you aren't a minister or a diplomat or a judge you're a ghost. Hell! You can be anyone in Bombay; as long as you've got brains and bluster, You've got it made. And then New Delhi's got the muddy Jamuna. Bombay's got the sea." (110)

Cyrus, Brit discovered, was also good at several other things. He was deeply interested in politics, economics and science. Brit listened with great enthusiasm whenever he talked about scientific phenomena. The friendship soon developed into one where Brit and Cyrus became partners in 'the serious business of living.' The basic feeling that Brit had for him was nothing other than lust which soon led to homosexual relations. When later Sera discovered this relation, she had to tell Sam that their son was a pervert.

When he was twenty-one, Brit thought that he had to keep reminding his parents about it. That was because they were always doing things like offering him their laps to sit on at the movies. Meanwhile Dolly left him on her getting married to Salim, a Muslim. Very often he had a strong feeling that loneliness was going to be his constant companion:

> I realized Sam was gone for now. So was Cyrus. And Ruby. I didn't have anyone left. Except Jeroo and Defarge, and they didn't add upto much. Sera—but she was just my mother. There was nothing to do. But jerk off. Even that was tough without thinking of Cyrus. I didn't want to think of Cyrus because I now knew how queer it felt in his arms. (151)

Meanwhile Brit had already become a writer. He wrote a story about a man who discovered he was the last leaf on the tree. And he was only twenty-one. That youngman was none other than Brit himself. He felt that it was 'dark ages' when Dolly left him. Light was immediately brought to his life when Zarthost entered his life. Brit liked Jerry (everyone called him so) very much. He liked him because he was ugly. He had enough money to buy out of the bookshop at the Taj which was what he seemed to be doing when he first saw him. Soon he had an irresistible temptation to step out. He had an inner feeling that it was time for him to know the real world, other people, people who were not like him:

> "I want to go somewhere i have never travelled," I said, remembering to keep the "i" small. (158)

Brit's meeting with Amy, Cyrus's friend was another turning point in his life. To begin with, Brit had to be satisfied with watching Cyrus and Amy 'locked together like one of Rodin's sculptures.' She expressed her desire to establish a friendship with Brit as she felt that they had a lot of things in common. Brit was angry which Cyrus as he could easily guess that he had told Amy about his gay past. To add to his misery, Cyrus also made jokes about his helplessness. He thought that though he had his faults, being declamatory as a bad politician was not one of them. As a natural consequence, he couldn't sleep well that night and looked around for books to read.

The next day he was woken up by his mother unusually earlier. That was to offer her first apology. A confused Brit was told that his father was no more:

> "I'm sorry because I know how late you went to sleep; I heard those books fall. But I had to tell someone. Sam is dead. Don't worry. We'll manage, I'm here to take care of you." And as usual, she smiled bravely, "I'm prepared." (165)

Suffering and death are two most loved motifs in the novel. As N.P. Sharma writes: "The centuries of suffering, segregation and loneliness have brought the Parsis to a vision of life where nothing is amiss and perhaps this is how they are ready even for their extinction." (335) Sam died in an accident when he was trying to cross on Fifth Avenue. It is ironic that the death occurred on the day of Dolly's marriage. Brit remembered how much Sam loved him and how much he hoped. He realized that he was trying to grow, 'trying—not grown enough.' In fact, Rati Davierwalla had told him that he was big in brain. His response was that he was small in body. He wanted to establish that he was not helpless. That was why he said it 'helpfully.'

Brit had already come to another phase in the process of growing up. It was when Amy told him with a smile that he was a man that he made an introspection: "A man? Who was she talking about? I was Brit Boy. But I had to admit she was right. Even if I didn't look much of a man. I had started shaving last month." (178-79)

He thought that he was lonely, as lonely as Robinson Crusoe before he found his Man Friday. At the same time, he proved that he was capable of reacting in a violent way. Once Esmero, his servant, tried to blackmail him and when things went beyond a limit he lifted a big book from the shelf on his left with one hand and smashed it on Esmero's head: "He groaned and fell back. I lifted the book from the floor and poised it over his bloated belly which dared to stare at me through his unbuttoned shirt." (180) Incidentally the book was *The Complete Works of Shakespeare*!

Slowly a stage came when he felt that he was absolutely healthy with his fine bones. But humiliation from the outside world continued to make him desperate. When he went for a movie he heard a little boy asking his father why the 'uncle' was so small. He made a fitting retort by asking what he was doing in a movie for adults only. Also, trying to grow meant leaving behind a lot of old habits like lying on his bed and getting powdered. Sera's request to leave Amy was taken more than as an insult by Brit:

> "And it would be so easy for me to agree with you and let Amy go," and I think I'm having a heart attack. Because there are things you don't say to your mother or school teacher or boss even if you are having your nails pulled out slowly. And I was about to say them now. "But, Sera, I've got to grow and get my heart broken if it must. You know that. You could have kept me safe in a soft bed all my life. But you didn't. You let me go around and break my bones and become as much like other people as was possible. And you took the pain everytime I broke my legs." (208)

Sera could take this only as mad notions. But Brit insisted on living like everyone else and feeling the things they did. He asked her if she had done it all those years why she should give up at that point of time. He had a strong conviction that people lived inside themselves and weren't their bodies only.

Sera did not live longer and she was literally crashing to death: "I saw her mouth fill with blood, the level rising slowly till it reached her teeth. Twice she gagged, tried to draw a breath and failed. Then she flung her head back and threw open her eyes. They were not the slightest bit afraid." (220) When her body was taken away to the well of death, Brit couldn't go along as it was very steep: "I was glad to be left with only Amy for company. Because I was crying like a rain cloud, thinking of my mother's dark brave eyes in a vulture's beak." (221) The unexpected visit of Dolly was the next important event in his life and she also complained that he had stolen Cyrus's girl.

Soon a day came when he had enough money—Dolly's, Sera's, Sam's and his own. He made it a habit to write at ten every morning. After lunch, he would count the pages he had written which went as high as one hundred. Soon we hear him telling Cyrus that Amy and he were finished. On the penultimate page of the novel, we are told that something strange began to happen in Brit's life. Sentences, paragraphs, pages began pouring into his head—fluent and clear and correct.

> I shivered with pleasure and went to the window, more out of habit than for a last glimpse of Amy. She must have walked away really fast. The causeway snaked, dry and deserted, into the distance. But I knew if I could see to the end of the road, I'd catch the moon in the white dome of the museum and the copper-pod and the flame trees shouting colour to the serene sky. (234)

He wondered if he could do without Amy why he should. He saw her arms going around Defarge's plump back. He watched himself sitting on the polished floor with his legs stretched out and blinked. He felt that there were things which couldn't be believed. The novel comes to a close with Brit's remark that he liked the way he looked. Jasbir Jain writes: "Natural surroundings, the flow of streams, the direction of winds affect creative imagination as well as the sense of identity. A sense of place, the architectures which the imagination encounters, the openness towards one's surroundings, these impart a sense of belonging and reduce the sense of being isolated."

To sum up, *Trying to Grow* can be looked at as a tale of the sensual and the adorable. Set in a Bombay Parsi middle class milieu, the novel unveils the apprehensions and desires of an osteo child Daryus Brit Kotwal. We find the growth of Brit from a child to a youngman, his struggles and dilemmas. The novel with its subtle humour mainly highlights the assertion of human dignity of the handicapped and his indomitable will to survive adversities. At the same time, the novelist does not forget to make us aware of the attitude of the society to the crippled persons which is very often humiliating and not becoming of a civilized group. What is significant is that the story is narrated without excessive sentimentality. The novel is also notable for its unique description of the sexual urges of a growing youngman, his desires, passions and lust. Also, the ethos of the middleclass society is effectively delineated where we get vivid pictures of families which suffer from all kinds of problems. The theme of marriage also gets sufficient focus through four important women characters who play a crucial role in the novel. The contradictions and divisions within the Parsi community come to the fore in the course of the development of the plot. In this respect, the novel can be read along with Rohinton Mistry's *A Fine Balance*. As Savita Goel says: "The rich culture, customs and traditions of the marginalised Parsi community are foregrounded and scenes describing the Parsi death rites and funeral ceremonies give the reader a glimpse into the Parsi world view."[7]

On the whole, the novel stands out as a wonderful piece of creation with its main focus on the efforts of a crippled youngman to fight against the odds and his unchallengable desire to be one among the normal human beings around him. Certainly,

Trying to Grow remains as a many-splendoured work with its serious theme and moving story.

NOTES

1. Rohinton Mistry, *A Fine Balance* (New Delhi: Rupa, 1996), p. 471.
2. Firdaus Kanga, *Trying to Grow* (New Delhi: Ravi Dayal Publishers, 1990), p. 4.
3. Novy Kapadia, "The Handicapped as Survivor in Firdaus Kanga's *Trying to Grow," The Postmodern Indian English Novel: Interrogating the 1980s and 1990s* (Bombay: Allied, 1996), p. 235.
4. Subhash Chandra, "Firdaus Kanga's *Trying to Grow," Fiction of the Nineties*, ed. Veena Noble Das and R.K. Dhawan (New Delhi: Prestige, Books. 1994), p. 141.
5. N.P. Sharma, "Parsi Culture and Vision in Rohinton Mistry's *Such a Long Journey* and Firdaus Kanga's *Trying to Grow:* A Comparative Study," *The Fiction of Rohinton Mistry: Critical Studies,* ed. Jaydipsinh K. Dodiya (New Delhi: Prestige, 1997), p. 37.
6. Jasbir Jain, "Geographical Dislocations and the Poetics of Exile: Ashis Gupta and Michael Ondaatje," *Writers of the Indian Diaspora,* ed. Jasbir Jain (Jaipur: Rawat 1998), p. 102.
7. Savita Goel, "A Literary Voyage to India: Rohinton Mistry's *A Fine Balance,*" *Writers of the Indian Diaspora*, ed. Jasbir Jain, p. 198.

Humour in Firdaus Kanga's *Trying to Grow*

S. RAMASWAMY

When you stop finding yourself funny, you're finished.
Firdaus Kanga

Trying to Grow[1] is unique among all the novels written in English in India. For sheer wit and humour, it is perhaps quite unparalleled. It is authentically and unmistakably a 'Parsi novel' firmly placed in Bombay. In this brief note, the focus is only on the very individualistic brilliant satire and humour which manifests itself from the first page to the last. The novel is generously punctuated with references to English literature, to dozens of British writers, Western classical music, Hollywood films, actors and actresses—in fact to many Western things. Bombay is evoked in all its glory, and vainglory surveyed from the Hanging Gardens down to Colaba. The entire narration is by a handicapped young man who is 'trying to grow.'

The introduction is given as it is necessary to put the entire narrative style, the tone and the attitude of the narrator who is 'trying to grow.' The novel is divided into two parts: "The Brave Act" and "Trying to Grow." The two parts are related by a statement like "So the brave act went on. Or maybe she was trying to grow. Without Sam." (194) There are a number of references to the title *Trying to Grow* within the novel itself making it a kind of self-reflexive novel. For example, "All I had to do was think; He wanted to hug me before he left and I didn't let him. Because I was trying to grow. Trying—not grown enough." (166) Another example: "Trying to grow meant leaving behind a lot of old habits like lying on my bed and getting powdered and I never could get myself dressed in the bathroom." (194)

Nothing seems to be outside the scope of Kanga's 'Critical Eye.' Everything under the sun is held up to ridicule one way or the other. There is sarcasm, satire, tongue-in-cheek irreverent blasphemy and sexual innuendoes in his hilariously humorous vision of the Bombay world. Just a few examples should suffice. One of the well-known comic devices is parody. There are so many examples of parody in the novel that unless the reader is familiar with the original, the parody loses its fun. For example, "Then she'd cry, 'Look at me!' and giving the Guide's three-fingered salute, she'd begin a robust death-dance stamping to the tune of 'John Brown's Baby's Got a Cold.'" (8) It makes funny reading when one remembers the original song "John Brown's body lies a moulding in the grave and his soul goes marching on!"

Exaggeration is another popular device in evoking laughter. The surging Bombay crowd at the rush hour near the Churchgate station is compared to the siege of the Bastille at the French Revolution. Since this illustrates the typical style of Kanga, the passage is quoted here:

> We had this elderly French lady, a pen-pal of Sera's, staying with us, when Sam had the weird idea of showing her the Churchgate Railway Station. So we went walking: this lady, Jacqui, Sera, Dolly, and Sam wheeling me; it wasn't that far from where we lived. We'd hardly arrived when, like her famous compatriot at the storming of the Bastille, Jacqui screamed, 'Riot!' rolling her 'r's like Peter Sellers playing Inspector Clouseau. And I, ever the show-off, gave Rochefoucauld's reply, 'No, it's a revolution!' Battalions of men and women surged towards us, faster and faster; even from a hundred yards away we could smell their sour sweat.
>
> 'Let's go!' shouted Jacqui quite hysterical, stamping her feet.
>
> 'Let's not!' I said, 'This is my first riot.'
>
> 'And if there's a baton-change it will be your last,' rolled Jacqui.

> 'OK. Break it up,' said Sam. 'You know as well as I that this is only the rush-hour crowd making for the trains. People come to South Bombay to work and in the evening they hurry north where they live,' he explained to Jacqui.
>
> 'I can't believe it!' she said. 'There cannot be so many commuting every day.'
>
> 'Not so many,' said Sam. 'Just a couple of millions use the trains. Another million or so go by bus.' (18)

There is even a joke about the Nobel Prize:

> 'Sure. Maybe I'll write about it one day.'
>
> 'And win the Nobel Prize for Literature.'
>
> 'They don't give the Nobel Prize,' said Sam, 'to writers who we can enjoy.' (21)

If charity begins at home, humour also begins at home as far as Kanga is concerned. There are many jokes against the Parsis themselves from a number of different points of view. Kanga makes fun of the Parsis as Anglophiles as well as "reluctant Indians":

> It happened at this sleazy restaurant called the Madras Cafe which served South Indian yummies; rice-cakes and paper-thin pancakes rolled up like giant calendars. Parsees have this nauseating habit of slumming whey they want to eat *Indian* food, which means non-Parsee food, since we are reluctant Indians. My family happily spent four hundred rupees at the Taj Mahal Hotel on an English meal, bland as an ulcer diet, but when it came to trying out some tongue-scorching, tasty food they made a bee-line for the cheapest joint they could sniff out. (27)

Parsi sophistication and a certain affectation is satirized by him:

> Her face bore an astonishing resemblance to Indira Gandhi's (who wasn't Parsee although she was the widow

> of one) with its hooked nose, pale skin and hooded eyes. Whenever she went to the villages to distribute grain or exercise books on behalf of one of the many societies of which she was chairperson, she would be surrounded by a hysterical mob of country folk screaming, 'Mother Indira!' in any one of India's seventeen official languages. Of course, she took great care to sport the long-sleeved cotton blouses, and white saris with colourful borders draped over her head that the Prime Minister wore on her village expeditions. She took even greater care to streak her hair white in the same place as Mrs. G. even though she was a quarter-century younger. (39-40)

Kanga doesn't spare even his father:

> Father often spoke then of the chaps at the bank because he was close to retirement and he knew he was going to miss them. He'd been forty-five year old when I was born. Young Parsee men have this inbuilt resistance to getting married; when they're about thirty-five they suddenly panic at the thought of a lonely old age (the Parsee old people's home being a cross between a loony house and the Lubyanka) and get married. Sam had fortuitously fallen in love at this dangerous age. (60)

Sometimes Kanga's humour gets out of hand and becomes bizarre as in the following account attributed to the narrator's sister Dolly who was working at the airport:

> Like the one about the veiled Arab lady who sat through a flight from Jeddah to Bombay cradling a baby in her lap. The air hostess found it very suspicious that the baby didn't wail or wake even once, so she alerted the customs officials who discovered the baby was dead, had been dead for the past so many hours. 'But,' said Dolly, leaning across the breakfast table, 'that isn't all. They found the baby's tummy slashed, and lying inside its tiny entrails was a little packet of the purest diamonds.' (60)

Another smuggling incident is seen through his father's eyes:

> What with foreign exchange restrictions allowing us to take just eight US dollars each, we couldn't stay much longer than eighteen days. Though Father knew all the tricks of smuggling out money. One night, he returned from a tryst with the black money-changer, his pockets pregnant with dollar notes. We had to hide them in our luggage. (61)

There is a hilarious account of the choosing of a bridegroom for Dolly at the fashionable Apollo Bunder where the narrator teases his sister:

> She returned, exulting, 'It's fixed! It's fixed! Apollo Bunder at six tomorrow evening. They'll be there. His mother will be in a shocking-pink sari, so you can spot her at once!' . . .
>
> I had to stop Dolly from walking into the Apollo trap, especially when I heard Defarge say, 'He's a handsome boy, a six-footer, and his body, he's built like a Mr. Bombay, big-big thighs and chest dark with hair.'
>
> I got the idea when I was about to slide into sleep that night. I shot up in my bed and intoned, like an oracle, just loud enough for Dolly to hear, 'Beware of Apollo!'
>
> Dolly jumped up and asked, 'Why? Why should I beware of Apollo Bunder? Are you dreaming, Brit?'
>
> 'A nightmare awaits you,' I said, pitching my cracking voice as low as I could. 'In the shape of Dinsu Dinshaw, your unchosen husband, Defarge's choice.' (66-67)

Kanga makes jokes about even death and this funereal humour becomes tawdry and grotesque:

> What do you suggest?' said Defarge. 'That we are burned to ashes, like those Hindus? Or chewed by worms like the Englishmen? I, for one, prefer to be eaten by vultures.

> 'Don't talk like that,' said Sera. 'It's bad luck.'
>
> The phone rang and I wheeled away to take it. 'Hello,' said a mock-Oxbridge voice, the kind that U-Parsees invariably affect. (73-74)

The 'sick joke' continues when he narrates the message contained in the blue envelope given to him by the dead teacher whose funeral he was attending:

> It was a short message my teacher had left for me: 'Sorry I couldn't stay. Shall miss you up there, MM.'
>
> And I'll miss you down here, I thought, my face screwing up though I was trying to keep it straight. Which was a bit like trying to walk. (78-80)

Thus his grotesque humour starts with himself and takes on a certain facetiousness. This 'trying to walk' is a part of the narrator's 'trying to grow.'

Firdaus Kanga's humour involves many well-known popular devices of poking fun. The Anglophilia and the snobbery of the Parsis is revealed in a quasi literary contest involving the British Royal Family:

> Jerry's mansion was not what I had expected it to be, a mini-Buckingham Palace. It was a biggish bungalow bang on the beach. It has that most Palestine of names, Mon Repos. 'First,' said Rati, 'when I got married it was called Davierwala House. I made it this because Duke of Edinburgh was born in a house of the same name. You knew where? Say!'
>
> 'Corfu.' She was always playing this kind of Trivial Pursuit with me. 'Where did Lord Byron expire?' she quizzed through the lay door. 'Can you say Victoria's nine offsprings' names?' she asked, a kind of historical alarm to get me out of bed, and I rolled them off backwards: Beatrice, Leopold, Arthur, Louise, Helena, Alfred, Alice, Edward, Victoria, sending her reeling with delight.
>
> Then there was Fill in the Blanks: 'Peter Pan and?'

> 'Wendy.'
>
> 'Sarah?'
>
> 'Churchill.'
>
> 'Mistake! Bernhardt. Never mind. Mrs.?'
>
> 'Miniver,' I said perversely.
>
> 'Simpson, silly boy. Lawrence?'
>
> 'Of Arabia.'
>
> 'Olivier. What has happened to you? Davier does not suit your head.'
>
> 'Suits the rest of me,' I said complacently. (196-97)

Even the 'Fun and games' in the novel are punctuated with authors and literary references. To mention just a few: R.L. Stevenson's character Long John Silver (27), to Dickens's Madame Defarge (29), which is incidentally a nick name that is given to a character that stays throughout the novel to 'perverted writers, which meant Oscar Wilde, Thomas Hardy and E.M. Forster but excluded Harold Robbins, since Jeroo hadn't heard of him' (35), to Enid Blyton, to James Bond 007, to Dylan Thomas (113), to the novel *All Quiet on the Western Front* (141), to a line from a famous poem 'The desire of the moth for the star' (145), Agatha Christie's 'Hercule Poirot' (149), to Jane Austen's *Pride and Prejudice*, to John Wain (161), to V.S. Naipaul, Shelley, Swinburne and Oscar Wilde (164), to Robinson Crusoe and his Man Friday (179), to Philip Roth, Irving Wallace and to the character, Tess of Thomas Hardy (198), to Connie and Mellors in D.H. Lawrence's *Lady Chatterly's Lover* (199) and of course to Shakespeare to whom he makes several allusions. Most of these literary references are used to create laughter by bringing in bathos, parody, anti-climax and such other devices. For example:

> 'Dolly,' said Sera, running her finger through the Shirley Temple curls, 'do you want your little brother to die?'
>
> 'Of course not!' cried Dolly. 'I love him!' And to prove it she dropped kisses all over my face faster than her lips could pucker.

> 'If you do that,' said Sera, 'the child will die. You are smothering him.'
>
> 'Like Othello smothered Desdemona!' cried Dolly, sending Sera and Sam flying with delight.
>
> 'We were right to buy her that frightfully expensive book, weren't we, darling?' said Sam.
>
> 'You mean that illustrated Shakespeare? I thought she'd never read it but she obviously did!' (26)

There are also brief references to Shakespeare's plays: 'Poor Dolly, if only she knew that a bottom-pincher compared with a blackmailer like the tooth fairy to Lady Macbeth,' (52) 'She had a girl friend in college whose hair teemed and when they put their heads together to study *Hamlet*.' (54) But the capital joke about Shakespeare is when his *Complete Works* is used as a weapon to hit the narrator's attacker written in a mock-epic style:

> Rage pumped through me till I felt it surge in my finger-tips. I lifted a big book from the shelf on my left with one hand and smashed it on Esmero's head. He groaned and fell back. I lifted the book from the floor and poised it over his bloated belly which dared to stare at me through his unbuttoned shirt. He opened his eyes and drew his legs in for protection. I let the book fall on his knee. He whined shrilly and began rolling towards the door. I pushed him, shoving my front wheels into his back, his torso, his shanks, till he was at the top of the staircase. I rolled the wheels into him and he tumbled down shrieking importantly seven times, till he thudded on the landing like a dead thing. . . .
>
> When I saw the book I had crashed on Esmero's head lying on the floor. It was so huge, I wondered how I'd ever managed to lift it with one arm, and that my left. I bent down and peered at the book's spine: *The Complete Works of Shakespeare*. (180-81)

Apart from funny references to literary works and authors,

many a time with twisted quotations, there are plenty of witticisms and puns like "Talking to you is like talking to a very intelligent woman,' the hero is told (118). A sort of 'Malapropism' sometimes is effectively employed:

> 'Yes, he was a Parsee Palestine. You know what a Palestine is, don't you?' I shook my head in surrender. 'A Palestine,' she said patiently, 'is a man who does not appreciate English culture.'
>
> 'Oh, of course,' I breathed, 'a philistine.'
>
> 'My Jerry is also a Palestine.' (173)

His comparisons are another source of humour. For example, "He was carrying a pile of books that hid his torso up to the chin; I could only see a nose that made mine look like Julie Andrews's. And thin slit eyes which hardly managed to stay open under the weight of fierce black brows that crossed his forehead like Hadrian's Wall. (154) "I liked talking about Cyrus more than a Marxist likes talking about Marx," (183) "I wouldn't take him if he were rich as the Birlas," (212) "I looked at the bottle of Coca Cola as if it were the last phial of smallpox stored up in some lab." (173) He makes fun of many kinds of Indian English. For example, Baba writes: 'Appli warm salt on legses,' (5) 'Veri good bones soft-soft now.' (12) He also makes fun of Europeans using English: "'Sit heem on my laap' said Father Ferra," (42) "Do you studee or do you read Tales from Toyland?,' (42) 'If he passes the tests I shall take heem like thees!' (43) 'Neverrr!' (43) 'No ees no!' (43) About one of the main characters in the novel, Kanga writes, 'She had this quaint habit of translating her native Gujarati idioms into English—like the time she had this chili-hot curry and asked for a sweet to repair her mouth.' (72) About another character, he says: 'He had a funny sort of accent that sounded as if he were speaking Hindi when he was speaking English.' (88) Sometimes he twists an English expression for comic purposes. After using 'On the other hand,' he uses the expression, 'And on the third hand!' (186)

Thus Firdaus Kanga, throughout the novel, uses the weapons of parody, the grotesque, the bizarre, jokes, puns, facetious expressions, funny comparisons, irreverent hilarity, wise cracks, witticisms etc., to write a unique Parsi novel which is eminently readable.

NOTE

1. Firdaus Kanga, *Trying to Grow* (Delhi: Ravi Dayal Publisher, 1990).

Honest Deceptions: Irony in Firdaus Kanga's *Trying to Grow*

INDIRA NITYANANDAM

Trying to Grow is a first-person narrative of a physically-handicapped boy growing into adolescence and manhood in the city of Bombay. In this first novel, Kanga recreates the world of this young man through his interactions with other characters as well as his own thoughts. In his travelogue *Heaven on Wheels*, Kanga admits: "Growing up in Bombay, my life had been unusual, so that when I wrote my fictional biography I had to leave out the strangest parts simply because they would have made the story unreal."[1] This novel celebrates the pain and embarrassment of being different. Mentally alert and intelligent, the protagonist realizes that physically he is obviously ugly: "I saw my neck squat as a toad's and my hollow shoulders, one higher than the other like Richard the Third's, my rib cage thrust forward so that it bulged in the centre and sloped down at the sides, and below that my legs thin as a famine child's, the shins bowed as if some kid had plastered on some clay as a joke or an afterthought."[2] This paper attempts to study Kanga's use of irony (as well as hyperbole and litotes) and to assess what purpose is achieved by it.

The importance of irony in literature is hardly ever questioned. Irony in European literature can be seen as early as Aristotle's *Poetics* where his concept of 'peripetia' or sudden reversal of circumstances can be interpreted as a form of dramatic irony. Irony in behaviour or irony in drama gradually came to be applied to deceptive use of language and hence a part of the rhetoric: "to blame by ironical praise or to praise by ironical blame."[3] In English literature it developed as a concept in Dryden's times through Donne and Swift to the twentieth century philosophical and aesthetic concept of irony. In Kanga's *Trying to Grow*, irony is seen in a wide variety and ranges from self-disparaging irony, non-verbal irony, or situational irony and the Catch 22 irony. The novel recreates the struggle of the handicapped Daryus Kotwal as he learns to grow up into manhood and come to terms with the facts of his life including his homosexuality. The novel never descends into melodrama or solemnity, bathos or tragedy mainly because the writer is able to view everything through the spectacles of irony and bring in a note of irreverence. Though it is not an autobiography, the author's personal experiences of life in Bombay have certainly coloured his perspective in the novel.

H.W. Fowler defines hyperbole as the "use of exaggerated terms" for the sake not of deception, but of emphasis.[4] Rhetorical exaggeration, in fiction, must obviously, be accompanied by some evidence that it is not to be taken at its face value. The literal meaning is necessarily refuted because we know that it is not only incredible but also impossible. Kanga uses the hyperbole frequently and appropriately: "Because I thought about it for a million minutes. . . . My heart was Zulu-dancing inside my chest." (83) "I was determined to have my knees turn to jelly . . . and my heart pound like a jungle drum." (82) It is doubly ironic that Brit's legs are lifeless. Here we realize that hyperbole is frequently concerned with personal values and sentiments: that is, with making subjective claims which, however exaggerated, we could not verify unless we are somehow able to get inside the cranium of the person about whom the claims are made. "You know Brit's getting more cautious as he is growing older; he's just had two fractures in the last three years" (6) would have no meaning if one were not aware that Brit has 'osteogenesis imperfecta' which meant that "He's never going to walk. He is going to grow toothless, and if he is lucky he'll only fracture his bones a dozen times before he is five. . . . He feels pain about four times as much as normal people do." (26)

If hyperbole is a trope of exaggeration, litotes is one of understatement. Leech describes it: "Litotes express an overt lack of commitment, and so implies a desire to suppress or conceal one's true attitude; but paradoxically this may, like hyperbole, be a mode of intensification, suggesting that the speaker's feelings are too deep for plain expression."[5] Kanga is able to use an absolutely matter-of-fact style to express quite shocking details—thus proving to be a master of understatement or a self-disparaging irony: "I saw to it that the doctor was proved right. I broke my legs eleven times before I was five years old. Mysteriously, the rest of me remained virtually uncracked." (26) And later: "I remember the dull weight of the plaster cast as if I had a wooden leg like Long John Silver" (27) or even: "She wanted to hug me but was afraid I'd break like that Sung dynasty vase." (74) Brit constantly indulges in self-disparaging irony very subtly: "Tina wasn't allowed to see movies rated 'Adult' till she was an adult. She was the only person in Bombay, apart from me (and that was because of my size) to have waited that long." (35) For a person who will never be able to grow beyond 4 ft., Brit shows a remarkable and constant sense of humour. Though Jeroo, Tina's mother, decided to protect Tina's innocence and ignorance as long as possible, Dolly and Brit planned it differently: "She [Jeroo] didn't know that Tina could have beat Masters and Johnson at a sex quiz." (35) Brit accepts his condition so easily and with such good grace that we begin to wonder how realistic such a portrayal could be: "I always saw people from down up: that was the view from my chair." (68) Time and again we realize that Brit has the capacity to tide over the difficulties caused by his handicap and Kanga never, not once, gloats over this strength: "Pain loses focus so quickly. The anguish I had squeezed into my plaster-hard-leg—what was the fuss about" (38) is Brit's reaction to another fracture even though it meant that he would have to endure, in addition to everything else, the boredom of not going out for six weeks.

Everytime Brit is reminded of his physical appearance he tries to tide over it and not to wallow in any form of self-pity or moody introspection. When Ruby tells him, "Brit, you're awfully ugly," (84) he tries to laugh it off by responding: "But

I've got litres of charm to pour over all that. So it doesn't matter." (84) However it is at night that the full impact is felt and he realizes that he can no longer smile "because I thought: I'll be alone in here ten or fifteen years from now." (48) The reader is never able to forget the physical condition of Brit because it is this that colours the entire novel: "I was scared of the way handicapped people looked . . . the hesitant gait and robot-stiff movements of the blind, the lolling head and strangulated speech of the spastics. Whenever I saw them I wondered if I seemed as ugly and pathetic. I'd shudder and turn my mind away." (32) The reader, however, can never turn his mind away because Brit's handicap is conspicuously present throughout the novel. The physical and sexual needs of Brit are underplayed very well but the reader feels the full depth and pathos of it all since he is obviously destined never to have them fulfilled.

The Parsis have always been an enigma, a paradox in India. Conspicuous even in their physical appearance (the Roman nose, the protruding chin), they have retained such a visibly different style of dress, speech and living so as to be easily caricatured both in Indian films and literature. As a dwindling community (marriages with non-Parsis being taboo), they have now become over-possessive and over-protective about their identity. Belonging to this community, Kanga is able to laugh at their foibles and eccentricities, at their own glorified notions of themselves: "So westernized you would think they were from *there*, and he looks like a Parsee" (141) says Sera believing that "to look like a Parsee" is a qualification in itself. Dolly knows that to her mother "Parsee guys are the cat's whiskers." (141) Pride in being a Parsi is brought home repeatedly: "I'm no gentle, fair-minded Britisher; I am Persian, pure Persian." (140) Parsis gloat in their uniqueness, even in names: "We delight in stretching, snipping and squashing given names out of all recognition, with a view to making them roll off the tongue easily and, perhaps, even sound English. So boys who are named Faredoon become Freddy, Nowroji becomes Neville, Adi becomes Eddy, and everyone is delighted with his new name and what he hopes is his new image." (22) The irony is apparent: aping the West, the Parsis have not yet achieved an identity apart from the colonizer. Even Parsi customs like leaving the corpse on the Tower of Silence is described ironically: "All those vultures and peacocks waiting to make a meal of poor Mr. Manekshaw." (73) When Dolly announces that she wants to marry Salim who is a Muslim, the parents are shocked. Their response is typical of a Parsi: "The Muslims are the traditional, nay, the historical enemies of the Parsees. And to give yourself to one of them is a shameful act of betrayal, nay, of High Treason," (139) says Sera. When Tina wants to marry Rohit—another non-Parsi—we notice the same closed attitude of the Parsis: "Tina's and Rohit's love was as surely doomed as the court dancer Anarkali's passion for Jahangir. We knew Jeroo would never, not on her frigid life, allow Tina to marry Rohit, though he was handsome, rich, working in his uncle's business, had a house in New Delhi. Because he wasn't a Parsee. When life came to solid things like marriage, everyone, even Sera and Sam, forgot how modern they are." (88) Her external sophistication and broad-mindedness are merely a sham seems to be the opinion of Kanga. Presented ironically, the Parsi community comes across as clearly as the novelist probably intended it to be.

Throughout the novel, Brit puts on a mask of irony—attemping to conceal what must be found out if the irony has to be effective. Seemingly indifferent to all his experiences and a bland acceptance of his difficult life and the ironic poses that Kanga's Brit assumes. The persona and the novelist overlap to form a single entity.

NOTES

1. Firdaus Kanga, *Heaven on Wheels* (New Delhi· Penguin, 1991), p. 11.
2. Firdaus Kanga, *Trying to Grow* (Delhi: Ravi Dayal, 1990), p. 195
3. D.C. Muecke, *Irony and the Ironic* (London and New York: Metheun, 1970), p. 16.
4. H.W. Fowler, *A Dictionary of Modern English Usage* (London: Oxford, 1926), p. 608.
5. Geoffrey N. Leech, *A Linguistic Guide to English Poetry* (London: Longman, 1969).

Dina Mehta: No Rushdie's Child

A.K. TRIPATHY

In this paper I propose to discuss a debut novel by a relatively older writer, Dina Mehta, who switched over to fiction after a successful career as a dramatist. I discuss this novel as offering a contrast to the recent trends in global fiction nominalised as postmodernism which have been successfully used by some recent Indian English novelists.

It is now a settled fact that with Salman Rushdie's *Midnight's Children* (1980) there has begun a new era in the history of Indian English fiction. In the early phase, the breakthrough appeared to the somewhat sporadic and spontaneous. Rushdie's novel was the first Indian manifestation of the international trend of postmodernist novel writing. Later developments confirm that in the Indian context, *Midnight's Children* was the major text to represent the spirit of the 'new novel' with regard to its form and content. It embodied a new sensibility—different, in a radical sense, from the earlier ones. In the earlier period, we have two major sensibilities, one represented by the generation of Anand, Narayan and Rao and the other represented by the generation of Anita Desai, Markandaya, Sahgal and Jhabvala. The sensibility of the first generation was determined by the ethos of the age of freedom movement whereas that of the second generation was shaped by a strong element of questioning about the validity of the major socio-political institutions of post-independence era. *Midnight's Children* projects a new perception and a vision of Indian social scene which is unmistakably post-independence, postcolonial and also neo-colonial in spirit and identity. We find it also as a postmodernist text with a strong modernist bias on the planes of both content and form of the novel. The novel, therefore, represents a breakthrough and has become a landmark not only in Indian English fiction but in English fiction as such.

After Rushdie, there came a host of new signatories who made their significant debut one after another in quick succession and each of their texts helped further as well as intensify the spirit generated by *Midnight's Children*. Amitav Ghosh Upamanyu Chatterjee, Allan Sealy, Shashi Tharoor, Farrukh Dhondy, Firdaus Kanga and Sunetra Gupta are the major writers with more or less similar elitist background and approach to contemporary Indian socio-political realities. In their fictional technique, they seem to belong to the contemporary international mainstream of novel writing. *The Circle of Reason* (1986), *English August* (1988), *Trotter Nama* (1988), *The Great Indian Novel* (1989), *Bombay Duck* (1990), *Trying to Grow* (1990), *Memories of Rain, The Glassblower's Breath* (1993) and *Moonlight into Marzipan* (1995) are some of their major texts which have given a radical orientation to Indian English novel which can now converse on equal terms with its American and European counterparts. The voices of the authors in these novels have been so authentic, natural, spontaneous, compulsive and full of confidence that the Indian intelligentsia who had been watching the socio-political realities of postcolonial India with a sense of indeterminacy of things and ambivalence of attitudes, frustration and unease found their true aesthetic articulation in these works. The Indian realities began to appear in these novels—determined and precisely defined. The writers, in a way, like the European modernists, were, on the deeper level, involved in the epistemological process to know, understand and communicate the Indian world of realities in the postcolonial period. In their aesthetic representation, they are highly innovative and apply in a sophisticated manner the modernist modes of expression by subverting the age-long fictional modes of portrayal in the classical-humanistic-realistic novel. They break up the narrative continuity, depart also from some of the standard ways of representing characters, and at times violate the usual syntax and coherence of narrative language by the use of stream of consciousness and other innovative modes of narration. Also like their English counterparts of the Twenties these novelists emphasize the dehumanized aspects of their characters, though of course in a different socio-politico-cultural context of modern India. Their *avant-gardism* is remarkable and vociferous in terms of Ezra Pound's call to "make it new."

The texts of these writers are also characterized by the elements of postmodernist fiction. The writers's representation of contemporary Indian reality is also ontological. It is ontological in its general as well as specific sense used by McHale, the writer of *Postmodernist Fiction*[1] as making of an autonomous world by a text best represented and professed by the French novelist Robbe-Grillet in his works. The texts present literary anomalies through a collating of literary genres, cultural and stylistic levels, the serious and the comic, in such a way that they resist classification in terms of the traditional literary modes of judgement.[2] All this is achieved by stretching the structure or form of the novel "as an elastic frame which expands obediently to contain every kind of subversion"[3] or as M.H. Abrams would call it, by a "free-wheeling narrative invention."[4] Again, in the philosophical context of their content these texts are postmodernist because they tend to "subvert the foundations of our accepted modes of thought and experience so as to reveal the "meaninglessness" of existence and the underlying "abyss," or "void," or "nothingness" on which any supposed security is conceived to be precariously suspended."[5] This idea is best illustrated by *English, August: An Indian Story*. We find thus that these novels represent Indian incarnations of 'modernism' and 'postmodernism' in literature. One is also reminded here that Indian English poetry and drama are lagging behind in this respect.

However, a careful survey of the fictional crop of the Eighties and Nineties reveals that parallel to the mainstream of modernist and postmodernist novel, there runs a stream of classical-humanistic-realistic fiction. *A Fine Family* (1990), *That Long Silence* (1989), *Such a Long Journey* (1991), *And Some Take a Lover* (1992), *A Suitable Boy* (1993), *Tara Lane* (1993), etc. are some of the major texts written in this tradition. They embody the basic characteristics of the traditional realistic novel. A realistic novel represents a comparatively stable world based on a system of values and codes of conduct sustaining and controlling individual being and thinking, human relationships and social institutions with all the inherent or manifest contradictions of a society in a given period. The realistic writers may attack, criticize or question the validity or relevance of the system of values and highlight the social anomalies and contradictions by an objective or impersonal rendering of facts in a fictional artifact, but they are not in search of an altogether new areas of faith as a substitute for the debunked value system in the manner of their modernist counterparts of the Twenties and Thirties of this century. Discussing the nature and scope of the realistic novel, Alison Lee, in her admirable study of the postmodern British fiction entitled *Realism and Power*, writes that the theoretical premise of Realism is that art should eschew the "idealist metaphysics (Becker 1963:6) of Romanticism, and portray instead "things as they really are, in the sense of actual life. (Kaminsky 1974, 217)"[6] The most common philosophy inherent in a realistic text is that of liberal humanism. M.H. Abrams presents a more familiar semblance of a realistic novel when he writes that it is "characterized as the fictional attempt to give the effect of *realism*, by representing complex characters with mixed motives who are rooted in a social class, operate in a highly developed social structure, interact with many other characters, and undergo plausible and everyday modes of experience." (132) The best example of this type of the novel may be seen, according to Abrams, in Defoe and Fielding in the eighteenth century, achieving high development in the master-novelists of the nineteenth century as Jane Austen, George Eliot, Anthony Trollope, and William Dean Howells in England and America; Stendhal, Balzac, and Flaubert in France; and Turgenev and Tolstoy in Russia. (132) We may say here with confidence that the Indian version of this type of the realistic novel is best represented by Dina Mehta and Vikram Seth among the Indian English novelists of today.

From thematic point of view, there is a strong element of

historical in a realistic novel. In the Indian English texts mentioned above, we have this in abundant measure. While *A Fine Family, That Long Silence, Such a Long Journey, Tara Lane* and *A Suitable Boy* embrace the socio-political realities of post-independence India beginning at times with the massive trauma of partition down to the perturbing realities of Indira Gandhi era, the story of *And Some Take a Lover* covers the year of 1940, a period of great socio-political significance in the history of modern India when the freedom struggle was rapidly heading towards a decisive phase and Gandhi's impact on the nation was maximum. We may dwell at some length to deal with this novel as a realistic text for it offers, by now, the most appropriate contrast of wholeness and integration both in form and content to the fractured aspects of the recent modernist and postmodernist texts mentioned earlier.

The locale of the novel is the city of Bombay. The protagonist is Roshni Wadia, a young and attractive Parsi girl. Intelligent and idealistic like a typical member of the Gandhian age, she is the product of the famous Elphinston College of Bombay. The entire story of the novel is told from her point of view in a straightforward horizontal manner. It is basically a love story unfolding a rich pattern of life in all its social, political and ideological (pertaining to value-system) implications. She wants to live a purposeful life in order to get all-round fulfilment. Though she maintains an anti-British attitude and feels fascinated by the freedom struggle, her immediate passion is love and she falls in love with a bright young and staunch Gandhian College fellow, Sudhir Mahipal. The lovers offer a unique contrast to each other. If Roshni's crowning passion is love, Gandhian politics occupies the place of central importance in the life of Sudhir. Roshni is drawn chiefly into the national struggle for independence in order to ensure Sudhir's love for her and thus to become his suitable life partner. Sudhir, on the other hand, has no desire to live an ordinary life of bourgeois aspirations because of his total dedication to the cause of national liberation under Gandhi's leadership. He has trained himself under the strict disciplines of Gandhian values and lives up to his ideals with a remarkable degree of success. Roshni is not able to understand why Sudhir will not accept her as his beloved partner. Sudhir on the contrary is fully aware of the fact that Roshni partakes of the national movement only to win over his love and that her commitment to the national cause is not wholehearted. In the course of the action of the novel, he leaves Bombay on Gandhian mission for social work and disappears temporarily. When we come to know his whereabouts again, we find that he has married a harijan girl with the blessings of Mahatma Gandhi. After having received this terrible blow, Roshni finds herself in a wistful state of a jilted woman and in a mood of self-loathing and self-torture yields to the pressures of extra-marital amorous demands of the hedonistic Rustom Bharucha, the wealthy husband of her friend, Mithu. However, in the heart of her hearts, she never accepts Rustom as a choice for a permanent bond of love. "She hated him. Would the pattern of revulsion and surrender be repeated endlessly? With a fastidiousness born out of despair her eyes travelled over the profile on the pillow, the symmetrical knit of muscles on the bare back, and she wanted to destroy him."[7] While in the throes of the shock caused by Sudhir's marriage, she happens to meet Douglas Archer, a pro-Indian American journalist, who has been deputed to India to post day-to-day information about Gandhi and Indian struggle for freedom. The meeting is arranged in connection with an interview pertaining to a murder. In the course of the interview, Roshni begins to have a genuine sense of love for the man as a resort. "For a long time Roshni stared at him as he sat brooding there. He was no more a stranger. She realized that they had been drawn into intimacy by imperceptible stages. She was glad . . . she wished she could respond to his confidence, give some token of acceptance, share with him something of herself." (250) She has yet another shock in store. The story ends before it begins properly, for Archer leaves India soon after that meeting.

Embedded in this main plot, there is also a convoluted and less powerful sub-plot involving Sabrina Jones, another college friend of Roshni, who is the daughter of an English spy and married to David Macaulay. She has an affair with Captain Ronald Brown who is murdered in her flat. Fazil Baig, a Congressman who has gone underground during the Quit India movement, is blamed for it. Although innocent, he is hunted and killed by the British police. The mystery of murder remains unresolved. The novelist employs in this part of the novel some of the devices of a detective novel and continues to weave the thematic as well as structural pattern filling it with varied dimensions of contemporary politics through a series of important national events centering round Roshni's life. The creation of suspense and revelation of the mystery is not of a high order and the novelist's art here is at its weakest.

Roshni is the most powerful and most victimized tragic character in the novel. Like a brave protagonist of a realistic novel, she struggles hard against the anomalies and odds in the broader social world to carve a rightful place for herself and live with a sense of freedom and fulfilment. She struggles on two fronts. In the family, she has to struggle against the strangulating hold of an orthodox middle-class Parsi family cocooned in its own conventions and attitudes to life. She longs and breaks in her own characteristic way the shackles of family environment to share life in the broader perspective of the freedom struggle, though ultimately she finds her priorities being in favour of love. Superior in intelligence and self-knowledge, Roshni offers a sharp contrast to her friends Mithu and Jer Marzban who live in tune with their family norms, get married and lead a happy life in the worldly, domestic sense. The parents of Roshni too fail to understand her essential nature. She has the problem of adjustment with the 'self-righteous and oppressive' father and conservative, tolerant and sympathetic mother and faces difficult situations from time to time. However, she does not break away and prefers to live with the family. Roshni is superior in being and thinking to her family members, friends and the Parsi suitors. She finds, however, a unique affinity with her moron aunt Gulestan who also appears to be out of tune with the Parsi norms of life. It is interesting to note that Roshni and Gulestan form a happy combination in their non-conformity to Parsi ethos in their own ways.

Roshni's struggle is more poignant in the larger social world outside the immediate surroundings of her Parsi community. She felt drawn into the national struggle for independence before she had met Sudhir but she became more and more involved into it along Gandhian lines for the sake only of her love for Sudhir. The centrality of the love-theme in the novel becomes eloquently pronounced at this juncture. The novelist portrays Roshni as a love-stricken young woman passing through a crucial stage in the typical process of man-woman relationship. This kind of love is typically Indian and perennially present as the central theme in the mainstream Indian literature since ancient times. The following passage makes it vividly clear:

> At home, too there was no rest for her. So absorbed was she in her love that Sudhir seemed to govern her even from a distance. She made her plans, bought clothes, accepted or rejected invitations, all in the light of whether Sudhir would approve or disapprove. She tried to read all the books he read. She subscribed to *Harijan* and read *Hind Namo* from cover to cover. Sometimes the power of her feelings for Sudhir amounted to a sickness. She looked pale and unwell. A capricious and infantile rebelliousness seized hold of her. She snapped at everyone. She disagreed with everyone. She had no patience with Gulestan. Her mother's heavy, martyr-like face irked her. She had no appetite. Her father noticed she was not eating well and assiduously passed her the dishes on the table. But his attentions merely served to irritate her. She felt guilty to receive any kindness from him. She was going to hurt him. There was no help for it. She was going to marry Sudhir. (186)

Roshni struggles hard to realize the wholesome and fulfilling aspect of love, in terms of man-woman relationship, in the male dominated Indian society and fails miserably. We find her in a state of utter helplessness as a victim both of Gandhian idealism represented by Sudhir and bourgeois materialism represented by Rustom. She is an idealist of love and represents the nobility of Indian womanhood in the modern context. Her urge for love is natural and rightful, but her failure to achieve this is not her failure; it is the failure of the society and the system. The life of Roshni is a touching tale of a wholesome and rounded personality confronted with a society in a ferment. She is a rare character in the plethora of dehumanized anti-heroes or heroines inhabiting the modernist and postmodernist worlds of the Indian novels in English published in the recent years for whom love is a concept of abnormality, for whom love means violence either cerebral or otherwise.

The book has twin themes of love and politics represented by Roshni and Gandhi, respectively. It goes to the credit of the writer that she vividly depicts Gandhi through his absence. Gandhi is more powerful in the impact and effects of his personality and values than in his presence as a character, as in R.K. Narayan's *Waiting for the Mahatma*. And this aspect of an absence operating so intensely and forcefully on a character is brought out by the closing lines of the novel. It is when Sudhir is no more that Roshni realizes what and how much he had meant to her. With Sudhir's death a vacuum occurs in Roshni's life, but she resolves to follow Sudhir's ideals which she had not been able to do when he was alive. With that one temptation now irretrievably gone, Roshni prepares herself for the greatest challenge of her life, the "challenge of having nothing, not even hopes." (317) The only possibility of achieving meaning is through action which is remote from self and is a mode of love. Thus, through her resoluteness to follow the path of selfless action, Roshni achieves a wholeness, dignity and nobility she had been thirsting for. The novel thus becomes a process of Roshni's education and individuation (a major characteristic of a realistic novel).

Parsi novel has developed as a sub-genre in the recent years within the English fictional tradition of the Indian subcontinent. Writers like Bapsi Sidhwa, Firdaus Kanga, Rohinton Mistry and Boman Desai have made significant contributions towards the growth and development of this sub-genre lending it distinctive characteristics. Dina Mehta's novel, according to Makarand Paranjape, marks a significant departure from the typical Parsi novel. For the writer makes the protagonist revolt against the largely pro-British ethos and attitudes of the Parsi community to participate in the country's struggle for freedom and share life in the broader socio-cultural perspective, providing it, thus, a broader canvas. This also suggests the participation of the entire Parsi community in the national cause, who have remained generally an alien Anglicised community in India. Makarand Paranjape's remarks in this context are very appropriate: "By making her heroine assume a pro-nationalist, anti-imperialistic stance, Mehta does well to reactivate, albeit unselfconsciously, a somewhat neglected, though major aspect of the Parsi heritage."[8] Politics apart, even from the point of view of life-philosophy, Roshni transcends her Parsi heritage and tries to embody the central Indian heritage of thought and action according to which man's highest and noblest attainment is *Nirvana* through *Karma Yoga* when one emerges from the domain of desire-stricken selfhood entering into the blessed realms of life devoid completely of any kind of desire. The novel ends with Roshni's spiritual sublimation. When '*Karma-Yogi*' Sudhir is no more physically alive as an object of temptation for her, she arises to achieve unison with him in spiritual terms:

> She scrambled to her feet with the force of a new temptation in her: To extricate herself from a net of wants. To prepare herself for the task and challenge of having nothing, not even hopes. To make life holy by her actions, to learn how to love. (317)

Vedanta and Buddhism form the crux of her resolution and Roshni thus acquires the wider dimension of an Indian woman; she does not remain only a Parsi woman. *And Some Take a Lover* is not a Parsi novel. It is an Indian novel admirably written in the classical-humanistic-realistic mode. Roshni becomes both an *arhat* and a *jeevanmukta*. The narrow confines of the self involuntarily shake off and there emerges before her a larger human significance which alone can give meaning and fullness to an individual's life.

NOTES

1. McHale, *Postmodernist Fiction* (London: Methuen, 1987), p. 10.
2. M.H. Abrams, *A Glossary of Literary Terms* (Bangalore: Prism Books, 1993), p. 120
3. Steven Connor, *Postmodernist Culture: An Introduction to Theories of the Contemporary* (Oxford: Basil Blackwell, 1989), p. 126.
4. Abrams, *A Glossary of Literary Terms*, p. 135.
5. *Ibid.*, p. 120.
6. Alison Lee, *Realism and Power: Postmodern British Fiction* (London: Routledge, 1990), p. 5.
7. Dina Mehta, *And Some Take a Lover* (Calcutta: Rupa, 1992), p. 88.
8. Makarand Paranjape, "Another Freedom," Review of *Some Take a Lover*, in *The Times of India*, 22 November 1992.

Significance of Structure in Dina Mehta's *And Some Take a Lover*

ALKA SAXENA

And Some Take a Lover is an absorbing novel about the conflicting loyalties of a Parsi family caught up in the political turmoil of the Quit India movement. It has a Parsi family at its nucleus and is set in the tumultuous background of the 1940s. On the wide canvas of the novel, the freedom struggle, Gandhian ideology, Naval Rating's Mutiny of 1946, riots, suspicious British characters and the British rule in India are effectively sketched. Betrayal, adultery, murder are boldly highlighted to build up an atmosphere of suspense and thrill. The central character of this novel is Roshni, a young Parsi girl, who feels rootless because of the complex surroundings. She is caught up in the traditions of her community, puzzled by the disappearance of her English friend Sabrina and involved in the political turmoil of the Quit India movement. But above all, the novel voices the acute feeling of rootlessness and alienation prevalent in the Parsi community of India.

Dina Mehta's novel can be studied and interpreted at various levels. The credit for making this novel interesting from different angles goes to Dina Mehta's captivating narrative technique. Dina Mehta has distinguished herself as a playwright for the stage, radio and television. A prolific writer, her collection of short stories was received very well. The same success came to her first novel *And Some Take a Lover*. Dina Mehta is a name to reckon with in contemporary women's writing not only in the Indian subcontinent but even in the west. She has emerged as a promising novelist gifted with a rare style, uniquely her own, among contemporary Parsi writers. Ethnicity has come up as an issue of great interest all over the world. In this context novelists like Bapsi Sidhwa, Dina Mehta, Rohinton Mistry and others have received wide acclaim.

Ethnicity, chaos and the theme of alienation are mentioned explicitly in the first chapter of the novel, *And Some Take a Lover*. The first chapter is excellent on various accounts and contains the essence of the novel. As the reader goes through the first chapter, he enters the traditional Parsi world. Roshni was dining with Mithu and Rustom Barucha at their visibly western style home. "Roshni looked round the room. Very grand it was, in a somewhat indeterminate fashion, with no Eastern colour in its decor, but not quite Western either despite Venetian glass vases, Dresden shepherdesses, and its Victorian mass and solidity."[1] The life-style, preferences and priorities of Parsis are inclined to imitate the west. Roshni knows very well that "the Parsi way of life was the most Westernized in India. More than the Anglo-Indians they could afford the tastes, the standards, the luxuries introduced by the alien rulers." (188) Even Rohsni's home has the western flavour. "She had wrinkled her brow in thought. Her home too was patterned on the western style. the toilet was of western mode." (188) The pictures that framed her walls were reproductions of western masters. A piano stood in the living room. Roshni knew that the piano was one of the drawing room accomplishments of every well brought up Parsi girl. A piano adorned the living room of the Baruchas as well.

The Parsis's fascination for the Englishmen is also conveyed in the first chapter. Mithu the hostess of the dinner looked "excessively pleased with herself, for she believed that anyone in this country would be dazzled to accept an invitation which carried with it the supreme distinction of sitting down to dinner with an Englishman." (11) Mithu devoted herself to the white sahib and she leaned towards him with a set smile and fluttering eyelashes, as he said something to her. All evening "she had camped beatifically within range" (15) of the English guest. Mithu's husband Rustom too paid special attention to the whiteman. He spoke sparingly and addressed his remarks to the white skin opposite him. Roshni observed that Indian sensibility was missing not only in the decor but also in the deep rooted ideas of the Parsis. Mrs Batliwala, one of the guests at the party, was definitely excited as she asked Daulat: "I hear you are going to study in Paris next year." (15) Mrs. Batliwala, the Parsi matriarch, examined Roshni with a fixed piercing eye. Roshni was 24 and not yet married, and this was a cause of concern for Mrs Batliwala. In her booming tenor, she questioned Roshni, "Your function in life should be that of a hen, to rear the young. How old are you?" (15) She further said that to be a woman and single was to defy the pattern of the world. It is ironical however, that the male of the species were exempted from her criticism. Her son Jangoo at 34 was still unmarried.

Roshni was a misfit in this gathering. She was a Parsi no doubt, but she had the Eastern inclination in her. Roshni's involvement with Sudhir, a young devoted Gandhian, the Quit India movement, her efforts to wear Khadi, were looked upon with scorn and disapproval from members of her Parsi community. They found Roshni ugly in khadi saris and failed to understand that she "meant them as a patriotic flourish." (16) The dinner party did not enliven the spirits of Roshni. She was as detached as the tigerhead on the wall. "On the wall above them glassy eyes in a tiger head took a dim view of the assemblage below." (15) Roshni, too, viewed dimly the glamorous presence of Englishmen, music and the rich food of the evening. As compared to the other guests and Mithu, who were enjoying the party, Roshni felt alone and uneasy. She hardly interacted with the guests. It was only when Rustom dropped her home in his car that she got opportunity to have a conversation with him.

Rustom stopped the car and expressed his loneliness to Roshni. He told her that he felt alienated in India. In deep anguish, he said, "what has this country to offer us? What kind of cultural life? We Parsis are aliens here. And our days are numbered after the British leave." (18) Roshni ventured to ask him 'where, then, do we belong?" (18) Rustom immediately expressed his very specific and strong notion, "I know where I belong. I was educated in England." (18) He broods over the quality of life he had in England. There is nothing he would like better than to go and live in England. But he had certain commitments in India and could not easily leave them. Although he lives in India, he knows that he belongs to England. He strongly desires to live the rich life in England. In India, he misses the "freedom, the dispassionate pursuit of knowledge, the concern for the well-being of the individual." (19)

In sharp contrast to Rustom's views, Roshni feels that after the war the situation in England would be grim. But Rustom pursues his own line of thought and is strictly governed by it. There has been trauma and stress in Roshni's personal life, and therefore she feels that Rustom is like her, in that he feels that he does not belong here. But their cases are quite different. Roshni feels more like a driftwood caught up in a swirl of the past two years of her association with Sudhir. But Rustom "stupidly believes he can come to the shore there?" (19) The similarity ends here. Roshni is certain that she "could not manage an infatuation with foreign climes." (19) Roshni and Rustom felt lonely and unhappy that evening, but the reasons for this ennui were entirely different. Rustom offered her a chance to be his friend. He wanted her consent so that they could discover each other. For Roshni, this friendship could only be a "temporary nymphomaniac madness." (20)

Roshni was reminded of her past relations with Sudhir, Lajwanti and Sabrina, all of whom had been swallowed by oblivion. She was drained of all emotional content and was left with only one longing: "to get rid of the void at the centre of her being, at whatever cost." (20) It is this feeling of being terribly lonely that brings Rustom and Roshni together. Roshni knew that perhaps she had arrived at a precarious new beginning. She was mature enough to understand that Rustom's wife, Mithu, was her friend and she would have to engage herself in a furtive frolic with Rustom. She could also sense that Rustom would have her submit to him as to the will of a maharaja. Her compunction would be to him sheer boredom. But ultimately, she did allow herself to be manouvered into an ugly trashy affair with Rustom. She had succumbed to Rustom and felt wretched and guilty. As she watched Rustom reaching for an ash-tray, "Roshni noted this second sacrilege; for a Zoroastrian to pollute fire by puffing at it was as heinous as dishonouring his marriage-bed." (24)

At the end of Chapter 1, Dina Mehta has outlined the various themes to be examined in the novel. Viewed critically, all themes seem to merge and symbolise the eternal friction between the East and the West. Both Rustom and Roshni are Parsis, the issue of ethnicity ends there and their different outlooks symbolise the struggle between the East and the West.

As the story develops further, Sudhir's character and his involvement with Roshni serve to determine the course of Roshni's life. It is evident that Roshni will not remain with Rustom and that their relationship will terminate. But it is not till the very end that Roshni's decision regarding her relationship with Rustom is clearly made. In chapter one she had stated that it was not her temperament to be infatuated with foreign climes. But still the possibility existed that she might marry Rustom and move to England.

Rustom showed his true colours when he said that he wanted to divorce Mithu because she could not give him a son. The desire for a male offspring crosses the barriers of caste and community. Here Dina Mehta's success as a novelist dealing with gender related problems is unmatched. The tragedy of Mithu is any woman's tragedy, hence she gets the sympathy of the readers. Dina Mehta deftly generalizes the crisis of marital disharmony through the particular case of Mithu, Rustom and Roshni triangle.

The last chapter of the novel is as significant as the first. It contains extracts from Sudhir's journal. During November 1946, Sudhir had been travelling in Bihar and Bengal. He wants to join Bapu but later decides: "No Bapu is carrying enough on his shoulders. I will not add to his burden. I will work alone." (284) Sudhir had sacrificed his love for Roshni because he was deeply committed to his cause. For him, life is a "stupendous yagna, sacrifice." (179-80) He is an austere Gandhian and patriotism fills his heart. As compared to the feeling of rootlessness of Roshni and Rustom, Sudhir's soul has its roots deep down in the Indian soil. The journal at the end is an imaginative reconstruction of Gandhi's Noakhali tour, a heroic one-man odyssey to quell the partition riots there. Sudhir undertook this mission in the true spirit of a patriot. He left behind his pregnant wife Gauri and dedicated his life in the service of the nation. At the Dattapara refugee camp, the conditions are appalling. The same is true of the refugee camps at Bhatialpur, Ramgunj and other places. The keystone of Gandhi's plan is demonstration of personal courage and Sudhir tried to follow it wherever he was. He remembered Gauri with reverence and affection. He had full faith that if she had been with him she would have carried his work with a glad passion of obedience: "Her loyalty is matchless. Entirely without guile, she is capable of self-less devotion. I would have sent for her, but she is with child." (296) When Sudhir was still a bachelor, he was attracted towards Roshni. She had set him dreaming of a different life but Sudhir had renounced it—"that dream I renounced at the cost of a thousand agonies." (296) Sudhir knew the basic differences that lay between them. He was correct in warning her, "Roshni, you will be cut off not only from your family, home, your way of life but also your emotional attitudes. . . . You will always be pulled in two ways." (190)

In the Journal, Sudhir had admitted that Roshni still appeared in his dreams. In his Journal, he made the entry: "I dreamed of Roshni. Even now I cannot banish her from my thoughts." (296) In the same note, he remembered the day almost two years ago when he had waited for her at the station and she could not reach there as her aunt had expired on that very day. Sudhir knew it was the end of the relationship. "As the bright scape rolled past the windows, I knew it was the end." (297) Now he only permitted her to come before him under the dark portals of a dream. He had written: "You will always remain a stranger to me. Only the dream of you hovers about my life, communicator of a destiny that can never be mine." (297)

Sudhir died soon after the last entry in the Journal. He developed malarial fever which carried him off in three days. After going through the Journal, Roshni's sorrow was tempered with a strange rejoicing because Sudhir did not fail himself. Even after his death, Sudhir's ideology, sacrifice and purpose in life were helpful in carving out Roshni's future path. After reading the manuscript, Roshni was "slowly invaded by a great wash of understanding." (316) The words of Sudhir had fallen "wild and unreal on her burdened soul." (316)

Rustom no longer seemed to her a fresh start or a spring-board into any sort of graceful life. She reached the wholesome decision to have it all over with Rustom. "Rustom was clearly dispensable and the last thing she wanted to do was to leave this country, the womb of gods." (317) She finally manages to keep herself away from the glamorous west and remain in her own country and with her own people. Her decision is symbolic of the victory of spiritualism over materialism, of East over West. There arose a new temptation in her to follow the path of Sudhir, the Karma Yogi. "To extricate herself from the net of wants. To prepare herself for the task and challenge of having nothing, not even hopes. To make life holy by actions, to learn how to love." (317)

At the end of chapter one, Rustom had physically overpowered Roshni. He made love to her with an intensity against which Roshni had no defences at all. She pleaded and begged him to let her go, but he "summoned her back for the plunder." (22) The taming of Roshni was a sign of victory for Rustom. The chapter emphasizes glamour, lust, unrest and frustration.

But in the last chapter of the novel Roshni proves to be stronger. Lust is replaced with restraint and disdain. With a new strength and confidence instilled after reading Sudhir's Journal, Roshni "scrambled to her feet with the force of a new temptation in her." (317) It is not the sexual temptation of chapter one. On the contrary, she prepares to detach herself from the net of wants. She discards Rustom and decides to dwell in India, the womb of gods.

NOTE

1. Dina Mehta, *And Some Take a Lover* (New Delhi: Rupa, 1992), p. 14.

Marriage, the Ultima Thule of Woman's Life: A Comparative Study of Dina Mehta's *And Some Take a Lover* and Bapsi Sidhwa's *An American Brat*

INDIRA BHATT

If the Nineties saw blossoming of Indian English fiction with Vikram Seth, Upamanyu Chatterjee and Amitav Ghosh, among many others, it also brought out an amazing number of women writers such as Shashi Deshpande, Githa Hariharan, Dina Mehta, Bapsi Sidhwa and Manju Kapur. Following the trend set by Salman Rushdie with his *Midnight's Children,* they experimented with both the stylistic innovation and thematic concerns. The women writers charted a path of their own with their concerns for acquiring space and place for their women protagonists in life and society. They attempt to trace the development of the protagonists trying to find a place of their own in the world at large either through rebellion or acceptance of realities.

Dina Mehta in *And Some Take a Lover* and Bapsi Sidhwa in *An American Brat* chart the progression of their protagonists, their self-awareness and relatedness to social norms with marriage as the core point of their dilemma. Both the novelists have marriage as the central issue, an ultima thule in their protagonists's life. One has Mumbai as the stage set for her protagonist, the other has Lahore and America where the action takes place. Dina Mehta chooses to tell the story of Roshni, the Parsi young woman of the Forties, of the Quit India Movement period. Sidhwa places her protagonist Feroza in Zia-ul-Haque's period of Islamic fundamentalism in Pakistan. The two Parsi writers depict the dilemma of choosing a husband for a Parsi woman and the restrictions imposed by their Parsi traditions, culture and faith. It appears that both Roshni and Feroza are thinking of marriage as the ultimate goal, conditioned as they are by their cultural heritage. Through this marriage motif the novelists have presented the paradoxes of life and their journey towards self-awakening and self-realization.

Dina Mehta's novel *And Some Take a Lover* opens with Roshni having an affair with Rustom who is her friend Mithu's husband. Her mother Shirinbai is worried about her marriage since Roshni is twenty-four years old, the right age for marriage. As Mrs. Batliwala pointedly tells Roshni: "If you have no contribution to make to the arts or the society in which you live . . . your function in life should be that of the hen to rear the young."[1]

The mother has some suitable boys for Roshni to choose from. And they are attracted by Roshni as she is quite different from other Parsi girls. Roshni is attractive and intelligent and is interested in Gandhi's Quit India movement and has fallen in love with Sudhir the Hindu young man who is a major figure in this movement in Mumbai. Shirinbai does not know this. She blames the college education for Roshni's refusal to choose a husband: "you learnt all these new-fangled notions in college." (39) She is worried that her child never deviated into good sense! Roshni is against marriage between cousins. Dina Mehta presents the dilemma of the Parsi woman who, tradition-bound, must not think of marriage outside the community and in that small circle, there is not much to choose from: "'What are you saying?' her mother sat up indignantly, 'that we should allow our girls to marry outside the community, mate with parjat?'" (37)

Roshni who is in love with the Hindu young man wonders what her mother would do if she knew about her choice of Sudhir as the only man she would ever consent to marry. Shirinbai would be shocked: "her cherished beliefs shaken to the core. Roshni to marry a Hindu! All her years of devotion wiped away, her prayers nullified, her family disgraced! and her Dad! Her father rose before Roshni on the white tiles, a small round scented presence . . . brown eyes sick with dismay over his daughter's declared passion. And would Pirozakaki have disowned her?" (38) They did not like her association with Gandhi's followers, her wearing Khadi and her working with them.

Roshni loves Sudhir and to be with him, she takes interest in Gandhi's freedom struggle. But the Parsis did not like to be involved in something that was against the British Raj. They identified themselves with the English and tried to remain in their company at parties in clubs. Yet there were Parsi leaders who devoted themselves to the cause of freedom. Dina Mehta tries to place the Parsi involvement in freedom struggle in proper perspective. Roshni's dilemma is resolved as Sudhir tells her about their social and cultural differences, their religion and style of living. Though he loves her equally well, he does not wish to make her miserable and unhappy. In his chosen way of life, she is likely to be a misfit, and her parents would never consent to her marriage to a Hindu. Sudhir clearly analyses the impact their marriage would make on Roshni: "You will be cut off not only from your family, home, your way of life . . . but also from your emotional attitudes, compulsions, even your memories. And they will never let you go. You will always be pulled in two ways, don't you see that, my Roshni?" (190) She knows that she lived on two levels, "midway between two worlds and that she did not belong to either. She was unwhole, because one set of loyalties in her, conflicted with another set of imperatives. And the choosing of one over the other, a decision on her future, involved a painful snipping, whittling operation." (190) Though prepared to make her choice to share his life, she knows that she is not as strong as Sudhir, that she needed him, and that wishing to share his life, she was "intent only on a personal salvation." She was not accustomed to a "vigorous intellectual self-support." The novelist clearly describes the chasm between them. Sudhir has his place and purpose in life whereas Roshni thinks only about her place in his life. She is trying to understand herself, find herself: "Could she really map out a future with him? Have him permanently by her side?" (192)

She fears that he would be gone, only the outer frame

would remain with her. Knowing full well the wide and deep chasm between them, their culture and religion, she feels that she is weak. This is the end to her love-life with him. Dina Mehta pointedly brings out the difference between the Parsi way of life, the westernized liberal life-style and the Gandhi-freedom struggle dedicated Hindu young man's way of living in a village. The question of cultural differences and faiths does not arise.

After Sudhir departs from Mumbai and from her life and marries a Harijan woman, Roshni's hope of Sudhir's return and their marriage is shattered. There is no possibility of fulfilment of her love-life. The news of his death further makes her up-rooted from the values she cherished so much in Sudhir's company. In her frustration, she has an affair with Rustom. But a change comes over her: "her soul came of age and with this prodigious blossoming she ceased to be a child." (200) Roshni faces a strange predicament. She gives up Sudhir and she cannot accept Rustom. "Her crisis consisted in the fact that her old self was dying and the new had not yet been born." (113)

Though she feels insecure of her future, she is determined to reject Rustom's offer of going to London. The novel is open-ended and one feels that the mature Roshni will make the right choice. But the thought of marriage and the right man remains paramount in her mind. This note of open-choice renders it a post-modern novel. Dina Mehta portrays realistically a woman's evolution and awakening against the political background. It is an awakening both on political and personal levels.

In almost similar way, Bapsi Sidhwa portrays the predicament Feroza in *An American Brat* faces, Sidhwa focusses on the issue of inter-faith marriage in Parsi community and highlights the Parsi traditions and culture, the orthodoxy of the elders and the priests and the double standards vis-a-vis the inter-faith marriage of the sons and daughters of the Parsi community.

Paradoxically, Feroza's parents are apprehensive about Feroza following the conservative Islamic code and her susceptibility of choosing a non-Parsi man as her husband. She is deeply influenced by the Islamic life-style and does not like her mother's dress of sleeveless blouse and saree. The parents find her conservative which threatens the liberal westernized way of living. They send her away to America to broaden her mind and expose her to a western life-style.

In this new world of America, Feroza acquires not only a free way of living but also falls in love with David. Bapsi Sidhwa charts her growth gradually, exposing her to varied experiences of life in the new world. She for the first time understands her body and open ups to the male-friendship. Feroza evolves from innocent, conservative and protected life in Lahore to the experiences of independent spirit and self-confidence.

With Zareen's arrival in America to discourage Feroza from her decision to marry David, the American Jew, the focus shifts from Feroza's predicament to the Parsi woman's plight if she marries outside the Parsi-fold. The novelist discusses in detail the unfair and unjust codes of marriage for the Parsi women. Zareen too feels that the Parsi-community must move with the time and permit equal rights to the women who marry outside the community. Even when Zareen considers the Parsi code to be as fundamentalist as the Islamic code, she does not dare to protest or speak up for her daughter Feroza. On the contrary, she manages to frighten David, and David's pact of marriage. Boman Desai in his novel *The Memory of Elephants*[2] and Firdaus Kanga in *Trying to Grow*[3] fully portray this issue of inter-faith marriage. In their anxiety for survival of the community, they advocate the inter-faith marriages to be accepted by the community and try to redefine and reposition this issue of the marriage.

With David turning away from her, Feroza finds herself depressed and frustrated, and tries to find comfort in her tradition, culture and faith. Her interest in her faith is renewed and she is determined to follow her faith. She is now confident of choosing the right man as her husband though he may or may not belong to her own faith: "It wouldn't matter if he was a Parsi or of another faith. She would be more sure of herself and she wouldn't let any one interfere."[4]

For her there is no going back to Pakistan. She would live a free life of a bird and would not be bound by the unjust rules of her community.

The novel ends on the note of freedom to choose for Feroza. It is the new mature Feroza fully understanding her predicament and the way to resolve it. This renders the novel a typically postmodern work.

Both the novels portray the marriage issue for the women protagonists and make it quite clear that marriage is their ultimate goal. Sooner than later, they will choose their husbands wisely and freely. Both Sidhwa and Mehta present their protagonists as women who acquire individuality and self-awareness. It is the postmodernist trend that the novelists follow and portray the marriage issue as a means of acquiring space in their protagonists's life, in their community and in society.

NOTES

1. Dina Mehta, *And Some Take a Lover* (New Delhi: Rupa 1992), p. 15.
2. Boman Desai, *The Memory of Elephants* (New Delhi: Penguin, 1992).
3. Firdaus Kanga, *Trying to Grow* (New Delhi: Ravidayal Publishers, 1990).
4. Bapsi Sidhwa, *An American Brat* (New Delhi, Penguin, 1994), p. 317.

A Song of Innocence: Ardashir Vakil's *Beach Boy*

V.L.V.N. NARENDRA KUMAR

> Bliss was it in that dawn to be alive,
> But to be young was very heaven.
>
> William Wordsworth, "The Prelude"

The Parsi novelists in English have made a noteworthy contribution to the canon of postcolonial fiction. They generally fall into two categories: stay-at-home writers and expatriates. B.K. Karanjia and Dina Mehta are stay-at-home Parsis who deal with westernized Parsi life whereas Farrukh Dhondy, Firdaus Kanga, Rohinton Mistry and Ardashir Vakil are expatriate writers. Bapsi Sidhwa's position is singular among Parsi writers in that she divides her time between Pakistan and America. In her there is no conflict whatsoever, which is perceptible, explicitly or implicitly, in most expatriate writers.

Though Rohinton Mistry (Canada), Boman Desai (America) Kanga, Dhondy and Ardashir Vakil (Britain) are expatriate writers, they continue to write about Indian life with their essentially Indian sensibility. At the same time, their works have a distinctive ethnic character to give them an identity of their own. In his first novel, *Trying to Grow*, Kanga does not depict expatriate experience. The novel is set in India; the action revolves round Brit, a thoroughly westernized invalid Parsi boy in Bombay whose quest for identity is, at the same time, a passionate struggle to grow, emotionally and psychologically, though there is virtually no growth at the physical level. Likewise, Mistry, now settled in Canada, writes about 'politics' in

India in *Such a Long Journey*, the victim of which is an innocent Parsi. The local colour in the narrative adds to the genuineness of Mistry's account. Vakil too gives expression to the juvenile experiences of a Parsi boy in Bombay whose zest for life is typical of the marginalized community of the Parsis.

Kai Nicholson, in his discussion of expatriate sensibility in Commonwealth fiction, raises a point: "However, Mistry's Indian world will stop growing unless he returns and plunges back into Bombay's hybrid culture. Of course, he could continue to write in the present vein, but after a while, the vividness of his world can start fading and imagination will replace realism."[1] Nicholson, however, does not discount the power and beauty of Mistry's imagination. His argument is that Mistry's imagination will be frozen to his time in India, since both *Such a Long Journey* and *Tales from Firozsha Baag* are full of documentation. Roshan Shahani observes: "Distance has given the author a certain lucidity of thought and a clarity of vision, tinged with nostalgia though it might be. It permits him to perceive certain 'home truths' about his old home and his people, a fact which sometimes eludes those too close to home."[2] Thus Shahani's argument highlights the advantages of expatriation. Nicholson focusses on the adverse effects of expatriation whereas Shahani regards expatriation as a creative source. What Nicholson and Shahani say of expatriate writers like Mistry holds water in the case of Vakil as well.

Beach Boy is a novel of education in the tradition of *Ice-Candy-Man* and *Trying to Grow*. The subject of a novel of education, according to M.H. Abrams, is the development of the protagonist's mind and character, in the passage from childhood through varied experiences and often through a spiritual crisis into maturity and the recognition of his or her identity and role in the world.[3]

Beach Boy is a rites-of-passage tale. Cyrus Readymoney, the central consciousness, is obsessed with films, food and sex. A young boy from the Parsi elite of Bombay, Cyrus is on the brink of adolescence. The narrative records his passage to selfhood. The ethnic identity of the protagonist is established in the very beginning:

> We are Zoroastrians. . . . We pray at agiryars . . . temples where the same flame has been kept burnt for hundreds of years—we offer up our dead to the vultures at the top of Malabar till in huge stadium-sized wells called the Towers of Silence. We come from Iran, even though my grandmother hates to admit it.[4]

Cyrus, like Brit, is detached and his stance is that of an outsider which is typical of westernized Parsis. He is indifferent to religious faith and the ritualistic aspects of Zoroastrianism.

Cyrus lives in a juvenile world of pleasures and sorrows. What sustains his existence is fantasy. He immensely enjoys films since they provide an escape route from bitter realities of domestic life. The dream world of films often crosses over into his real life. He says: "this world, the world on our doorstep, the world on the street, the world on the hundreds of billboard advertisements around the city was as alien and as repellant as the underworld of rats in the sewers of the city." (52)

Films thus constitute an illusion, which, at least for Cyrus, is life sustaining. At the theatre, he tries to make a ball. He says to himself after his failed attempt: "But there was something in the process of making that ball that I never forgot. An acknowledgement, perhaps, of the futility of human endeavour." (54) Though he is too young to understand the implications of his own gesture, Cyrus begins to perceive the dichotomy between the ideal and the real. His experience at the shooting of Dev Anand's film *Heera Panna* is an eye-opener: "Going to see a picture is so much better than all this shooting nonsense. It was the opposite kind of experience." (123) Ennui is the problem of westernized Parsis in the postcolonial period. Cyrus's passion for films and food is an adolescent's quest for pleasure.

Minoo, Cyrus's father, and Mr. Krishnan, their Malayali neighbour, are drawn in contrast. Mr. Krishnan is a simple and industrious man whereas Minoo is rich and aristocratic. Yet there is no organization in his life; he misses his flights, comes late to marriages, and is unpunctual. Cyrus records in his diary one day: "The Krishnans' existence is happily circumscribed. I like the routine in their lives—the order it offers, as compared to the chaotic freedoms of my own home." (31) When he finds himself alone, Cyrus unlocks his heart to himself. His dreams and fantasies do not sustain him for long, emotionally. He wants something to cling to; hence his attachment with the Krishnans.

His father's affair with an air hostess sets the cat among the pigeons. In vengeance, Mehroo, his mother, starts a liaison with a prosperous man. Ten years of successful marriage thus comes to an end with his father's betrayal. After the separation of his parents, he remarks: "My life too had been transformed. My parents had split up." (112)

Thus nostalgia creeps into an otherwise buoyant life of Cyrus. The Krishnans, on the other hand, continue to live together happily. He receives from their family what he craves for at home—love and affection. Cyrus's family lives in a glass house facing the sea. Vakil perhaps seems to suggest that it stands for the fragile and delicate status of the Parsis which they earned during the colonial period.

Cyrus is emotionally attached to his mother. The Oedipal urge in him is so intense that it leads to a crisis of loyalty in his being. He and his father are kindred souls. He says of the similarity: "There was something special between him and me. He recognised a similar vagabond, vulnerable spirit in his son, a recklessness rushing towards ruin." (105) He begins to understand his father's misery, loneliness and frustration: "For years his past had lurked underground. Now it was beginning to claw its way to the surface. An old ugliness was dragging him down, forcing him to revisit his former lives." (101) Thus, Minoo, like Sam in *Trying to Grow*, is a failed romantic.

In Vakil's *Beach Boy* too, Parsi women are portrayed as strong beings, holding the family together. Mehroo faces her husband's death with courage. She reclaims her position of assurance and control in the family. Cyrus, who does not shed a single tear, realizes the need for crying: "And now I was beginning to feel the need to cry, not just for the world outside, but for myself. To maintain my sanity, to be able to say something to someone, to be able to say something to myself."

(200) Mehroo even fulfils her husband's last wish—to sprinkle his ashes over the sea.

Like most adolescents, Cyrus is too eager to grow. At the same time, however, he is aware of his limitations: "That's what I am like. I think of a good reason to do something and then I don't do it." (80)

His fascination for the Maharani of Bharatnagar is typical of a growing boy. She is a mystery to many but he finds her accessible. He observes once: "this woman's life represented a hidden world outside my own, a world in which I might play a part." (71) She displays genuine enthusiasm for his views. She, like Madame Manekshaw in *Trying to Grow*, makes him look at life from a different perspective. He admires her as she is the only person who treats him like an adult. The Maharani is a reminder of the Raj; her aristocratic life is out of tune with the realities of Indian life in the post-Independence context. It is she who, with her words of assurance, helps him to progress step by step in his journey to selfhood.

Like Brit in *Trying to Grow*, Cyrus too is impatient to do all things done by adults. He reads Kafka's *Diaries*. His impatience is clearly perceptible:

> Sometimes though, being the odd one out, the bad egg, the rotten apple, the black sheep or the white sheep, had its advantages. These became my focus of influence and power. The embarrassment of being on display turned into the egotism of showing off, of procuring things I wouldn't otherwise be able to get, of proving myself worthy of recognition, especially by those older than me, while pretending to play the joker. (35)

But Cyrus's assessment of adults is precise. He muses:

> It seemed to me that all these adults were after was tears and sadness. Toothing away at their hearts was a sadness of their own which they dare not admit to, a pain they could expiate only by flogging someone. There was one lesson to be learnt by the victim: display the correct emo-

> tion at the right time. Say thank you when someone gives you a present, cry when you are beaten. (88)

Like most Parsi novelists, Vakil too gives graphic descriptions of various dishes specialised by the Parsis. Cyrus, an adolescent brimming with enthusiasm, is fond of food. Most of the time he eats and drinks outside, in the neighbours' houses. He is regarded as a free boarder. He swallows the insults of Mrs. Krishnan very often. He admits:

> I considered these insults a fee one had to pay for eating their food, for demanding their friendship, for sleeping in their beds, partaking of their quarrels, sharing their holidays, walking their dogs, making love to them, even sharing in their dreams. Generosity is often spiked. Hospitality has its limits. (16)

However, Cyrus enjoys their reluctant benevolence since he receives there what he fails to get at home—attention. He refers to the last supper of Jesus and says of his neighbours: "My neighbours were like Jesus. They liked to give, they wanted to share, but they couldn't resist the temptation to make me feel guilty, to make me suffer, to make me feel ashamed of my family, to pretend that I was a deprived child to whom they provided succour." (17) Cyrus thus enjoys several 'guilt-ridden' meals. He draws a contrast between his own family which is in doldrums and the neighbours like the Krishnans in whose existence there is order and stability.

In *Beach Boy*, Vakil employs first person narration. Cyrus is the narrator and also a participant in the proceedings. He is both an insider and outsider; an insider in the Parsi community, he tells about the Parsi cuisine, customs and westernized social life of the community. As an outsider, he observes with detachment the life of non-Parsis like the Krishnans and the Maharani. By employing a single narrative voice, Vakil follows the tradition already set by Bapsi Sidhwa in *Ice-Candy-Man* and Kanga in *Trying to Grow*.

Though the Zoroastrian worldview is not explicitly perceptible in the narrative, its implicit purpose assumes significance. Vakil, though apparently indifferent to the antiquity of Zoroastrian history, does not question the validity of certain tenets in the Zoroastrian worldview as Dhondy does in *Bombay Duck*. Cyrus's stance is that of a detached observer on the periphery, though he is a Parsi. For instance, he is amused at the fire temple where prayers are held for his dead father. Vakil touches upon the aspect of charity in *Beach Boy*. Cyrus being young, does not realize the significance of charity. When Horace, his friend takes his bag and keeps it, he struggles to get it back and succeeds eventually. He confesses honestly: "I wasn't sure what charity meant." (46) But he realizes the import of charity only after his father's sudden death. Bhagwan, a servant in Cyrus's home, tells him: "He left everyone something, you know. He left me a lot, Cyrus." (208)

In *Beach Boy* too, as in *Trying to Grow*, the conflict between Good and Evil is internalized. From a child who is at the mercy of the generous neighbours, Cyrus grows into a self-reliant being. His new-found confidence is reflected in the words of Maharani: "Never mind, Cyrus, you will survive. These things happen." (210) Maharani covertly refers to the setbacks, disappointments and heartburns which are part of adult life. Thus *Beach Boy* ends on a note of affirmation with Cyrus adapting himself to the new clime which is the result of his father's death.

NOTES

1. Kai Nicholson, "Are we Expatriates?" *The Commonwealth Review*, Vol. IV, No. 2, 1992-93, p. 11.
2. Roshan Shahani, "On the Periphery of the City," *Indian English Fiction: 1980-90: An Assessment*, ed. Vilas Sarang and Nilufer Bharucha (New Delhi: B.R., 1994), p. 37.
3. M.H. Abrams, *A Glossary of Literary Terms* (Bangalore: Prism Books, 1993), p. 132.
4. Ardashir Vakil, *Beach Boy* (Penguin Books, 1997), pp. 17-18.

The Triumph of Ashavan: Farishta Murzban Dinshaw's *Discovering Ashavan*

NOVY KAPADIA

Discovering Ashavan, by the Karachi based author, Farishta Murzban Dinshaw is a novel in which myth, magic and history are astutely inter-twined into a tension-filled story. A story of many layers, the novel is appealing with its universal themes of the battle between good and evil, of friendship and alienation and the search for one's own self. The author Farishta Murzban Dinshaw consciously makes use of history to present the spellbinding story of the despised, outcast stable boy Ashavan and his friendship with the young Zarathushtra who befriends him. Zarathushtra, the prophet of the Zoroastrians or Parsis as they are known in India, is depicted in this novel, as a young boy. His questioning mind, loyalties to his physically challenged friend Ashavan and interest in abstract and philosophic matters is aptly revealed. The novel starts when Ashavan, an orphaned stable boy disparaged by his peers because of his deformed leg, gets into a midnight brawl to save a dying dog. This impulsive act by the fourteen-year-old Ashavan, snowballs into an alarming chain of events as he fights to clear his name of charges of sorcery cast on him by the cruel foreman of the stableyard. Both Ashavan and the foreman worked in the stableyard of the chief judge of the area. It is set in the pre-Zoroastrian area in ancient Iran, known as Persia. The tribes discussed are the Mazdayasnis and their highest god is Mazda. According to legend, Mazda was perceived as most wise. The Mazdayasnis in those days were polytheistic and other gods were also worshipped. They believed in the pantheon of Gods. The most charismatic god was Mithra, the god of light who rode a golden chariot across the sky. He was also the god of bountiful harvests, thus a very important deity for an agricultural community. The Aryans also invoked other gods and goddesses such as Anahita, the beautiful goddess of water, Rashnu the goddess of truth and Adar the angel of fire. As Farishta Dinshaw says in her author's note, "It is interesting to note that the beings that the Aryans deified reflect their priorities—wisdom, truth, warmth and water."[1] Later, Zarathushtra singled out the highest and most wise God, Mazda, as the only God.

An interesting aspect of *Discovering Ashavan* is that it aptly portrays the era of superstition and irrationality that pervaded ancient Iran four millenia ago. The vindictive foreman spread the canard that Ashavan indulges in sorcery. The superstitious and fearful community believes these malicious charges because Ashavan is deformed. He becomes an outcast. It is Zarathushtra who befriends him and gives him the courage to resolve the fears within himself and take a stand for what he believes. Zarathushtra's struggle against irrationality and the superstitions of his tribe get highlighted in the novel. The contemplative and questioning mind of Zarathushtra gets aptly reflected in the novel. The novel in fictional form reveals the Prophet of the Zoroastrians in his adolescent and developing stage of life. We read about him at a stage of his development when he did not possess all the answers and was in search for the divine truth. During a heated discussion, he candidly tells Ashavan, "I do not have all the answers, Ashavan. All I have are a lot of questions." (16) Zarathushtra is presented as an earnest young boy in search of the truth. He explains to Ashavan, "I know it sounds silly, but it is as if there is a spark inside me that becomes shiny and warm when I do what must be done." (16) Such frank revelations of his inner self, friendship with the lame Ashavan, instinctive reactions against hypocrisy and oppression of the weak and arguments with his father Pourushaspa make Zarathushtra very accessible and human. History records that Zarathushtra grew up to be a kind, considerate and thoughtful boy. Noted Zoroastrian scholar, Piloo

Nanavutty records that suffering and the plight of the poor always perturbed Zarathushtra. When there was famine in the land, he begged his parents to share their wealth. So in this novel, we see the human side of the prophet Zarathushtra. The author Farishta Dinshaw has explained the reason, which inspired her to write this story. She said in her author's note, "I wanted people to see our prophet Asho Zarathushtra differently. For the few who have read the Gathas he is a visionary philosopher, but for many of his followers he is simply a portrait on the wall. I wanted people to recognise him for what he really was—"

According to legend, Zarathushtra became contemplative and philosophical at the age of fifteen years and renounced worldly life at the age of twenty years: "At the age of fifteen, Zarathuhstra turned away from all worldly pleasures and devoted himself day and night to the worship of Ahura Mazda. When he was twenty, he bade farewell to his parents and went to meditate in a cave. His father wished to load him with gifts. but the lad only accepted the Kusti, as a momento."[2]

Befittingly this novel ends with Zarathushtra as an adolescent, questioning existing precepts and religious teachings and searching for the infinite. He is known throughout the novel as "the trouble maker who disturbs the priests with the questions." (20) The parents Pourushaspa and Doghdova are anxious at what they consider as "the strange obsession for arta which consumes him." (78) By arta is meant the quest for what is ethically right or the path of righteousness. They think that marriage with the fair Havovi will make their son more worldly wise. In the closing pages of the novel, there is a poignant scene when the friends Zarathushtra and Ashavan have to depart. Ashavan who has an instinctive rapport with horses, is going to work as a foreman with Doghdova's father, Frahimurva who raises stallions. As Ashavan departs, he turns to look back at Zarathushtra for the final time.

> Maybe it was the veil of tears that was responsible. or perhaps it was a trick of the light from the setting sun.

> but Ashvan saw Zarathushtra bathed in a radiant glow that spread and shimmered all around him. In that heartbeat, Ashavan knew for certain that Zarathushtra would one day find the answers he was seeking. And just as Zarathushtra had touched his life and changed him, so would countless other lives be changed forever after. (82)

So in the concluding pages of the novel, the author hints that the young Zarathushtra will soon receive the divine spark and become a prophet. It shows him at the age of fifteen years spending long hours on the hillside in contemplation of the divine and the single-minded thirst for truth and righteousness.

It is the first English novel of the Karachi born Parsi author, Farishta Murzban Dinshaw. Previously she had written three plays and numerous skits as fund-raisers for charity. She had also co-authored several handbooks for teachers.

Homi Meherhomji aptly illustrates this compact novel with a pacy narrative and gripping story line. The characters are well developed and the author cleverly uses history and legend as a backdrop to this novel. She is the first Parsi author to use the Prophet as a character in her work of fiction. Of the characters in the book, "only Asho Zarathushtra, his parents Dughdova and Pourushaspa, his cousin Maidyomah, his wife Havovi and Jamaspa are known to have existed. All other characters, including Ashavan are fictitious." (Author's Note, 86)

The author deconstructs legends and myths and uses history to present a fascinating fictional account of the early life of the Prophet Zarathushtra. It is this use of early Zoroastrian history and Zarathushtra's family as the main characters, which makes this novel quite unique. The use of ancient legends in Parsi fiction was almost non-existent. So the author Farishta Murzban Dinshaw is a trend-setter in this respect. Besides this, the author is also to be complimented for her meticulous research and presentation of alternative history, especially the economic conditions and social life of society amongst the Mazdayasnis. For instance we learn about the role of the judges who were the leaders of society. Ashavan also works as a stable boy for a judge. Priests also acted as judges because judgements were according to the rules and regulations of religious beliefs. So, as regards subject matter and theme, Farishta Dinshaw's novel is a direct contrast to the fiction of recent Parsi authors.

The Parsi novelists of the twentieth century have tended to focus on contemporary issues. Most of the Parsi novels of the current era can be viewed as either distinctive for sociological reasons, or as a part of the genre of Indian writing in English or in the context of creative alienation. In India and Pakistan as is reflected in the works of Rohinton Mistry, Bapsi Sidhwa, Dina Mehta, Firdaus Kanga and Boman Desai, this minority community has to cope with hegemonic forces, identity crises and the struggle to create their own space. All the concerns of the community, declining population, brain-drain, late marriages, inter-faith marriages, funeral rites, attitude to the girl-child, urbanisation, alienation, modernist vs traditionalist attitude to religion and the existence or non-existence of ethnic anxieties are aptly delineated in the works of the Parsi authors. Recent Parsi fictional writers like Ardeshir Vakil and Meher Pestonji focus on the marginalisation of the Parsis in the 1990s, dilution of values, isolation in the urban scenario, hybrid personality traits, the struggle to preserve identity in a multi-cultural society and the influence of massive commercialisation on the Parsi psyche.

Boman Desai in his novel, *The Memory of Elephants*[3] refers to the decisive battle of Ghadessiah, which took place in 637 A.D. In this battle, the Arab forces conquered the Persians and the Zoroastrians, the worshippers at the Fire-temple either fled to India or got converted to Islam. However the era of the prophet Zarathushtra has not been used in Parsi fiction. So Farishta Murzban Dinshaw has tread on new ground. According to tradition, Zarathushtra was born in the city of Rai near Tehran. As per the Gathas, his father's name was Pourushaspa, owner of many horses, of the clan of Spitama. His mother's name was Dughdova, milkmaid and she came from the clan of the Hvogas. He lived during the reign of King Kae Vishtaspa of the Kayanian dynasty. There is controversy as to the date of Zarathushtra. There are three main traditions. The first, favoured by Western scholars, is a late Sassanian tradition stating that Zarathushtra lived "258 years before Alexander." (Nanavutty,

12) The second tradition regarding the date of Zarathushtra is that he was born 6,000 years before Plato. (Nanavutty, p.12) The third tradition is based on a linguistic comparison between the Gathas and the Rig Veda and on the split between the Aryan tribes, which led to one branch migrating to India and the other remaining in Iran. This tradition asserts that Zarathushtra lived about 2,000 B.C. or earlier. (Nanavutty, 12) It is the third tradition, which is widely accepted by scholars as the era in which Zarathushtra lived.

Basically the novel is the story of two boys. It is the story of Zarathushtra, the boy who searched for the Eternal Truth and his friendship with Ashavan, who is lame and a social outcast. Ashavan works as a stable boy in the household of an eminent judge. He is initially depicted as a shy and lonely fourteen-year-old boy. The author states that the boy was diffident for two reasons because he was an orphan and because he was lame. Farishta writes:

> In the fourteen summers of his life Ashavan had mastered the art of paling into the background. In a time when muscular strong bodies were prized, his deformed leg left him open to taunts and blows. There was no one to protect him. His family had perished in a skirmish with the marauders who had swooped down from the mountains when he had been a nursling. (2)

The reference to the marauders conveys some important historical facts and beliefs of the Mazdayasnis or believers of Mazda. The Mazdayasnis who stayed in settlements, were often attacked by marauding tribes from the North who looted their belongings and caused death and destruction. This established the belief that demons resided in the North. These raiding tribes were known as Devayasnis or believers in demons.

Ashavan first gets into trouble when he attacks the foreman who had kicked a bitch about to litter. The author shows that in those days, crimes against animals were one of the five categories of crime punishable by Law. In her author's note, Farishta writes, "In those days, dogs were integral to a well-ordered and safe life, and rigorous punishment was prescribed to those who ill-treated dogs. A man who would not give shelter to a bitch about to litter with the result that the young perished was liable to be sentenced for willful murder." (85) Severe punishment for mistreating a bitch is stressed in the novel also. Ashavan narrates the tale to Zarathushtra's parents Pourushaspa and Dughdova, of why he left his job as a stable boy at the judge's house. After listening to the story, Pourushaspa at once reacts, "Ashavan do you realise what you have said about the foreman is very serious? Ill treating a bitch about to litter is a crime punishable by seven hundred strokes of whip." (11)

It is important to note that the dog plays a significant part in the rituals of the Parsis till the middle of the twentieth century. The dog is used in death ceremonies. After a person is declared dead, his or her body is washed, wrapped in white clothes and laid on stone. A dog is then brought to see the dead. In recent days it is just a custom but in ancient Iran this move had sound ecological reasons. Explaining these motives, T.R. Sethna in his book, *The Teachings of Zarathushtra*, says that, "if the person was not dead, a dog would remain at a distance and bark."[4] He also explained how such a ritual became a custom. Sethna writes, "During the prayers that are offered before taking the body for the final rest the dog is brought in to see the corpse three times, only to be sure that the person is dead." (64) Thus it can be seen that the foreman had committed a serious crime by kicking this pregnant bitch. He was infuriated that he had been spotted by Ashavan and curtly ordered him to depart and carry the bitch away from the stables.

A desolate Ashavan cradles the whimpering bitch and departs from the settlement. He finally leaves the bitch to die on a stony ledge. Tired and dispirited Ashavan walks away in search of shelter. It is in this state of despair that he meets Zarathushtra the camel-herder's son who promptly befriends him and invites him home. This is the start of the unusual friendship. For Ashavan it is a relief that he now has food and shelter and the protection of an important household. Above all for him it is a psychological satisfaction, that he is being acknowledged and treated with respect by Zarathushtra and that his lame leg is not looked upon as a symbol of evil. The invitation to the house and Zarathushtra's warmth provides solace to Ashavan and the utmost despair changes to rising hopes.

For Ashavan, joy is only short lived. Pourushaspa considers the act of carrying the corpse of the dying bitch alone as a capital offence. It is an act of pollution and in those days penalties for endangering public health were severe. Ashavan was supposed to have cleansed himself and offered purification before entering the house. He is taken to the judge for the violation of rules and being a possible threat to public health. Due to the candid nature of Ashavan's revelation of the incident in the stable yard and his overall bravery, his punishment is not severe. He is ordered bodily purification and the payment of one stallion to the cleanser. The detailed description of the bodily purification indicates the importance given to ritual and superstition in the daily lives of the Mazdayasnis. The higher purification rituals meant separation for ten days in a secluded room in a temple, bathing with bull's urine after the third, sixth and ninth night. Investigations reveal that the foreman was guilty and he was formally charged with "kicking a bitch about to litter." (23) As penance, the foreman had to feed "twice nine pious men with sumptuous food and drink." (23)

The happiest period in Ashavan's life is when he stays in Zarathushtra's house and works as a helper with the camels. For Zarathustra, his young companion becomes a sounding board for questions and doubts on the universe, ethics and justice. Several philosophic questions are raised in the rambling conversation between these two friends. Zarathushtra has already developed the reputation of an iconoclast because of his strange questions to the priests. Ashavan knows that people look on his deformed leg with disgust and even with fear. Such thinking reflects the prejudices and irrational superstitions of that age. Deformity as an adjunct of evil is a deep-rooted obsession or fixation, as the author indicates. Ashavan also raises this issue when he tells his friend that "the foreman said that the gods only gathered men who walked straight and upright. That I must be a creature of the dark Forces from the North." (27) Later in the novel, Zarathushtra's cousin, Maidyomah also echoes the popular sentiment that Ashavan is "not of god's making. That he is fashioned by the Forces of the North." (34) In the novel, it is Zarathushtra who challenges such orthodoxy and rigid superstitions of the priests. He makes Ashavan realise that such views are mere superstition, based on ignorance. He explains that symptoms like not having fever are a sign of good health and not an indication of sorcery or witchcraft. In an age, when medical facilities were negligible and life expectancy limited, illness was seen as inevitable. A lame boy like Ashavan who never had fever in his life, was seen as evidence that he had links with the devil. He challenges the view that deformity was a sign of divine displeasure. He cites examples from nature, like comparing different types of leaves or the contrast between an apple and a grape to show that differences are inevitable. It is the young Zarathushtra, seeking an answer to philosophic questions, like the cause of suffering and the creation of the universe, who provides solace to Ashavan. Zarathushtra rightly says, "But I know that Mithra shines on him with as much warmth as he does on me. If he can so without passing judgement, so can I." (35) By raising questions, Zarathushtra plays the role of an iconoclast, challenging existing dogma. The Aryans of that era believed that if someone broke an oath, then the charismatic God, Mithra the God of Light, struck them with a disability like blindness or limp. The fact that Ashavan was born with a limp and deformed leg would understandably multiply the superstitious fear attached to his disability. Deformities were abhorred as they were seen as the outcome of sin. The Aryans prized a vigorous body and lifestyle. By his forceful questioning and raising of doubts, he makes Ashavan realise that deformity is not a punishment or a retributive act by God. Zarathushtra, by his repeated queries, also challenges the existing orthodoxy that all suffering is retributive. The global puzzle of the reason for suffering thus becomes one of the significant subsidiary themes of Farishta Dinshaw's novel. In her presentation of the theme of suffering, the author is similar to the questions and doubts raised by the biblical character Job, in the Old Testament, *The Book of Job*.

The wealthy patriarch of Uz, Job raises the universal mystery of misery unmerited, during the course of his intense suffering and discussions with his three friends or comforters, Eliphaz, Bildad and Zophar. In Dinshaw's book, the youthful Zarathushtra, because of the spirit or 'arta' to do the right thing expresses similar doubts. When the Law clerk and the foreman accuse Ashavan of sorcery, an agitated Zarathushtra speaks out loudly, "How can the gods and priests who have given the world hatred, wrath and woe be good guides." (60) Throughout the community, Zarathushtra is known as the "one who asks the questions." (70) He questions orthodoxy, superstition, the belief in sorcery, witchcraft and the notion that deformity was a sign of evil.

Celebrating the feast of Mithra, a six-day event, further cements the friendship of Ashavan and Zarathushtra. During this feast, there is also an indication of the growing intimacy between Zarathushtra and the young girl, Havovi, who also developed an interest in the higher branches of literature and law. She also questioned "the priest's dictat that only men will know Paradise." (39) But during this feast, comes news of the next crisis. There is danger of famine as the granaries have not been filled for winter. The famine affects both people and cattle. Even Zarathushtra loses his equanimity, at the sight of distress. During this period of famine, we witness the generosity of Zarathushtra. He shares the family oats and grain with the poor. At first, Ashavan, who has known hunger, does not realise why Zarathushtra is indulging in such philanthropy. But gradually he comes to appreciate his friend's gesture and shares food with the poor. Ashavan had often stored uneaten apples, currants and grapes. When he is told that Jarovanhu's young friends are unwell because of hunger, he shares his stocked food with them. He is now moved at the sight of misery and joins Zarathushtra in compassion for the suffering and organising relief work. The practical nature of Ashavan is also seen in small gestures. He offers suggestions to make the process of apportioning rations speedier.

Later Ushtavaiti's young son, who had been constantly crying out of hunger, attaches himself to Ashavan and starts chewing the tassle of his belt. Ushtavaiti looks upon this act as an omen. However, the practical Ashavan says, "There was no magic involved in stopping that child from crying. It is obvious that the little boy is teething. He will not cry as long as he has something soft like my leather tassle to chew on." (54) At this stage in his life, it does seem that Ashavan is finally integrated into the community and his deformity is no longer being seen as a sign of divine displeasure. He feels wanted and appreciated as a person who is honest, kind and brave. However his days of happiness are short-listed. The foreman from the judge's stables and the young law clerk accuse Ashavan of sorcery. His act of generosity of feeding apples to Jarovanhu gets mis-interpreted. The young boy falls ill and Ashavan's enemies seize this opportunity to malign him. They state that, "Jarovanhu has been taken by seizure and high fever after eating the food you gave him. It is obvious to the townsmen that you have deliberately cast your evil spell upon him." (59) He is accused of hypnotising the young boys. The material he used to make cherry-wood whistles for them are being mis-interpreted and mis-represented as "defiled bones." Pourushaspa realises that "with the famine the men and women of the settlement are not in their best minds. I must speak to the priests before these shallow stories reach them. They will guide the people." (60)

The author, to vividly portray the era of superstition and irrationality that pervaded ancient Iran four millennia ago, used such incidents to illustrate her point. Ashavan becomes a victim of jealousy and politicking. His rivals capitalise on his helplessness and deformity to defame him in society. Again it is the young Zarathushtra who remains loyal to his friend. Indignant at his friend being needlessly maligned, Zarathushtra in a rare outburst says, "At every turn, I see the mayhem caused by superstition and deceitful actions. Will there never be a saviour who will free us from this?" (61) This outburst is a bit ironic also as Zarathushtra himself is going to be the saviour in the near future. The foreman and the judge's clerk have stirred the people against Ashavan. The judge's clerk had even convinced the people that Ashavan was responsible for the famine. There was even the fear that the crowd could be incited to attack him. The sympathy and understanding he gets from

Zarathushtra, his cousin Maidyomah and the girl Vohu, encourage him to act bravely and face the trial at Jarovanhu's house. A Diviner from the King's Court and his son were journeying through and the Council had asked them to foretell the extent of the famine. The Diviner is at Jarovanhu's house, when Ashavan acts heroically and goes there to face the trial. A hostile crowd at Jarovanhu's house meets him. But an inspired Ashavan lives upto his name, which means doer of righteousness.

The reason for such heroism is twofold. Firstly Zarathushtra had inspired in him a sense of righteousness and willingness to act against evil forces and superstition. Another reason is the affection and respect that Jarovanhu and his friends had given him. As Ashavan explains:

> All my life people have looked on me with pity or fear. I accepted it because I could not fight it, and I did not expect anything more. But Jarovanhu and his friends gave me affection and respect without question. I cannot let people think I would harm them. (68)

Ashavan, despite the hostility of the crowd, takes the oath by the fire of Mazda as a witness to his truth and good mind. The Diviner believes in his confession and act of courage and for all time cleared his name of any attachment to evil. Instead the Diviner blames the "hand of malice that shapes these accusations." (69) The law clerk and the judge's foreman are accused of maliciously spreading rumours and orders are given for their severe punishment. The triumph of Ashavan is seen as an allegorical victory for the forces of good over evil. Ashavan's life becomes more settled now. He is accepted in the community. Once it is learnt that Zarathushtra is soon to be wed to Havovi, there is again a new direction in Ashavan's life. He leaves the household to work as a foreman with stallions in the household of a Mazdayasni who is known to Dughdova's father Frahimurva. Ashavan thus has a settled life. His skill with animals is recognised and he is doing the job he loves, working with horses. Zarathushtra's sense of righteousness had helped him overcome the dogmatic beliefs and animosity of society. The triumph of Ashavan is thus seen allegorically as the triumph of good over evil and irrationality and of the search for one's self. The novel ends on a clairvoyant note. Zarathushtra is seen seated on a hillside, in a contemplative mood. There is a radiant glow that spread and shimmered all around him. As he was departing, Ashavan saw this scene and instinctively understood that one day Zarathushtra will find the answers he is searching for. So the novel has a prophetic ending.

NOTES

1. Farishta M. Dinhaw, *Discovering Ashavan* (Karachi: Zarthisti Banu Mandal, 2000), p. 85.
2. Piloo Nanvutty, *The Parsis* (Delhi: National Book Trust, 1977), p. 14.
3. Boman Desai, *The Memory of Elephants* (New Delhi: Penguin, reprint, 1992).
4. T.R. Sethna, *The Teachings of Zarathushtra* (Karachi: Times Subscription Agency, 1966), p. 64.

Contributors

NILUFER E. BHARUCHA	University of Bombay Mumbai
INDIRA BHATT	C.U. Shah Science College Ahmedabad
KEKI N. DARUWALLA	Eminent poet and writer New Delhi
R.K. DHAWAN	Shaheed Bhagat Singh college University of Delhi
JAYDIPSINH DODIYA	Saurashtra University Rajkot
RUSTOM S. GAE	Senior Advocate Supreme Court of India
AMALENDU GUHA	Eminent Economist and Journalist
PALLAVI GUPTA	M.Phil., University of Delhi Now Ph.D. Scholar, USA
NOVY KAPADIA	S.G.T.B. Khalsa College University of Delhi
DINA G. MCINTYRE	Trustee Gatha Studies Trust, USA
PESI MUNCHERJI	Editor, Quarterly House Magazine Shree Parsi Panchayat, Vadodara

PILOO NANAVUTTY (JUNGALWALLA)	Author of *Parsis: The Gatha of Zarathustra*
V.L.V.N. NARENDRA KUMAR	Govt. Polytechnic for Women Ethamukkala
S.D. NARGOLWALA	Ex-ICS Officer Former President, Parsi Anjuman
INDIRA NITYANANDAM	S.R. Mehta Arts College Ahmedabad
R.S. PATHAK	H.S. Gour University Sagar
S. RAMASWAMY	Bangalore University Bangalore
ALKA SAXENA	D.A.V. College Kanpur
HOMI D. SETHNA	Renowned Journalist and Broadcaster
FATIMA SUGARWALA	KSNKM Arts & Com. College Rajkot
K.V. SURENDRAN	Govt. Brennen College Tellicherry
A.K. TRIPATHY	Banaras Hindu University Varanasi